D0708584

Lisbon

Julia Wilkinson

Lisbon

1st edition

Published by
Lonely Planet Publications
Head Office: PO Box 617, Hawthorn, Vic 3122, Australia
Branches: 155 Filbert St, Suite 251, Oakland, CA 94607, USA
              10a Spring Place, London NW5 3BH, UK
              71 bis rue du Cardinal Lemoine, 75005 Paris, France

Printed by
Colorcraft Ltd, Hong Kong

Photographs by
Julia Wilkinson
Bethune Carmichael
Tony Wheeler

Front cover: Nun descending red steps, Steve Niedorf (Image Bank)

First Published
April 1998

Although the authors and publisher have tried to make the information as accurate as possible, they accept no responsibility for any loss, injury or inconvenience sustained by any person using this book.

National Library of Australia Cataloguing in Publication Data

Wilkinson, Julia
Lisbon.

1st ed.
Includes index.
ISBN 0 86442 550 3

1. Lisbon (Portugal) - Guidebooks. I. Title.

914.6904

Julia Wilkinson

Julia set out with her first backpack at the age of four in a moment of tempestuous independence and has been hooked on travel ever since. After finishing university in England in 1978, she headed for Australia but got sidetracked in Hong Kong, where she worked in publishing and radio until going freelance as a writer and photographer. Since then she has travelled throughout Asia, writing for various international magazines. She has contributed to guidebooks on Hong Kong, Tibet and Laos, and authored others on Portugal and Thailand. In 1994 Julia updated the Portugal chapter for LP's *Western Europe* and *Mediterranean Europe* guides and again in 1996 with her husband, LP author John King. At this time, too, they researched and wrote LP's first *Portugal* guide and *Portugal Travel Atlas*. When Julia wants to get away from it all she takes to the skies, flying hot-air balloons.

From the Author

My thanks must first go to my husband, John King, whose meticulous research and text for the Lisbon chapter of LP's *Portugal* guide provided a rock-solid foundation on which to build this guide.

Pilar Pereira of ICEP London once again came up trumps with logistical support and Miguel Gonzaga of Lisbon's Town Hall Tourism Department proved patient beyond words in dealing with my stream of queries.

Amélia Paulo Vieira at Sintra's *turismo* was again invaluable, not least because she found a perfect child-minder for my three-year-old son, Kit: thanks to Ana Valente, he had a great holiday while I pounded the streets of Lisbon. Similar thanks are due to Neliza Rumbaua back home in Hong Kong, for helping to take care of our one-year-old daughter, Lia.

Obrigada to EXPO '98's Press Office Manager, Teresa Casal Ribeiro, and Press Officer, Tomas Colares Pereira, for their time and information; to Goncalo Diniz of Associação ILGA-Portugal for his excellent press bulletins; and to various organisations in the UK including Campus Travel, Beehive Communications, AB Airlines, Connex and KTA International for their efficiency in dealing with my requests and enquiries.

Finally, a toast of the best vintage port to LP editors Adrienne Costanzo and Sarah Mathers and designer Lyndell Taylor who have been a pleasure to work with once again.

From the Publisher

This 1st edition of Lisbon was edited at the Lonely Planet head office in Melbourne by Sarah Mathers and proofed by Tom Smallman. Lyndell Taylor produced the maps and took the project through layout while Kerrie Williams produced the index and Margaret Jung designed the cover.

Warning & Request

Things change – prices go up, schedules change, good places go bad and bad places go bankrupt – nothing stays the same. So, if you find things better or worse, recently opened or long since closed, please tell us and help make the next edition even more accurate and useful.

We value all of the feedback we receive from travellers. Julie Young coordinates a small team who read and acknowledge every letter, postcard and email, and ensure that every bit of information finds its way to the appropriate authors, editors and publishers.

Everyone who writes to us will find their name in the next edition of the appropriate guide and will also receive a free subscription to our quarterly newsletter, *Planet Talk*.

The very best contributions will be rewarded with a free Lonely Planet guide.

Excerpts from your correspondence may appear in new editions of this guide; in our newsletter, *Planet Talk*; or in updates on our Web site – so please let us know if you don't want your letter published or your name acknowledged.

Contents

Introduction

Lisbon is an enticing tangle of times past and present. It's funky and old-fashioned, unpretentious and quirky, and booming with new money and new confidence. Its position on seven low hills beside the Rio Tejo (River Tagus) was the main attraction for traders and settlers in centuries past, and it's still a stunning site. Add to that today's cultural diversity, its laid-back ambience and a time-warp of architecture, and you've got one of the most enjoyable cities in Europe. And, despite recently rising prices, it's still an economical destination, worth considering as a base for several nearby day trips after you've meandered around Lisbon itself.

Apart from its muscle-aching hills – tackled by a bevy of funiculars and half a dozen cranky old trams that hiss and zing through the streets – Lisbon is a manageable city that's small enough to explore on foot (don't even try to drive: the traffic jams and one-way streets are a nightmare). At its heart are wide, tree-lined avenues graced by Art Nouveau buildings, mosaic pavements and street cafés, while the Alfama district below Castelo de São Jorge is a warren of narrow old streets redolent of Lisbon's Moorish and medieval past. Seen from the river – one of the city's many great viewpoints – Lisbon is an impressionist picture of low-rise ochre and pastel, punctuated by church towers and domes.

But Lisbon has also been hit by massive redevelopment in recent years. Although the Alfama and Chiado districts have seen some sensitive restoration projects, many fine old buildings have been destroyed in commercial areas where office blocks are in demand. Sleepy old Lisbon is no more: it's now on a helter-skelter ride towards modernisation as it experiences new wealth and new international prestige, thanks to EXPO '98.

The resulting contrasts can be startling: among the jackhammers and new high-rises are still the seedy backstreets of Alfama and Cais do Sodré where you'd be wise not to wander alone at night. And though the traffic is increasingly frenzied, the main squares still maintain a caravanserai character, with lingering lottery ticket-sellers, shoe-shiners, itinerant hawkers and pavement artists.

Such contrasts give a buzz and vitality to pre-millennium Lisbon. You'll still find plenty of history and culture, from the magnificent Manueline masterpieces at Belém to the world-class Calouste Gulbenkian Museum. But there are pulsating new rhythms too, most noticeably in the African

clubs popping up everywhere as the refugees who flooded into Portugal from the country's former African colonies in 1974-75 respond to a growing demand for their music. Nothing could be further from the soul-searing strains of the uniquely Portuguese *fado* songs (which originated here, in the Alfama district). Traditionalists may be disappointed, but this is a city on the move.

When you're ready to get away, you have the option of day trips to the massive monastery at Mafra or the rococo palace at Queluz, seaside frolics in Sesimbra or Cascais, or walks in the wooded hills of Sintra.

Facts about Lisbon

HISTORY

Legend has it that Lisbon was founded by Ulysses but it was probably the Phoenicians who first settled here some 3000 years ago, attracted by the fine harbour and strategic hill of São Jorge. They called the city Alis Ubbo ('delightful shore'). Others soon saw its delightful qualities too: the Greeks kicked out the Phoenicians and were in turn booted out by the Carthaginians.

In 205 BC the Romans arrived in the city known then as Olisipo, managing to hold on to the place for the next two centuries. Julius Caesar raised its rank (and changed its name to Felicitas Julia), making it the most important city in Lusitania – the western region of the Iberian Peninsula. After the Romans, a succession of northern tribes – Alans, Suevi and Visigoths – occupied Lisbon, but in 714 the powerful Moors arrived from Morocco. They fortified the city they called Lissabona and fought off occasional attacks by Christian forces for the next 400 years.

Finally, in 1147, after a four month siege, the Christians under Dom Afonso Henriques recaptured the city with the help of a ruffian bunch of Anglo-Norman crusaders. Just over a century later, in 1255, Afonso III asserted Lisbon's pre-eminence by making it the country's capital in place of Coimbra.

Since then, Lisbon has had more than its fair share of glory and tragedy: in the 15th and 16th centuries it became the opulent seat of a vast empire after Vasco da Gama discovered a sea route to India. In the 17th century, gold was discovered in Brazil, further boosting Lisbon's importance. Merchants flocked to the city from all over the world, trading in gold and spices, silks and precious stones. Under Dom Manuel I, the extravagant style of architecture that came to be called Manueline – typified by the Mosteiro dos Jerónimos at Belém – complemented Lisbon's role as the world's most prosperous trading centre. But the extravagance was short lived: the massive earthquake of 1755 turned everything to rubble and Lisbon never regained its power and prestige.

After Napoleon's forces occupied the city in November 1807 (they were repulsed from Portugal in 1811 by a joint British and Portuguese force), Lisbon declined with the country into political chaos and military insurrectionism. In 1908, at the height of the turbulent republican movement, Dom Carlos and his eldest son were assassinated as they rode in a carriage through the streets of Lisbon. Over the next 16 years there were 45 changes of government, another high-profile assassination (President Sidónio Pais, at Rossio station in 1918), and a cloak-and-dagger period during WWII when Lisbon (which was officially neutral) developed a reputation as a nest of spies.

Two bloodless coups (in 1926 and 1974) later rocked the city, but it was the influx of refugees from Portugal's former African colonies (Angola, Cape Verde, Guinea-Bissau, Mozambique and São Tomé e Príncipe) in 1974-75 that had the most radical effect on Lisbon. This influx strained its housing resources, but introduced an exciting new element.

The 1980s and 90s have finally seen Lisbon revitalised. Membership of the European Community in 1986 coincided with a stable, centre-right government which lasted a record 10 years. Massive European Union (EU) funding has boosted redevelopment projects (especially welcome after a major fire in 1988 destroyed the Chiado district) and Lisbon returned to the limelight again as European City of Culture in 1994. Its next high-profile appearance, as host of EXPO '98, confirms its re-emergence on the world stage, albeit in a less glorious role than in Vasco da Gama's day.

GEOGRAPHY

Lisbon has a superb position on the north bank of the Rio Tejo, some 15km inland from the Atlantic Ocean. Just east of the city's

Prince Henry the Navigator

Henrique, Infante de Portugal (Prince of Portugal), was born in Porto in 1394, third of four half-English sons of João I and Philippa of Lancaster. By the time he died 66 years later, he had almost single-handedly set Portugal on course for its so-called Age of Discoveries, turning it from Spain's little brother into a wealthy maritime power. In the process, Portugal's groping, semi-random process of seaborne exploration was transformed into a near science.

At the age of 18, Henry and his older brothers, Duarte and Pedro, keen to prove themselves in battle, convinced their father to invade Ceuta in Morocco. The city fell with ease in 1415 and Henry was appointed its governor. Though he spent little time there, this stirred his interest in North Africa, and with several ships now at his disposal, he began to sponsor exploratory voyages. Two of his protégés discovered the islands of Porto Santo and Madeira (actually rediscovered them, as Genoese sailors had already stumbled across them in the 14th century).

In 1419 Henry became governor of the Algarve, moved to the south coast and began collecting the best sailors, map makers, shipbuilders, instrument makers and astronomers he could find in order to get Portuguese explorers as far out into the world as possible. The usual story is that he did this at Sagres, and while he did found the new town of Vila do Infante there, much of the work may actually have gone on at Lagos, where many of his expeditions sailed from.

The next year, at the age of 26, Henry was made Grand Master of the Order of Christ, which superseded the crusading Knights Templar, and his efforts went into high gear thanks to money available through the order. His strategy was indeed as much religious as commercial, aimed at sapping the power of Islam by siphoning off its trade and ultimately, as it were, by finding a way around it by sea, all the while converting newly 'discovered' peoples. All his ships bore the trademark red cross of the Order of Christ on their sails. Henry took no vows, though he lived simply and chastely, and remained single all his life.

One of the major accomplishments of Henry's sailors during the reign of his brother Duarte as king was psychological as much as physical: the rounding of Cape Bojador on the West African coast by Gil Eanes in 1434, breaking a maritime superstition that this was the end of the world. The newly designed, highly manoeuvrable Portuguese caravel made it possible.

In 1437 Henry and his younger brother, Prince Fernando, embarked on a disastrous attempt to take Tangier. The defeated Portuguese army was only allowed to leave on condition that Fernando remain behind as a hostage. Fernando died six years later, still in captivity, a source of lifelong guilt for Henry and probably an added incentive for his work.

He carried on under the regency of his brother Pedro and the rule of his nephew Afonso V. In 1441, as unease was mounting over his lavish spending on exploration, ships began returning with West African gold and slaves. Within a few years the slave trade was galloping, and Henry's interest gradually began to turn from exploration to commerce. He founded his own trading company in Lagos, having been granted by Afonso the sole right to trade on the coast of Guinea.

The last great discovery to which Henry was witness was of several of the Cape Verde islands by the Venetian Alvise Cá da Mosto and the Portuguese Diogo Gomes. The furthest his sailors got in his lifetime was present-day Sierra Leone, or possibly the Ivory Coast. His last military adventure, at the age of 64, was the capture, with Afonso, of Alcácer Ceguer in Morocco. Two years later, on 13 November 1460, he died at Sagres – heavily in debt in spite of revenues from the slave and gold trade. ■

Ponte de 25 Abril, the Tejo broadens into a bay 11km wide called the Mar de Palha (Sea of Straw) which forms Portugal's finest natural harbour.

With the Tejo on its southern and eastern flanks and the Atlantic to its west, Lisbon is very much an 'aquatic' city, its finest panoramas taking in views of the shimmering Mar

Lisbon's Great Earthquake

It was 9.30 am on All Saints' Day, 1 November, in 1755 when the Great Earthquake struck. Many residents were caught inside churches, celebrating High Mass, as three major tremors hit in quick succession. So strong was the earthquake that its effects were felt as far away as Scotland and Jamaica. In its wake came an even more devastating fire – helped on its way by the flickering church candles – and a tidal wave that submerged the quay and destroyed the lower town.

At least 13,000 of the city's 270,000 people perished (some estimates put it at three times as many) and much of the city was devastated. Although Lisbon had suffered previous earthquakes – notably in 1531 and 1597 – there had been nothing on this scale.

Portugal's European neighbours immediately offered aid and commiseration. England sent food and pickaxes. In France there arose a lively exchange between Voltaire and Rousseau on the doctrine of providence: Voltaire's *Poème sur le désastre de Lisbonne* was followed by an account of the earthquake in his philosophical novel *Candide*, published in 1759. Dom João I's minister, the redoubtable Marquês de Pombal, proved to be the man of the moment, efficiently handling the catastrophe (though it was actually the Marquês de Alorna who uttered the famous words 'we must bury the dead, and feed the living') and rebuilding the city in a revolutionary new 'Pombal' style.

Lisbon recovered, but many of its glorious monuments and artworks had gone. It lost its role as Europe's leading port and finest city. Once revered by Luís de Camões as 'the princess of the world ... before whom even the ocean bows', the city had finally bowed before the sea, and its power no longer shone. ■

---

da Palha. The stunning vistas are possible thanks to seven low-lying hills on which the city is built, each providing splendid *miradouros* (viewpoints).

The city lies over several geological fault-lines, causing earthquakes during the 14th and 15th centuries, and most disastrously in the 18th (see the boxed aside, Lisbon's Great Earthquake). There have been only slight seismic tremors this century.

On excursions from Lisbon, you'll find enormous varieties of landscape: to the south, the vast sandy coastline of the Costa da Caparica and the inland Mediterranean woods and thickets of the Serra da Arrábida; to the north-west, the craggy cliffs of the Cabo da Roca (the westernmost point of Europe) and the lush forested hills of the Serra de Sintra.

CLIMATE

Unique among European cities, Lisbon falls in both the Atlantic and Mediterranean climatic zones, thereby enjoying a pleasantly temperate climate year round. Its mean annual temperature is 17°C, with average temperatures in the winter of 13°C and 27°C in the summer. Even when summer temperatures reach the mid-30s, the proximity of the Atlantic ocean ensures some cooling breezes.

The city receives an average of 666mm of rain annually (not bad, considering the national average of 1100mm), most of it falling during the winter months. July and August are the hottest, driest months whilst November to February are the wettest and coldest.

If you're taking a trip to Sintra (see the Excursions chapter), be prepared for some dramatic changes in temperature: the granite Serra de Sintra, capturing both the Atlantic winds and rains and the Mediterranean weather system, hosts a series of climatic phenomena which have created perfect conditions for some fabulous parks and woods.

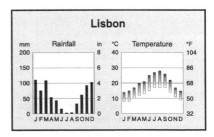

But they also result in considerably cooler, damper conditions than in Lisbon, with frequent mists even in mid-summer.

ECOLOGY & ENVIRONMENT

Before Portugal joined the EU in 1986, Lisbon was one of the most run-down and degraded cities in Europe, its streets littered and pot-holed, its sewage system a health hazard, and several old residential areas such as the Alfama and Bairro Alto suffering almost medieval living conditions. Some places (eg around Cais do Sodré) are still pretty bad, but massive EU funding, increased demands from tourism, and the infrastructure improvements necessary for EXPO '98 have recently cleaned up much of the city. And although environmental issues are low on the agenda of most Portuguese, many *lisboêtas* are now becoming more aware of their urban environment and demanding improvements.

Unfortunately, their concern doesn't extend to restricting the use of private cars: growing wealth in recent years has led to a surge in Lisbon's traffic. On some humid summer days the air pollution is noticeably oppressive. And though drivers may do their bit by using unleaded petrol (now widely available) they have yet to find the crowded public transport system an attractive alternative.

Added to this is the dust and dirt created by pre-EXPO '98 works – from highway and hotel improvements to metro extensions – which are likely to continue throughout 1998. At least the site itself can claim to be something of an environmental success story: once a dangerously polluted and degraded factory area, it had a two-year clean-up before EXPO '98 participants moved in to build their pavilions. Soon the site will be the focus of Expo Urbe (see the following boxed aside), the largest urban regeneration project in Portugal and one which will help alleviate some of the city centre's problems.

The exposition itself – which is dedicated to preserving the oceans (it coincides with the United Nations' International Year of the Oceans) – will put the environmental spotlight firmly on Lisbon throughout 1998. In addition to building the biggest oceanarium in Europe, Portugal is planning to use the occasion to boost its world role in the management, study and preservation of the oceans. In particular, it's hoping to win the bid to provide a headquarters in Lisbon for a major international organisation concerned with marine resources (for more on EXPO '98, see the Things to See & Do chapter).

Compared with Lisbon itself, the nearby coastal resort of Estoril and the World Heritage Site of Sintra have taken some notable environmental steps forward. Estoril's once-notoriously polluted Praia de Tamariz is now so clean it's got an EU Blue Flag bill of health; and Sintra, which has already banned tour buses from its historical centre and reinstated an eco-friendly tram, is now planning a traffic-free zone and electronic buses.

Environmental Organisations

The most active environmental group in Lisbon (and throughout Portugal) is Quercus: Associação Nacional de Conservação da Natureza (National Association for the Conservation of Nature, Map 6; ☎ 01-353 05 40; fax 01-315 20 39), 139 Rua do Salitre 3-A (open only from 3 to 7 pm Monday to Friday). Established in 1986, it now has some 10,000 members and branch offices all over the country as well as an environmental education centre (Centros de Educação Ambiental) in Setúbal and elsewhere farther afield. In addition to carrying out studies of Portugal's flora, fauna and ecosystems, its members also bring environmental issues to the attention of the public and government through regular campaigns. The Lisbon office occasionally organises field trips for around 1000$00 per person. Call for details. If you read Portuguese, you'll find Quercus' monthly magazine, *Teixo*, packed with the latest environmental horror stories.

Another group worth contacting if you're interested in joining like-minded locals in weekend trips to environmentally special areas is GEOTA: Grupo de Estudos de Ordenomento do Território e Ambiente ᵈᵈᵈᵈᵈᵈᵈᵈᵈᵈᵈᵈᵈᵈᵈᵈᵈᵈᵈᵈᵈᵈᵈᵈᵈᵈᵈᵈᵈᵈᵈᵈᵈᵈᵈᵈᵈᵈ

Expo Urbe

Once EXPO '98 closes its doors on 30 September 1998, will the weeds start to grow again on the once-degraded site? No way. Expo Urbe, the largest urban regeneration project ever seen in Portugal, is working to ensure that the entire 60-hectare EXPO site will be incorporated into a vibrant new riverside area. Included in the 340-hectare project are residential, office and commercial buildings, with housing for 5000 people, a recreational harbour for some 900 craft and an 80-hectare park (the Tejo & Trancão City Park), transformed from a former refuse landfill site.

By the time EXPO '98 opens, Expo Urbe will already have built 1850 homes, two hotels and various company offices. And when the exposition ends, the North International Area will be transformed into Lisbon's new Exhibition Centre; the Oceans Pavilion will remain as Europe's largest Oceanarium, and the Utopia Pavilion will become a Multipurpose Pavilion for major shows and concerts.

The project will continue until 2009, when housing and work opportunities will be available for up to 20,000 people. ∎

ᵈᵈᵈᵈᵈᵈᵈᵈᵈᵈᵈᵈᵈᵈᵈᵈᵈᵈᵈᵈᵈᵈᵈᵈᵈᵈᵈᵈᵈᵈᵈᵈᵈᵈᵈᵈᵈᵈ

(Study Group of the Environment, ☎ 395 61 20; fax 395 53 16), Travessa do Moinho de Vento 17. The cost of these trips ranges from 5000$00 to 10,000$00 per person, depending on the location. There are no trips in August.

Less obviously active environmental organisations include Liga para a Proteção da Natureza (League for the Protection of Nature, ☎ 778 00 97), Estrela do Calhariz de Benfica 187; and Associação Portuguesa de Ecologia e Amigos da Terra (Portuguese Association of Ecology & Friends of the Earth, ☎ 395 18 66), Calçada Marquês de Abrantes 10, 3/f.

FLORA & FAUNA
Flora

Although Lisbon has concentrated its efforts more on architecture than gardens over the centuries, there are several places where greenery dominates. The largest is the Parque Florestal de Monsanto, a densely wooded area west of the city centre thick with European pines and oaks. Several smaller parks or gardens in the city centre offer a surprising variety: Lisbon, like most of Portugal, supports a mixture of Atlantic and Mediterranean (or European) floral species, as well as many other species of foreign origin, introduced during Portugal's colonisation era or in the 18th or 19th centuries when it was fashionable to sport a thuja fir or two in your back garden.

The charming, subtropical Jardim Botânico (Map 6), established in 1874, is a classic example, with cacti and palms filling its small hillside site. And in the extensive Parque Eduardo VII (Map 3), right at the heart of the city, you'll find two greenhouses dedicated to exotic species and rare tropical plants, from palms and poinsettias to pineapple plants. Other areas of greenery worth seeking out are the Jardim da Estrela (Map 5) and the private garden belonging to the Palá dos Marquêses da Fronteira, which is famous for its box-hedges.

Not far from the city are several areas which will delight botanists: the Parque Natural da Arrábida, in the southern part of the Setúbal peninsula (see the boxed aside in the Excursions chapter) is a richly wooded area of limestone hills featuring oaks, bush heather and Mediterranean thickets. The sandy coastline here is also renowned for its profusion of seaweed, with more than 70 identified species. To the north-west of Lisbon the Parque Natural de Sintra-Cascais (see the boxed aside in the Excursions chapter) hosts some exuberant vegetation, thanks to its humid microclimate.

Around Sintra itself the Serra de Sintra comprises wooded hills of oak and pine, birch and yew, sycamore and sweet chestnut. Some trees and ferns are of colossal size. The parks of Pena and Monserrate feature exotic imported species such as enormous sequoias and araucarias. Even along the rocky coast there are all kinds of flora, from lichens and ferns and phoenician juniper to rock samphires, dianthus and the lovely but rapacious kaffir fig (originally from South Africa) which is gradually ousting the natural vegetation.

Fauna

As with many European cities, Lisbon is plagued by the scruffy urban pigeon. Parks such as Jardim da Estrela and the huge Parque Florestal de Monsanto (Map 1) offer more variety, of course. But for birdlife on a grand scale, head for the Reserva Natural do Estuário do Tejo, just up the river from Lisbon.

A vitally important wetland area, it hosts around 40,000 migrant wading birds during the winter including avocets and teals. Also common are black-tailed godwits, grey plovers and redshanks. The reserve's headquarters (☎ 234 16 54) are in Alcochete, accessible from Montijo (a ferry ride from Lisbon's Praça do Comércio terminal).

South of Setúbal, the Reserva Natural do Estuário do Sado (see the boxed aside in the Excursions chapter) is great for spotting storks and little egrets as well as migrant flamingoes. Among the many mammal and mollusc species resident here, the most famous is a fast-disappearing dolphin species, *tursiops truncatus*. Easier to catch sight of are the birds of prey in the Setúbal peninsula's Parque Natural da Arrábida. If you're into insects you'll love this place: there are some 450 species of beetles in the park as well as around 300 species of butterfly. Mammal life includes the wild cat, mongoose and bat.

The Parque Natural de Sintra-Cascais also hosts a variety of birdlife: along the rocky coast and beaches are razorbills, ganets, herring gulls and shags. In winter, puffins, purple sandpipers and cormorants can also be spotted here. In the park's hills are woodpeckers, jays, coal tits and robins while the wilder parts of the Serra de Sintra host buzzards and tawny owls. Animal species are less varied, though there are plenty of foxes and rabbits, snakes and lizards.

Wolves

It's thought that there are fewer than 200 Iberian wolves left in Portugal (out of an estimated 1500 in the entire Iberian Peninsula). Most of these are believed to live in the Parque Natural de Montesinho in north-east Trás-os-Montes. Fully protected by law, the wolf is still illegally shot, trapped or poisoned

(an estimated 20 wolves are illegally killed every year). As elsewhere in the world, it is widely feared and hated for supposedly attacking cattle and domestic animals (though in fact many of these attacks are by wild dogs).

Now in danger of extinction in Portugal the wolf has at least some friends working on its behalf: Grupo Lobo, an independent, nonprofit association established in 1985, wins support for the wolf and the preservation of its habitat by publishing booklets and pamphlets and operating a travelling exhibition. It also helps run a Centro de Recuperação do Lobo Ibérico (recuperation centre) for some 22 wolves in Malveira, about 40km north of Lisbon, although this is reportedly now becoming very commercialised (see the boxed aside in the Mafra section of the Excursions chapter).

For more information on Grupo Lobo, contact the Departamento de Zoologia e Antropologia, Faculdade de Ciências, Bloco C2, Campo Grande (☎ 757 31 41, ext 2213; fax 759 77 16). ■

Cruelty to Animals

Bullfighting Although not as popular in Portugal as in Spain, bullfighting is still considered by many Portuguese to be a spectacular form of 'entertainment' and a noble cultural tradition dating back 2000 years. At least 300 *touradas* or bullfights are held every March to October (traditionally from Easter Sunday to All Saints' Day), many in tourist areas such as Cascais (which boasts the country's biggest bullring). To alleviate foreigners' distaste, the posters for these events often carry the headline, 'The bull isn't killed!'. Don't be deceived – the bulls do suffer. And they are killed. You just don't get to see the final fatal blow.

Bullfighting supporters point out that the Portuguese *tourada* is far less brutal and bloody than the Spanish version. There's a good deal more horse-riding skills, more artistry, more valour and bravado. The most obvious differences are that the bull is initially fought by a man on horseback, then by a team of young men who tackle it by hand; and the fight is not to the death – at least, not in public (see the following boxed aside). Another difference is that the bulls' horns are covered in leather or capped with metal balls.

However, none of this can disguise the fact that bullfighting is basically a cruel sport. The anti-bullfighting lobby in Portugal is vocal but small. Most Portuguese are either impartial or simply surprised at the protests. If you feel strongly enough, you could write to the *turismo* (tourist office) and *câmara municipal* (town hall) of places which hold touradas.

GOVERNMENT & POLITICS

The Área Metropolitana de Lisboa (AML, metropolitan area of Lisbon; population 2.5 million) extends over an area of 3128 sq km, stretching as far north as Azambuja and as far south as Sesimbra. Like Portugal's other 18 districts, the AML is headed by a civil governor who is appointed by the central government. The district is divided into 18 *concelhos* or municipal councils, nine in the north and nine in the south. These concelhos are run by an assembly (a mayor and 16 other members), elected for a four year term by popular vote by every resident adult aged 18 and over. Within these councils are 210 smaller *freguesias* or parish councils (the City of Lisbon alone has 53). These, too, are governed by an assembly elected by popular vote under a system of proportional representation. The ruling left-of-centre Socialist Party (Partido Socialista, or PS) under Prime Minister António Guterres, currently controls most of the councils.

The Cidade de Lisboa, or City of Lisbon

The History of Bullfighting

The first recorded mention of bullfighting in Portugal is from the Roman historian Strabo, who wrote in the 1st century that 'the peoples inhabiting the coastal regions of the Peninsula like to challenge isolated bulls which in Hispania are very wild'.

Developing their hunting into a sport, the Celtiberian people used to hold games in Baetica (later known as Andalusia), where wild animals were killed with axes or lances. Combats with bulls were common, too, in ancient Crete, Thessaly and imperial Rome: several amphitheatres were rebuilt for bullfights in the dying days of the Roman Empire.

Portugal's modern version of the bullfight was originally conceived in the 12th century, when the tourada was developed as a method to maintain military fitness and prepare kings and nobles on horseback for battle. By the 16th century, the increasing popularity of the bloody spectacle had aroused such indignation in the Vatican that Pope Pius V decreed in 1567 that 'exhibitions of tortured beasts or bulls are contrary to Christian duty and piety'. The penalty for violating this decree (which has never been repealed) is excommunication. Only the gory death of a Portuguese nobleman, Count dos Arcos, in 1799, resulted in a less blatantly cruel version of the tourada in Portugal: from then on, public slaughter of the bulls was prohibited. Today's *cavaleiro* still wears a black handkerchief around his neck in remembrance of the count. ∎

(population 610,880) is obviously the most important and densely populated concelho within the AML. It covers an area of 84 sq km, extending to the suburb of Charneca in the north, Benfica in the west, and all along the Rio Tejo estuary in the east. The concelho's responsibilities include road maintenance, waterworks and sanitation as well as urban redevelopment and care of the city's architectural heritage.

Its current mayor, João Soares, has been in office since 1993: as elections loomed in December 1997, many urban improvement projects were being pushed to completion to win the popular vote.

ECONOMY

Not so long ago, Portugal was among the poorest nations in Europe, its economy a shambles, its inflation and unemployment rates appalling, its trade deficit a nightmare, and its workforce thoroughly demoralised. Now its growth rate is among the highest in Europe (between 2.5 and 3%), its unemployment (7.1%) one of the lowest, and its inflation tamed to a mere 4% or so. Lisbon, as the country's largest commercial and financial services centre, with one of its most important ports, has benefited from this dramatically.

The turnaround started in 1985 when the austere economist Aníbal Cavaco Silva and his centre-right Social Democratic Party came to power. The following year Portugal joined the EC (now the EU). Over the next decade the government introduced a wide range of structural reforms, extensively deregulating and liberalising the economy and launching an ambitious privatisation programme (now accelerated even further, despite the new socialist government). The EU pumped massive funds into its poor relative (an astounding US$12.8 million a day for the rest of this century) and, helped by falling oil prices, political stability and sound monetary policy, Portugal's economy started to revive.

After the tough recessionary years of the early 1990s, the future economic picture looks encouraging: further economic expansion is predicted, driven by export market growth and a rebound in domestic demand. Showing the most promising growth is the services sector (real estate, banking and tourism): it now employs 56% of the population (compared with 35% a decade ago) and its GDP has been increasing at an average rate of 5.4% a year. Lucky Lisbon accounts for almost a third of the national activity in this sector.

Lisbon's port, too, is thriving. With its docks, warehouses and quays stretching some 20km along the Tejo riverside, it handles millions of tons of traffic a year, including major imports of cotton, grain and coal. The city's manufacturing sector still features some important traditional industries, such as metal products and machinery. More recent additions have included electronics and diamond cutting. The biggest industrial development is now focused south of the Tejo, all the way down to, and including Setúbal, 50km south of Lisbon. Here are factories of steel, cork and plastics and one of the world's largest cement plants.

Most of the headline-grabbing action these days, however, is in the huge new industrial parks with massive manufacturing projects funded by foreign investment. The most high-profile example is the Ford-Volkswagen AutoEuropa plant just north of Setúbal. This massive US$3 billion joint venture, which opened in 1995, is manufacturing some 180,000 'multi-purpose vehicles' per year, employing some 3900 workers and supporting up to 10,000 others in related services.

But all these healthy developments also mask some dismal realities. The years of rapid growth have seen the gulf widen between rich and poor. Despite the prime minister's electoral promises of improvements in health care, welfare and education, there's little chance of them being fulfilled soon: the government is under heavy pressure to maintain rigorous control of public finances so that Portugal can be among the first wave of European Monetary Union entrants in 1999.

POPULATION & PEOPLE

The metropolitan area of Lisbon has a population of some 2.5 million, almost a quarter of the national population. Around 10% are under 24 years old and 13% over 54. The City of Lisbon accounts for only 610,000 of this number. And although it has a population density of some 7200 per sq km, it's actually experiencing a decline in its population (in 1981 there were more than 807,000 residents).

The migration to the suburbs (or even further afield) is due to lack of housing within the city centre, the cost of existing housing and the growing dissatisfaction with Lisbon's run-down residential areas. Some major urban regeneration and housing projects, such as Expo Urbe (see the boxed aside earlier in this chapter) will help alleviate the problem, but the mayor of Lisbon is also resorting to some novel ideas, such as all-expenses-paid, high-publicity weddings (see the following St Anthony's Brides boxed aside), to lure youngsters to stay in the city.

The biggest recent jump in Lisbon's population occurred in the mid-1970s when nearly a million refugees arrived in Portugal following the 1974-75 independence of Portugal's African colonies. Several hundred thousand of these immigrants settled in Lisbon and now make up the city's major ethnic groups (the Cape Verdeans are the biggest single group). On the whole, they have integrated well into Lisboan and Portuguese society; indeed, African music is now all the rage in many of Lisbon's nightclubs. Incidents of racism do occur, however. And as the new era of wealth exacerbates social divisions, immigrants may well face tougher times.

ARTS
Music

Lisbon's most internationally famous style of music is the bluesy, melancholic chants known as *fado*. They are said to have their roots in troubadour songs (although African slave songs have had an influence, too), and are traditionally sung by one performer accompanied by one or two guitarists playing the 12-string Portuguese guitar. Fado first emerged in the 18th century in Lisbon's working-class districts of Alfama and Mouraria. A more academic version developed later in the university town of Coimbra.

The big name among fado performers is Amália Rodrigues, although her 55-year singing career ended in 1995 after a lung operation. Pick up a copy of her best album, *O Melhor* to hear what fado should really sound like before heading to the Bairro Alto clubs to hear a live performance (the Entertainment chapter suggests a number of fado clubs).

Both fado and traditional folk songs – and, increasingly, 'foreign' strains from Europe and Africa – have had a major influence in shaping Portugal's modern folk music scene (now generally known as *música popular*). This first began to attract notice in the 1960s when contemporary musicians such as José Afonso joined forces with modern poets to start a new musical movement, singing about social and political issues. Often censored during the Salazar years, its lyrics became overtly political after the 1974 revolution, with many singers using their performances

---

St Anthony's Brides

Lisbon's mayor, João Soares, has recently revived a charming Lisbon tradition, the Noivas de Santo António (literally 'Brides of St Anthony'), offering couples the chance to marry around St Anthony's day (13 June) in the Igreja de Santo António. With expenses paid by the municipal authorities and commercial sponsors, the 1997 mass wedding, held on 12 June, attracted 17 couples ranging in age from 17 to 64.

In the past, the free marriage was offered only to less-well-off couples (and to virgin brides!). These days, the idea behind the revival is to lure youngsters back into living in Lisbon rather than heading for the suburbs: two of the requirements for the free 1997 wedding was that the bride or groom had to be living in Lisbon and that they would live in the city once they were wed. ■

to actively support the various revolutionary factions. Today's música popular has gone back to its traditional roots, and is increasingly popular, thanks to several outstanding singer-songwriters and instrumentalists such as Carlos Paredes. Some of the more notable groups include Brigada Victor Jara, Trovante and the widely known Madredeus (whose blend of traditional and contemporary music has been described as a 'window into the Portuguese soul').

Another style of music that is now very popular in Lisbon is contemporary African jazz and rock. Dozens of new African nightclubs pulsate with the rhythms of Portugal's former African colonies. Cesaria Evora is the name to look for among Cape Verde performers; Geum from Angola; and Kaba Mane from Guinea-Bissau.

Sculpture

Sculptors excelled in many periods of Portugal's history. Among the first memorable creations are the carved tombs of the 12th to 14th centuries, such as the beautifully ornate limestone tombs of Inês de Castro and Dom Pedro in Alcobaça Abbey. During the Manueline era, sculptors including Diogo de Boitaca (see the following Architecture section) went wild with uniquely Portuguese sea-faring fantasies and exuberant decoration. At the same time, foreign influences were seeping in: first, a Flemish style, followed in the 16th century by Flamboyant Gothic and Plateresque styles (named after the ornate Spanish work of silversmiths or plateros) from Spanish Galicia and Biscay. The Biscayan artists João and Diogo de Castilho created the most outstanding work during this time, often combining their native styles with Manueline.

During the Renaissance period, it was the turn of the French: several French artists who had settled in Coimbra, including Nicolas Chanterène and Jean de Rouen, excelled in sculpting doorways, pulpits, altarpieces and low reliefs. Foreign schools continued to influence Portuguese sculptors in the 18th century baroque era when Dom João V, taking advantage of all the foreign artists

helping with the construction of the Convento do Mafra, founded a school of sculpture. Its first principal was the Italian Alexander Giusti, but its most famous Portuguese teacher was Joaquim Machado de Castro (who crafted José I's statue in Praça do Comércio). A century later, the work of António Soares dos Reis reflects similar French and Italian influences, although Soares also tried to create something uniquely Portuguese (and impossibly intangible) by attempting to portray in sculpture the melancholic feeling of saudade (see the boxed aside later in this chapter). At the turn of the 20th century, two names were prominent: Francisco Franco, and the prolific sculptor António Teixeira Lopes (Soares dos Reis' pupil), whose most famous works are his series of children's heads.

Architecture

There's relatively little original pre-18th century architecture left to admire in the city centre, due to the devastating earthquake of 1755. Among the few major monuments that did survive (albeit with later restoration work) the most notable are the Sé (cathedral), a squat Romanesque building dating from 1150; the Igreja de São Vicente de Fora, built by the Italian Renaissance master Felipe Terzi in the early 17th century; his other work, the Igreja de São Roque; and the Casa dos Bicos, largely reconstructed during the 1980s in its unique 16th century style. The best testimony to the earthquake itself are the formidable Gothic ruins of the Convento do Carmo in the Chiado district.

The most outstanding architecture is found at Belém, 6km west of the city centre. Here is one of the country's finest expressions of the Manueline style. This uniquely Portuguese style marked the transition from Gothic to Renaissance and flourished during the reign of Dom Manuel I (1495-1521) when Vasco da Gama and his peers were exploring the seas as far as India and discovering new lands and new wealth for Portugal. The confidence of this Age of Discoveries was expressed in sculptural creations of extraordinary inventiveness, drawing heavily on nautical themes: ropes, coral and anchors in twisted stone topped by ubiquitous armillary spheres (Dom Manuel's emblem) and the cross of the Order of Christ (the former Knights Templar organisation, which largely financed and inspired Portugal's explorations). The Mosteiro dos Jerónimos at Belém (masterminded largely by architects Diogo de Boitaca and João de Castilho) is a supreme example of the artform, its portals dense with sculptures and its cloisters adorned with intricately carved arches.

Nothing could possibly match the Manueline's imaginative flourish but, in terms of flamboyance, the baroque style surpassed it. Financed by the 17th century gold and diamond discoveries in Brazil, and encouraged by the extravagant Dom João V, local and foreign artists created baroque masterpieces of mind-boggling opulence. The Convento do Mafra (39km north-west of Lisbon) was so immense it took 13 years and 15,000 workers every day to complete. A hallmark of the architecture at this time was the awesome use of *talha dourada* (gilded woodwork), which was lavished on church interiors throughout the land. Lisbon's finest examples are inside the Igreja de São Roque and the Igreja de Nossa Senhora da Madre de Deus.

Only when the gold ran out did the baroque fad fade. At the end of the 18th century, architects quietly returned to the classical style (exemplified by Mateus Vicente's Queluz Palace, 5km north-west of Lisbon). After the 1755 earthquake, even more simplicity followed. The Marquês de Pombal invited architect Eugenio dos Santos to rebuild the city in a revolutionary new 'Pombal' style marked by plain houses and wide avenues. Walk through the Baixa district and you'll see Pombal's influence everywhere. A similar architectural opportunity has recently been given to Portugal's leading architect, Álvaro de Siza Vieira (winner of the prestigious Pritzger Prize) who is restoring the historic Chiado shopping district following a major fire in 1988.

Among the more impressive pieces of contemporary architecture are the Palace of Justice and the startling 'post-modern' Amoreiras shopping complex, designed by Tomás Taveira. Several of EXPO '98's buildings are also remarkable, notably the Pavilhão de Portugal (Portuguese National Pavilion), designed by Siza Vieira. The most stylish engineering feat is the Elevador de Santa Justa, built in 1902 by Raul Mésnier (a colleague of Gustave Eiffel).

Literature

Portuguese literature has been moulded by foreign influences since the 13th century: first, by the Provençal songs of the medieval troubadours, then by Castilian court poetry and Italian Renaissance poetry, and for the longest time of all, by Spain's literary styles and standards. Nonetheless, Portuguese literature retains a distinct temperament and individuality. Two major styles dominate: lyric poetry and realistic fiction. And no figure dominates the whole more than Luís Vaz de Camões (1524-80). This 16th century poet enjoyed little fame or fortune during his lifetime. Only after his death in 1580 was his genius recognised, largely thanks to his epic poem, *Os Lusiadas* (The Lusiads). Ostensibly, the poem relates the historic sea voyage by Vasco da Gama to India in 1497, but it is also a superbly lyrical song of praise to the greatness of the Portuguese spirit, written at a time when Portugal was still one of the most powerful countries in the western world. When it was first published in 1572 it received few plaudits. Over 400 years later, it is considered the national epic, its poet a national hero.

Traditional lyric poetry continued to flourish in the wake of Camões (and still does), but in the 19th century a tide of romanticism swept the Portuguese literary scene. The chief figurehead of the movement was poet, playwright and novelist Almeida Garrett (1799-1854), who devoted much of his life to stimulating political awareness in Portugal through his writings. He initially became politically active in the liberal cause, eventually leading to his exile in 1823 to Europe where he encountered the Romantic literary movement. Garrett's most notable works include two long nationalistic romantic narrative poems, *Camões* and *Dona Branca*, and the novel *Viagens na minha terra* (Travels in My Homeland) in which he mixes fiction and fact in a romantic episode that serves as an allegory of contemporary political events. He was also an important playwright (the best since the 16th century court dramatist, Gil Vicente) and wrote several plays with the aim of establishing a national repertoire.

Towards the end of the 19th century several other notable writers emerged, among them José Maria Eça de Queirós, who introduced realism to Portuguese literature with his powerful 1876 novel, *O Crime do Padre Amaro* (The Sin of Father Amaro). His other outstanding works include the entertaining narratives of 19th century life *Os Maias* (The Maias) and *A Illustre Casa de Ramires* (The Illustrious House of Ramires).

José Maria Ferreira de Castro continued the realism trend in the early 20th century with his novels *A Selva* (The Jungle), based on his experiences in Brazil, and *Os Emigrantes* (The Emigrants). Fernando Pessoa (1888-1935), author of the 1934 *Mensagem* (Message), is posthumously regarded as the most brilliant poet of his generation.

But the Salazar dictatorship that spanned much of this era suppressed both creativity and freedom of expression. Several notable writers suffered during this period, including Maria Velho da Costa, one of the three authors of *Novas Cartas Portuguesas* (The Three Marias: New Portuguese Letters), whose modern feminist interpretation of the 17th century *Letters of a Portuguese Nun* so shocked the Salazar regime that its authors were put on trial.

Today's post-Salazar literary scene is dominated by figures such as António Lobo Antunes and José Saramago. Saramago's international reputation has been based on impressive works, such as *Memorial do Convento* (Memorial of the Convent), which combines an astute realism with poetic fancy. Of the several novels of his available

in English translation, the award-winning *Death of Ricardo Reis* is well worth tracking down. Another author high on the list of Portugal's best contemporary writers is José Cardoso Pires, whose finest novel is *Balada da Praia dos Cães* (Ballad of Dog's Beach), a gripping thriller based on a real political assassination in the Salazar era.

Painting

Among early Lisbon artists, the most outstanding was the 15th century court painter Nuno Gonçalves, whose polyptych of the *Adoration of St Vincent* (now in the Museu Nacional de Arte Antiga, Map 5) is a unique tapestry-style revelation of 15th century Portuguese society.

The Manueline school of the 16th century also produced some uniquely Portuguese paintings, which were remarkable for their delicacy, realism and luminous colours. Although the biggest names in the school – Vasco Fernandes (known as Grão Vasco) and Gaspar Vaz – both worked from Viseu, Lisbon also boasted artists such as Jorge Afonso (painter to Dom Manuel I), Cristóvão de Figueiredo and Gregório Lopes.

The Renaissance era produced more notable sculpture than painting, but the 17th century saw a female artist, Josefa de Óbidos (based at Óbidos, 82km north of Lisbon) make waves with her rich still lifes. In the late 18th century, Domingos António de Sequeira produced wonderful portraits. The 19th century saw an artistic echo of the Naturalist and Romantic movements, expressed particularly strongly in the works of Silva Porto and Marquês de Oliveira, while Sousa Pinto excelled in the early 20th century as a pastel artist.

Naturalism continued to be the dominant trend this century, although Amadeo de Souza Cardoso struck out on his own impressive path of Cubism and Expressionism, and Maria Helena Vieira da Silva became noted as the country's finest abstract painter (although she lived and worked in Paris most of her life). Other eminent artists in the contemporary art world include Almada Negreiros (often called the father of

Azulejos

There's no question which decorative art is Portugal's finest: painted tiles, known as *azulejos* (probably after the Arabic *al zulaycha*, which means 'polished stone'), cover everything from church interiors to train stations, house façades to fountains, all over Portugal. While the Portuguese can't claim to have invented the technique – they learnt about it from the Moors, who picked it up from the Persians – they have certainly used azulejos more imaginatively and consistently than any other nation.

Some of the earliest 16th century tiles to be found in Portugal (for instance, at Sintra's Pálacio Nacional) are of Moorish origin and are geometric in style. But after the Portuguese captured Ceuta in 1415, they began to investigate the art more thoroughly for themselves. The invention of the majolica technique by the Italians in the 16th century, enabling colours to be painted directly onto the wet clay, over a layer of white enamel, gave the Portuguese the impetus they needed, and the azulejo craze began.

The first truly Portuguese tiles started to appear in the 1580s, gracing churches such as Lisbon's Igreja de São Roque. Initially, these azulejos were multicoloured and mostly geometric, reflecting carpet or tapestry patterns, but in the late 17th century a fashion began for huge azulejo panels in churches and cloisters and on houses and public buildings, illustrating everything from cherubs to picnics, saints to bucolic landscapes. Every nobleman had to have his azulejo hunting panel or poetic allegory (as in the Pálacio dos Marquês da Fronteira), every church its life of Christ or the saints. Indeed, such was the growing azulejo craze that the quality of production and colouring eventually suffered and the blue-and-white tiles produced by the Dutch Delft company were able to take over the market.

But with the 18th century arrived the great Portuguese azulejo masters António de Oliveira Bernardes and his son Policarpo, who revived the use of both blue-and-white and polychrome Portuguese tiles, producing brilliant panels that perfectly complemented their surroundings. Rococo themes and flavours also appeared, decorating fountains, stairways and sacristies (such as the Convento da Madre de Deus). Only towards the end of the century did a simpler style and colour scheme emerge, reflecting the neoclassical movement in architecture. By then, the industrial manufacture of azulejos had started to cause another decline in quality, as did the rapid need for huge quantities of azulejos after the 1755 Lisbon earthquake.

New, imaginative uses of azulejos still appeared in the 19th century – among them, the large azulejo figures in restaurants such as the Cervejaria da Trindade in Lisbon. The Art Nouveau and Art Deco movements took the art of azulejo even further into the public domain, with some fantastic façades and interiors for shops and restaurants, kiosks and residential buildings created by Rafael Bordalo Pinheiro, Jorge Colaço and others. Azulejos still have their place in contemporary Portuguese life: Maria Keil and Júlio de Resende are two of the leading artists, responsible for creating some stunning wall mosaics and murals.

For the complete history of this uniquely Portuguese art, visit the Museu Nacional do Azulejo in the Convento da Madre de Deus. See the Things to See & Do chapter for more details. ■

Portugal's modern art movement) and Guilherme Santa-Rita. Their works and many others can best be seen in the Centro de Arte Moderna.

Performing Arts, Cinema & Puppetry

Although a few film directors such as Manual de Oliveira have made an international reputation for themselves (his latest film stars Catherine Deneuve and John Malkovich), Portugal's film industry is basically nonexistent. Even classic theatre is still finding its feet after the repressive Salazar years, though many small theatres both in Lisbon and the provinces are now flourishing, thanks largely to the support of the generous Gulbenkian Foundation.

Far more exciting are the 'fringe' performing arts, such as Lisbon's circus school (see the Chapitô boxed aside in the Entertainment chapter), the puppet shows performed at the Museu da Marioneta and the contemporary dance and theatrical displays performed outdoors during the Lisboa Mexe-me Festival (see Music Festivals under Public Holidays & Special Events in the Facts for the Visitor chapter).

Handicrafts & Indigenous Arts

Although Portugal's finest handicrafts are

mostly produced in the provinces (especially the Algarve, Alentejo and Minho), Lisbon's *artesanato* shops (see the Shopping chapter for details) stock items from practically everywhere. The artesanato shops of nearby Sintra are particularly strong in azulejos (painted tiles), an art form in which its artistans have specialised for generations.

But it's the ceramics which are perhaps the most impressive handicraft. Look out for the style of pottery from Estremoz which features jugs and bowls often encrusted with marble chips; the brightly coloured pots and cockerels from Barcelos in the Minho; predominantly green and geometric wares from Coimbra; huge amphora jars from the Algarve; and the popular cabbage leaf designs originating from nearby Caldas da Rainha.

Hand-embroidered linen is a flourishing handicraft in both mainland Portugal and Madeira, and widely available in Lisbon. Lace and filigree jewellery, often crafted in the northern Minho province, are also fine examples of Portuguese craftwork.

A more rustic kind of handicraft is baskets made from rush, willow, cane or rye straw, for both practical use and decoration. Cleverly crafted wooden toys and miniature boats are other specialities, and tiny straw figures dressed in traditional rural costume are widely made for decoration or souvenirs.

Two of the best occasions to see and track down these regional handicrafts is the annual Feira do Artesanato (Handicraft Fair) held every summer in Estoril and the smaller version in Sintra (see the Excursions chapter for details).

SOCIETY & CONDUCT
Traditional Culture

Thanks to a strong Catholic influence and decades of repression under Salazar, Portugal remains a largely traditional and conservative country. Although Lisbon is far less religious than the northern provinces, it still honours certain religious customs and festivals – none more so than the Festa de Santo António (see Public Holidays & Special Events in the Facts for the Visitor

Saudade

It's been described as a great nostalgia for the glorious past, a fathomless yearning, and a longing for home, but unless you're Portuguese you'll probably never really grasp the uniquely Portuguese emotion of *saudade*. Its musical base is the aching sorrow expressed in fado songs – a melancholic submission to the twists and turns of fate. In Portuguese and Brazilian poetry it's a mystical reverence for nature, a brooding sense of loneliness that became especially popular among 19th and early 20th century poets who cultivated a cult of *saudosismo*. In tangible form it's the return of thousands of émigrés to their home villages every August, drawn not just by family ties but by something much deeper – a longing for all that home and Portugal represents: the heroism of the past, the sorrows of the present and wistful hopes for the future. ■

chapter), which features solemn religious processions as well as music, dancing and all-night revelries.

It doesn't take much of an event, either, to feature some traditional folk dancing: Lisbon often imports leading groups from the provinces to spice up a festival since some of the best groups come from the northern Minho or central Alentejo provinces.

The only modern activity to rival the popularity of the folk dance is football (see Spectator Sport in the Entertainment chapter): when a big match is being played you'll find customers in bars and restaurants glued to TV sets. It even puts a temporary stop to the menfolk's traditional activity of lingering in squares or at outdoor cafés, gossiping and watching the world go by.

Dos & Don'ts

Portuguese politeness is delightful, because it is by no means purely artificial, but flows in a great measure from a natural kindness of feeling.
Lord Carnarvon, 1827

Portuguese everywhere share characteristics of friendliness and an unhurried approach to life: in other words, expect smiles and warmth (especially if you speak some Portuguese) but don't expect punctuality or brisk efficiency. This lassitude can drive business travellers and tourists mad with frustration at times, particularly in banks and post office queues, but, as in Asia, displays of anger are unlikely to get you anywhere.

Travellers may also experience another face-saving technique when Portuguese offer information: if you're asking directions (or even for information in the turismo) you'll rarely hear the simple answer, 'I don't know'. Portuguese people like to appear confident, which means their answers may not always be correct. Get a second judgement if the answer required is important.

Portuguese pride comes into play with language, too: Spain may be their neighbour, but after centuries of rivalry and hostility the last thing they want to hear spoken to them is Spanish. Try English, French, or even German instead. Best of all, of course, is an attempt (however clumsy) at Portuguese. Politeness is so highly valued in this society that simply addressing someone in Portuguese *(senhor* for men and *senhora* for women, or *senhora dona* followed by the Christian name for an elderly or respected woman) will earn you lots of Brownie points.

How you dress can be a sensitive issue even in Lisbon in certain situations. While beachwear (and even nudity on some beaches) is acceptable in coastal resorts, such as nearby Cascais, if you're visiting a church, you'll find that shorts and skimpy tops are definitely frowned upon. And if you're visiting the authorities (eg police or immigration office), you'll stand a far better chance of cooperation if you're well dressed.

You'll probably know if you've upset a Portuguese in any way – they're not shy of showing their emotions, whether it's anger at an obnoxious motorist, sadness at a farewell or simply grumpiness at the rainy weather.

RELIGION

As freedom of religion is part of the constitution there is no state religion in Portugal, but Roman Catholicism is the dominant faith and is adhered to by roughly 95% of the population. Lisbon, however, shows a growing trend (especially among the young) to ignore many religious practices such as going to church. Civil marriage and divorce are accepted more easily here than elsewhere in the country. Other Christian denominations represented include Anglicans, Evangelists, Baptists, Congregationalists, Methodists, Jehovah's Witnesses and Mormons. There are also small communities of Muslims and Jews in the city.

Christianity has been a major force in shaping Portugal's history. The religion first reached Portugal's shores in the 1st century AD, thriving even among pagan invaders.

St Anthony

Although St Vincent is officially Lisbon's patron saint, lisboêtas show far greater affection for St Anthony, despite the fact that he spent most of his life in France and Italy. Born in Lisbon in 1195 and baptised in the cathedral, he first joined the Augustinian Order in the Convent de São Vicente de Fora before switching to the Franciscans (in 1220) in Coimbra. After illness forced him back from an African trip, he divided his time between France and Italy, dying near Padua in 1231.

Revered in Italy as St Anthony of Padua, or simply Il Santo, his humanistic preachings and concern for the poor made him internationally famous. Less than a year after his death he was canonised. Many miracles are attributed to him but he's especially renowned for his help in fixing marriages: many single women still ask for his help in finding husbands and newly wed couples leave gifts of thanks at the Alfama's Igreja de Santo António, built in 1812 allegedly on the site of his birthplace, and containing a museum devoted exclusively to the saint's life.

Elsewhere in the Alfama you'll notice many houses decorated with azulejo panels depicting the miracles he performed. But the best time to feel the fervour of affection for this saint is during the Festa de Santo António on 12 to 13 June. See Public Holidays & Special Events in the Facts for the Visitor chapter for details. ■

After the Muslims invaded in 711, Christianity lost its foothold. During the 12th century, the Christian Reconquista (Reconquest) picked up speed. Christian crusaders en route to the Holy Land from Europe frequently helped the kings of Portugal boot out the Moors – notably at Lisbon in 1147.

Other Christian forces that influenced Portugal's development at this time were the powerful Christian military orders such as the Knights Templar. It was the wealth and vast resources of this organisation that largely financed Portugal's overseas explorations in the 15th century.

But Christianity has also been responsible for some of Portugal's darkest moments, notably the Inquisition, which was started in the 1530s by João III and his strictly Catholic Spanish wife. Thousands of victims, including many Jews, were tortured, imprisoned or burnt at the stake at public sentencing ceremonies known as *autos-da-fé* (in Lisbon, these were held in the Rossio). The terror was only really suppressed in 1820.

Today's Catholic Church is still powerful and highly respected. One of Europe's most important centres of pilgrimage is at Fátima (about 120km north of Lisbon), where up to 100,000 pilgrims congregate for two days every May and October (see Public Holidays & Special Events in the Facts for the Visitor chapter). Lisbon itself shows its religious colours every June when it celebrates with gusto the Festa de Santo António.

LANGUAGE

Like French, Italian, Spanish and Romanian, Portuguese is a Romance language, that is, closely derived from Latin. It is spoken by over 10 million people in Portugal, 130 million in Brazil, and it is also the official language of five African nations (Angola, Mozambique, Guinea-Bissau, Cape Verde and São Tomé e Príncipe). Visitors to Portugal are often struck by the strangeness of the language, which some say sounds like Arabic. However, those who understand French or Spanish are often surprised to see how similar written Portuguese is to the other Romance languages.

The most useful language to speak in Portugal (after Portuguese, of course) is French. English and Spanish follow, and are equally useful. German can be handy too.

Pronunciation

Pronunciation of Portuguese is difficult; like English, vowels and consonants have more than one possible sound depending on position and stress. Moreover, there are nasal vowels and diphthongs in Portuguese with no equivalent in English.

Vowels Single vowels should present relatively few problems.

Nasal Vowels Nasalisation is represented by an 'n' or an 'm' after the vowel, or by a tilde (~) over it. The nasal 'i' exists in English as the 'ing' in 'sing'. For other nasal vowels, try to pronounce a long 'a', 'ah', 'e' or 'eh' while holding your nose, so that you sound as if you have a cold.

Diphthongs Double vowels are relatively straightforward.

Nasal Diphthongs Try the same technique as for nasal vowels. To say *não*, pronounce 'now' through your nose.

ão	nasal 'now' (owng)
ãe	nasal 'day' (eing)
õe	nasal 'boy' (oing)
ui	similar to the 'uing' in 'ensuing'

Consonants The following consonants are specific to Portuguese:

c	hard, as in 'cat', before **a**, **o** or **u** or soft as in 'see', before **e** or **i**
ç	as in 'see'
g	hard, as in 'garden', before **a**, **o** or **u**, soft, as in 'treasure', before **e** or **i** or hard, as in 'get', before **e** or **i**
h	silent at the beginning of a word
j	like the 's' in 'treasure'
lh	like the 'll' sound in 'million'
m	silent in final position (it simply nasalises the previous vowel)

nh like the 'ni' sound in 'onion'

qu like the 'k' in 'key' before **e** or **i** or like the 'q' in 'quad' before **a** or **o**

r at the beginning of a word, or **rr** in the middle of a word, is a harsh, guttural sound similar to the French *rue*, Scottish loch, or German *Bach*; in some areas of Portugal this **r** is not guttural, but strongly rolled. In the middle or at the end of a word the 'r' is a rolled sound stronger than the English 'r'

s like the 's' in 'see' (at the beginning of a word), like the 'z' in 'zeal' (between vowels) or like the 'sh' in 'ship' (before another consonant, or at the end of a word)

ss like the 's' in 'see' (in the middle of a word)

x like the 'sh' in 'ship', the 'z' in 'zeal', or the 'ks' sound in 'taxi'

Word Stress Word stress is important in Portuguese, as it can change the meaning of the word. Many Portuguese words have a written accent and the stress must fall on that syllable when you pronounce the word.

Remember also that Portegese has masculine and feminine forms. These two forms appear separated by a slash, the masculine first (eg *obrigado/a*). When using a verb or adjective in the first person, the masculine and feminine forms vary according to the speaker. Thus, if you are a man you will say *obrigado*, 'thank you', if you are a woman you will say *obrigada*.

Basics

Yes/No.	*Sim/Não.*
Maybe.	*Talvez.*
Please.	*Se faz favor/Por favor.*
Thank you.	*Obrigado/a.*
That's fine/ You're welcome.	*De nada.*
Excuse me.	*Desculpe/Com licença.*
Sorry/Forgive me.	*Desculpe.*

Greetings

Hello.	*Bom dia/Olá/Chao.*
Good morning.	*Bom dia.*
Good evening.	*Boa tarde.*
Goodbye.	*Adeus/Chao.*
See you later.	*Até logo.*

Small Talk

How are you?	*Como está?*
I'm fine, thanks.	*Bem, obrigado/a.*
What is your name?	*Como se chama?*
My name is …	*Chamo-me …*
Where are you from?	*De onde é?*
I'm from …	*Sou de …*
Australia	*Austrália*
Japan	*Japão*
the UK	*os Reino Unido*
the USA	*os Estados Unidos*

Language Difficulties

I understand.	*Percebo/Entendo.*
I don't understand.	*Não percebo/ entendo.*
Do you speak English?	*Fala inglês?*
Could you write it down?	*Pode escrever isso por favor?*

Getting Around

I want to go to …	*Quero ir a …*
What time does the next … leave/ arrive?	*A que horas parte/chega o próximo …?*
boat	*barco*
bus (city)	*autocarro*
bus (intercity)	*camioneta*
metro	*metro*
train	*combóio*
tram	*eléctrico*
How long does it take?	*Quanto tempo leva isso?*
Where is …?	*Onde é …?*
the bus stop	*a paragem de autocarro*
the metro station	*a estação de metro*
the train station	*a estação ferroviária*
the tram stop	*a paragém de eléctrico*

Is this the bus/train to …? — *E este o autocarro/comboio para …?*

I'd like a one-way ticket. — *Queria um bilhete simples/de ida.*

I'd like a return ticket. — *Queria um bilhete de ida e volta.*

1st class — *primeira classe*
2nd class — *segunda classe*
left-luggage office — *o depósito de bagagem*
platform — *cais*
timetable — *horário*

I'd like to hire … — *Queria alugar …*
  a car/motorcycle/bicycle — *um carro/uma motocicleta/bicicleta*
  a tour guide — *uma guia intérprete*

Fill it up (ie the tank, with petrol). — *Encha a depósito, por favor.*

Directions
How do I get to …? — *Como vou para …?*
Is it near/far? — *É perto/longe?*

What … is this? — *O que … é isto/ista?*
  street/road — *rua/estrada*
  suburb — *subúrbia*
  town — *cidade/vila*

Go straight ahead. — *Siga sempre a direito.*
Turn left/right … — *Vire à esquerda/direita …*
  at the traffic lights — *no semáforo/nos sinais de trânsito*
  at the next corner — *na próxima esquina*

north — *norte*
south — *sul*
east — *leste/este*
west — *oeste*

Around Town
Where is …? — *Onde é …?*
  a bank/exchange office — *um banco/câmbio*

the city centre — *o centro da cidade/da baixa*
the … embassy — *a embaixada de …*
the hospital — *o hospital*
my hotel — *do meu hotel*
the market — *do mercado*
the post office — *dos correios*
the public toilet — *sanitários/casa de banho pública*
the telephone centre — *da central de telefones*
the tourist office — *do turismo/posta de turismo/junta de turismo*

What time does it open/close? — *A que horas abre/fecha?*
I'd like to make a telephone call. — *Queria usar o telefone.*
I'd like to change some money/travellers cheques. — *Queria trocar dinheiro/uns cheques de viagem.*

Accommodation
I'm looking for … — *Procuro …*
  a camping ground — *um parque de campismo*
  a youth hostel — *uma pousada de juventude/albergue de juventude*
  a guesthouse — *uma pensão*
  a hotel — *uma hotel*

Do you have any rooms available? — *Tem quartos livres?*
I'd like to book … — *Queria fazer uma reserva para …*
  a bed — *uma cama*
  a cheap room — *um quarto barato*
  a single room — *um quarto individual*
  a double room/with twin beds — *um quarto de casal/duplo*
  a room with a bathroom — *um quarto com casa de banho*
  a dormitory bed — *cama de dormitório*

for one night/two nights	*para uma noite/ duas noites*
How much is it per night/per person?	*Quanto é por noite/ por pessoa?*
Is breakfast included?	*O pequeno almoço está incluído?*
Can I see the room?	*Posso ver o quarto?*
Where is the toilet?	*Onde ficam os lavabos (as casas de banho)?*
It is very dirty/ noisy/expensive.	*É muito sujo/ ruidoso/caro.*

Food

breakfast	*pequeno almoço*
lunch	*almoço*
dinner	*jantar*
dish of the day	*prato do dia*
food stall	*quiosque de comida/ uma bancada*
grocery store	*mercearia*
market	*mercado*
restaurant	*restaurante*
supermarket	*supermercado*
Is service included in the bill?	*O serviço está incluído na conta?*
I'm a vegetarian.	*Sou vegeteriano/a.*

Shopping

How much is it?	*Quanto custa?*
Can I look at it?	*Posso ver?*
It's too expensive.	*É muito caro.*
bookshop	*livraria*
chemist/pharmacy	*farmácia*
clothing store	*boutique/confecções*
laundrette	*lavandaria*
newsagency	*papelaria*
department store	*hipermercado*

Time & Dates

What time is it?	*Que horas são?*
When?	*Quando?*
today	*hoje*
tonight	*hoje à noite*
tomorrow	*amanhã*
yesterday	*ontem*
morning/afternoon	*manhã/tarde*

Monday	*segunda-feira*
Tuesday	*terça-feira*
Wednesday	*quarta-feira*
Thursday	*quinta-feira*
Friday	*sexta-feira*
Saturday	*sábado*
Sunday	*domingo*

Numbers

1	*um/uma*
2	*dois/duas*
3	*três*
4	*quatro*
5	*cinco*
6	*seis*
7	*sete*
8	*oito*
9	*nove*
10	*dez*
100	*cem*
1000	*mil*
one million	*um milhão (de)*

Health

I need a doctor.	*Preciso um médico.*
Where is a hospital/ medical clinic?	*Onde é um hospital/ um centro de saúde?*
I'm diabetic/epileptic/ asthmatic.	*Sou diabético/a; epiléptico/a; asmático/a.*
I'm allergic to anti- biotics/penicillin.	*Sou alérgico/a a antibióticos/ penicilina.*
I'm pregnant.	*Estou grávida.*
antiseptic	*antiséptico*
aspirin	*aspirina*
condoms	*preservativo*
constipation	*constpaçao*
contraceptive	*anticoncepcional*
diarrhoea	*diarreia*
dizzy	*vertiginoso*
medicine	*remédio/ medicamento*
nausea	*náusea*
sanitary napkins	*pensos higiénicos*
tampons	*tampões*

Emergencies

Help!	*Socorro!*
Call a doctor!	*Chame um médico!*
Call the police!	*Chame a polícia!*
Go away!	*Deixe-me em paz!*
I've been robbed.	*Fui roubado/a.*
I've been raped.	*Fui violada/*
	Violarem-me.
I'm lost.	*Estou perdido/a.*

Further Reading

Lonely Planet's *Western Europe phrasebook* is good for the basics. For more detail, the Chambers *Portuguese Travelmate* is a useful hybrid of phrasebook and pocket dictionary. For each English word it gives the usual literal translation and a variety of possible English-language contexts and phrases for this word, and the corresponding Portuguese translations of these idioms.

Facts for the Visitor

WHEN TO GO

Portugal's climate is temperate, and you'll find agreeable weather in Lisbon almost year-round, though the winter months can be damp. The best time to come is probably spring (late April to June) and early autumn (late September and October), though even in high summer the city's proximity to the Atlantic ensures some cool breezes. Party-goers may want their visit to coincide with Lisbon's most important and enjoyable holiday, the Festa de Santo António (Saint Anthony's Festival) on 13 June (see Public Holidays & Special Events later) when the whole city celebrates.

Peak tourist season is roughly mid-June through August or September. *Pensões* and hotels are at their most expensive during this time and are often full: book ahead if you can (especially for middle or top-end accommodation). But outside peak season, crowds thin out, rooms are plentiful and prices may drop by as much as 50% (prices in this book are for peak season).

During August, when many *lisboêtas* go on holiday, the city falls relatively quiet. Some shops, restaurants and theatres close and cultural events are limited. On the plus side, there are some great summer sales, offering up to 50% discounts.

If you're keen to see EXPO '98 (see the Things to See & Do chapter), you'll have to time your visit between 22 May and 30 September 1998.

ORIENTATION

Lisbon nestles against seven hills on the northern side of the Rio Tejo. The hills – Estrela, Santa Catarina, São Pedro de Alcântara, São Jorge, Graça, Senhora do Monte and Penha de França – are fine places for bird's-eye views of this photogenic city. São Jorge is topped by Lisbon's famous *castelo*, and each of the others by a church or a *miradouro* (lookout).

Other places to get your bearings and shoot off film are the Elevador de Santa Justa (Map 9) and Parque Eduardo VII. The city's highest point (at 230.5m) is within the military fortress in the huge Parque Florestal de Monsanto (Map 1), west of the centre.

At the river's edge is the grand Praça do Comércio (Map 11), the traditional gateway to the city. Behind it march the latticework streets of the Baixa ('lower') district, up to the twin squares of Praça da Figueira and Praça Dom Pedro IV – the latter known to virtually everybody as Rossio or Largo Rossio.

Here the city forks along two main arteries. Lisbon's splendid 'main street', Avenida da Liberdade – more a long park than a boulevard – reaches 1.5km north-west from Rossio and the adjacent Praça dos Restauradores to Praça Marquês de Pombal and the huge Parque Eduardo VII (Map 3). The other fork is Avenida Almirante Reis (which becomes Avenida Almirante Gago Coutinho), running arrow-straight north for almost 6km from Praça da Figueira (where it's called Rua da Palma) to the airport.

From the Baixa it's a steep climb west, through a wedge of up-market shopping streets called the Chiado, and over Rua da Misericórdia, into the pastel-coloured mini-canyons of the Bairro Alto, Lisbon's centre for food, traditional entertainment and antique shops. Eastward from the Baixa it's another climb to the Castelo de São Jorge (Map 12) and the ancient, maze-like Alfama district around it.

River ferries depart from Praça do Comércio and Cais do Sodré to the west. Lisbon's four long-haul train stations are Cais do Sodré (for Cascais and the Estoril coast); Santa Apolónia, 1.5km east of Praça do Comércio (for northern Portugal and all international links); Rossio (for Sintra and Estremadura); and Barreiro (for southern Portugal), reached by ferry across the Tejo.

The city's main long-distance bus terminal (Map 3) is on Avenida Casal Ribeiro, near Picoas and Saldanha metro stations. A cluster of other bus companies runs from Rua dos Bacalhoeiros, a few blocks east of Praça do Comércio.

In addition to the metro and a network of city bus lines, ageing trams clank picturesquely around the hills, and spiffy new ones run 6km west from Praça da Figueira, past the port district of Alcântara, to the waterfront suburb of Belém.

With the exception of Belém, Lisbon's main attractions are all within walking distance of one another, and public transport (when you need it at all) works well. Streets are generally well marked and buildings clearly numbered. Note, however, that the names of many smaller streets, and some big ones, change every few blocks.

Lisbon is connected across the Tejo to the Costa da Caparica and Setúbal Peninsula by the immense Ponte 25 de Abril, Europe's longest suspension bridge. Were you only permitted to stop and look from its 70m-high deck, the bridge would provide the finest panoramic view of the city from anywhere except the *Cristo Rei* monument, on the other side of the Tejo (see Cacilhas in the Excursions chapter).

Map References

The exact location of most museums, hotels, restaurants etc mentioned in this guide is indicated on one of the colour maps, 1 to 15, found at the back of the book. Each address includes the reference number of the relevant map, usually after any translation and right before the telephone number.

MAPS

The main *turismo* (Map 8; tourist office) at Praça dos Restauradores hands out a (free) microscopic city map, though most Portuguese tourist offices abroad have a far better 1:15,000 *Lisboa* map. Decent maps for sale in bookshops and kiosks include the glossy 1:16,000 Rand McNally *City Flash* map (1000$00), with a boxed aside showing bus routes; the Fota-Vista 1:13,400 *Lisboa* map showing major roads and attractions; and the

detailed Kümmerly & Frey 1:15,000 *Lisboa* map (990$00), which has bus and metro routes marked. The oblique-perspective *Lisbon City Map – Vista Aérea Geral* (1100$00), is great for spotting landmarks. A good place to track down these maps is Emílio Braga Papelarias (Map 12) at Rua da Madalena 42.

For map junkies and long-term residents there's the 230-page *Guia Urbano* city atlas, which noses into every corner of the city at about 1:5300; it's 1800$00 from bookshops or the turismo at Restauradores. Also available from the turismo is the glossy *Mapas Turísticos* booklet for 1200$00, which packs in adequate maps on Lisbon, Oeiras, Cascais and Sintra as well as lists of accommodation, restaurants, bars and museums.

Map Sources

A variety of road maps and army and civilian topographic maps is available from mail-order map shops abroad. Probably the widest range of Portugal maps is available at GeoCenter ILH (☎ 0711-788 93 40; fax 0711-788 93 54; geocenterilh@t-online.de), Schockenriedstrasse 44, D-70565 Stuttgart, Germany. Other reliable mail-order firms are:

Stanfords (☎ 0171-836 1321),12-14 Long Acre, Covent Garden, London WC2E 9LP, UK
Michael Chessler Books (toll-free ☎ 800-654-8502, ☎ 303-670-0093), PO Box 2436, Evergreen, CO 80439, USA
The Travel Bookshop (☎ 02-9241 3554; fax 02-9241 3159), 6 Bridge St, Sydney 2000, NSW, Australia
Omni Resources (☎ 910-227-8300; fax 910-227-3748; complete catalogue on the World Wide Web at www.omnimap.com), 1004 S Mebane St, PO Box 2096, Burlington, NC 27216-2096, USA

TOURIST OFFICES
Local Tourist Offices

The state's umbrella organisation for tourism is ICEP (Investimentos, Comércio e Turismo de Portugal), with its administrative headquarters (☎ 793 01 03; fax 794 08 26; www.portugal.org) at Avenida 5 de Outubro 101. It runs a large turismo in the Palácio Foz on

Praça dos Restauradores (a block north of Rossio train station). The turismo (Map 8; ☎ 01-346 63 07) is open daily from 9 am to 8 pm; information supplied from this office is not 100% reliable, so get a second opinion if your query involves a long trip across town. The staff can advise on accommodation and will call about availability, but they won't make bookings.

Useful free publications worth picking up (you may have to ask for them) include a Lisbon edition of the *TIPS* booklet, packed with all kinds of information; *Lisboa em ...* (month of publication) which gives a rundown of bars, clubs, shops and events; the monthly *What's On in Lisbon and the Estoril Coast*; and the town hall's monthly cultural diary, *Agenda Lisboa Cultural*. Also on sale here is the slightly outdated but still useful *Real Lisbon* guide (1850$00).

There is another turismo (☎ 849 43 23, ☎ 849 36 89) at the airport; it's open daily from 6 am to 2 am. Turismo kiosks, open during summer only, can also be found at the Castelo de São Jorge and at the southern end of Rua Augusta in the Baixa.

Lisboa Card Lisbon's municipal tourism department has a switched-on office (Map 9; ☎ 343 36 72) with polite staff at Rua Jardim do Regedor 50, across Praça dos Restauradores from the turismo; it's open daily from 9 am to 6 pm. Here you can buy a Lisboa Card, which provides free travel on nearly all city transport, including the metro; free admission to most of the city's museums and monuments; and discounts of 15 to 50% at more museums, on bus and tram tours and river cruises. There are 24, 48 and 72-hour versions for 1500$00, 2500$00 or 3250$00 respectively (600$00, 900$00 or 1250$00 for children from five to 11 years old) – excellent value if you plan on cramming lots of sights into a short stay.

The Lisboa Card is also available at several other outlets, including the Mosteiro dos Jerónimos and the Museu Nacional dos Coches in Belém (Map 13) and the central post office (Map 11) on Praça do Comércio.

Tourist Offices Abroad

ICEP-affiliated trade-and-tourism offices abroad include the following:

Brazil
(☎ 011-288 87 44; fax 011-288 28 77), Avenida Paulista 2001, Suite 901, 01311-300 São Paulo

Canada
(☎ 416-921 7376; fax 416-921 1353), 60 Bloor St West, Suite 1005, Toronto, Ontario M4W 3B8
(☎ 514-282 1264; fax 514-499 1450), 500 Sherbrooke St West, Suite 940, Montreal, Quebec H3A 3C6

France
(☎ 01 47 42 55 57; fax 01 42 66 06 89), 7 Rue Scribe, 75009 Paris

Germany
(☎ 069-23 40 94; fax 069-23 14 33), Schäfergasse 17, 60313 Frankfurt-am-Main

Japan
(☎ 03-54 74 44 00; fax 03-34 70 71 64), Regency Shinsaka, Suite 201, Akasaka, 8-5-8 Minato-ku, Tokyo 107

Netherlands
(☎ 070-326 4371; fax 070-328 0025), Paul Gabriëlstraat 70, 2596 VG, The Hague

South Africa
(☎ 011-484 3487; fax 011-484 5416), 4th floor, Sunnyside Ridge, Sunnyside Drive, PO Box 2473 Houghton, 2041 Johannesburg

Spain
(☎ 01-522 9354; fax 01-522 2382), Gran Via 27, 1st floor, 28013 Madrid

UK
(☎ 0171-494 1441; fax 0171-494 1868), 22-25a Sackville St, London W1X 1DE

USA
(☎ 212-354-4403 or toll-free in the USA ☎ 800-PORTUGAL; fax 212-764-6137), 590 Fifth Ave, 4th floor, New York, NY 10036-4704
(☎ 202-331-8222; fax 212-331-8236), 1900 L St, Suite 310, Washington, DC 20036

DOCUMENTS
Passport

Check your passport's date of expiry – you may have trouble getting a visa if it expires during or soon after your proposed visit. Most passport offices and embassies abroad can provide you with a new passport, or insert new pages in your present one, fairly quickly.

Police in Portugal are empowered to check your ID papers at any time: always carry your passport with you.

Visas

Nationals of all EU countries, as well as of Ireland, USA, Canada, Australia, New Zealand and Israel, can stay in Portugal for up to three months in any half year without a visa. Some others, including nationals of South Africa and Singapore, need a visa from a Portugal consular office, and must produce evidence of financial responsibility, eg a fixed sum of money plus an additional amount per day of their stay (the amounts vary depending on nationality), possible evidence of travel insurance, unless they are the spouses or children of EU citizens.

The general requirements for entry to Portugal also apply to the other signatories of the 1990 Schengen Convention on the abolition of mutual border controls – at least those who have put the agreement into effect (Belgium, France, Germany, Italy, Luxembourg, Netherlands and Spain). In fact, you can apply for visas for more than one of these countries on the same form, though a visa for one does not automatically grant you entry to the others.

Visa Extensions

To extend a visa after arriving in Lisbon, you'll need to contact the Foreigners' Registration Service, called Serviço de Estrangeiros e Fronteiras (Map 3; ☎ 346 61 41, ☎ 352 31 12), at Avenida António Augusto de Aguiar 20. It's open on weekdays only, from 9 am to 3 pm. As entry regulations are already liberal, you'll need convincing proof of employment or financial independence, or a pretty good story, if you're asking to stay longer.

In theory a simpler option might be to leave Portugal, then return and get a new permit, though at present the only entry points where you'll find anybody to give you one are at Lisbon, Porto and Faro airport arrivals!

Photocopies

It's wise to carry photocopies of the data pages of your passport and visa to ease the paperwork headaches should they be lost or stolen. Other copies you might want to carry are of your credit card and travellers cheque numbers, airline tickets, travel insurance policy and birth certificate.

Keep the copies in a separate place from the originals. To be doubly secure, leave copies with someone at home too.

Travel Insurance

However you're travelling, it's worth taking out travel insurance to cover theft, loss and medical problems. EU residents are covered only for *emergency* medical treatment throughout the EU on presentation of an E111 certificate, though charges are likely for medications, dental work and secondary examinations including x-rays and laboratory tests. Ask about the E111 at your national health service or travel agent at least a few weeks before you go. In some countries you can get an E111 by post.

Even with an E111 or private medical insurance you'll usually find in Portugal that immediate cash payment is expected. Make sure you keep all documentation, in case you have to make a claim later. Check that the policy covers ambulances or an emergency flight home.

A wide variety of travel insurance policies is available: your travel agent will have recommendations. The international policies handled by STA Travel and other youth/student travel agencies are good value. Check the small print: some policies specifically exclude 'dangerous activities' such as scuba diving, motorcycling or even trekking. If these are on your agenda, get another policy or ask about an amendment (for an extra premium) that includes them.

Driving Licence & Permits

Nationals of EU countries need only their home driving licences to be allowed to drive – and hire – a car in Portugal. Others should consider getting an International Driving Permit as well, through an automobile licensing department in their home country. If you're stopped by the Portuguese police, you probably won't be allowed to go back to your hotel to fetch your licence. Carry it with you whenever you're driving. If you hire a

Top: Lisbon & the Rio Tejo from Castelo São Jorge, with the Cristo Rei monument in the background.
Bottom Left: Elevador de Santa Justa
Bottom Right: Casa dos Bicos in the Alfama district

Top Left: Vintage tram in the Baixa district
Top Middle: A Brasileira café, Rua Garrett
Top Right: Postboxes
Bottom: Torre de Belém

car, the hiring firm will furnish you with registration and insurance documentation, plus a rental contract.

Useful Cards

The *pousadas de juventude* (youth hostels) in and around Lisbon are part of the Hostelling International (HI) network, and an HI card from your hostelling association at home entitles you to the standard cheap rates (see the Hostels sections in the Places to Stay chapter).

Numerous discounts – eg for domestic and international transport, museum admission, accommodation and in some cases restaurant meals – are available to full-time students and to those who are under 26 years of age or 60 and over. Refer to Money in this chapter for more information.

The Camping Card International (formerly known as a Camping Carnet) serves as an ID card which can be presented instead of your passport when you register at camping grounds affiliated with the Fédération Internationale de Camping et de Caravanning (FICC). See the Camping Card International boxed aside in the Places to Stay chapter for details.

EMBASSIES
Portuguese Embassies

Portuguese embassies abroad include the following. Where they are known, we list consular offices rather than ambassadorial headquarters:

Argentina
(☎ 01-312 3524), Avenida Cordobe 315, 1023 Buenos Aires
Australia
(☎ 02-6290 1733; fax 02-6290 1957), 23 Culgoa Circuit, O'Malley, ACT 2606
Brazil
(☎ 061-321 3434), Avenida das Nações, lote 2-CP, 70402 Brasilia
Canada
(☎ 613-729 0883; fax 613-729 4236), 645 Island Park Dve, Ottawa, Ontario K1Y OB8 – plus consulates in other cities
France
(☎ 01 47 27 35 29; fax 01 44 05 94 02), 3 Rue de Noisiel, 75116 Paris

Germany
(☎ 0228-36 30 11; fax 0228-35 28 64), Ubierstrasse 78, 5300 Bonn 2
Ireland
(☎ 01-289 4416; fax 01-289 2849), Knock Sinna House, Knock Sinna, Fox Rock, Dublin 18
Israel
(☎ 03-695 6361; fax 03-695 6366), Beit Asia, 4 Veizman St, 64239 Tel Aviv
Japan
(☎ 03-34 00 79 07; fax 03-34 00 79 09), Olympia Annex, apt 304, 31-21 Jingumae, 6-chome, Shibuya-ku, Tokyo
Netherlands
(☎ 070-363 0217; fax 070-361 5589), Bazarstraat 21, 2518 AG, The Hague
New Zealand
(☎ 09-309 1454; fax 09-308 9061), 85 Forte St, Remuera, Auckland 5
South Africa
(☎ 012-341 2340; fax 012-443071), 599 Leyds Street, Muckleneuk, 0002 Pretoria
Spain
(☎ 91-261 7808; fax 91-411 0172), Calle del Pinar 1, 28046 Madrid
UK
(☎ 0171-581 3598, premium-rate recorded message ☎ 0891-600202; fax 0171-581 3085), 62 Brompton Rd, London SW3 1BJ
USA
(☎ 202-328 8610; fax 202-462-3726), 2125 Kalorama Rd NW, Washington, DC 20008 – plus numerous consulates in other cities.

Foreign Embassies in Lisbon

Foreign embassies and consulates in Lisbon include the following:

Argentina
embassy: (Map 3; ☎ 797 73 11), Avenida João, Crisóstomo 8
consulate: (Map 3; ☎ 353 17 57), Rua dos Açores 59
Austria
embassy: (Map 5; ☎ 387 41 61), Rua das Amoreiras 70, Rato
Belgium
embassy: (Map 3; ☎ 354 92 63), Praça Marquês de Pombal 14
Brazil
embassy: (Map 2; ☎ 726 77 77), Estrada das Laranjeiras 144
consulate: (Map 10; ☎ 347 35 65), Praça Luís de Camões 22
Canada
embassy: (Map 6; ☎ 347 48 92), Edifício MCB, Avenida da Liberdade 144

Denmark
  embassy: (Map 6; ☎ 54 50 99), Rua Castilho 14-C
Finland
  embassy: (Map 5; ☎ 60 75 51), Rua Miguel Lupi 12
  consulate: (Map 10; ☎ 347 35 01), Cais do Sodré 8
France
  embassy: Rua Santos-o-Velho 5 (☎ 60 81 21)
  consulate: (Map 5; ☎ 395 60 56), Calçada Marquês de Abrantes
Germany
  embassy: (Map 6; ☎ 352 39 61), Campo dos Mártires da Pátria 38
Greece
  embassy: (☎ 301 69 91), Rua Alto do Duque 13 (Belém)
Ireland
  embassy: (Map 5; ☎ 396 15 69), Rua da Imprensa à Estrela 1
Israel
  embassy: (Map 3; ☎ 357 02 51), Rua António Enes 16
Italy
  embassy & consulate: (Map 6; embassy ☎ 354 61 44, consulate ☎ 352 08 62), Largo Conde de Pombeiro 6
Japan
  embassy: (Map 6; ☎ 352 34 85), Rua Mouzinho da Silveira 11
Luxembourg
  embassy: (Map 5; ☎ 396 27 81), Rua das Janelas Verdes 43
Netherlands
  embassy: (Map 5; ☎ 396 11 63), Rua do Sacramento à Lapa 6
Norway
  embassy: (Map 13; ☎ 301 53 44), Avenida Dom Vasco da Gama 1, Belém
South Africa
  embassy: (Map 3; ☎ 353 50 41), Avenida Luís Bívar 10
Spain
  embassy & consulate: (Map 6; embassy ☎ 347 23 81, consulate ☎ 342 26 54), Rua do Salitre 1
Sweden
  embassy: (Map 5; ☎ 395 52 24), Rua Miguel Lupi 12
Switzerland
  embassy: (Map 5; ☎ 397 31 21), Travessa do Patrocínio 1
Turkey
  embassy: (Map 1; ☎ 301 42 75), Avenida das Descobertas 22 (Belém)
UK
  embassy: (Map 5; ☎ 396 11 91), Rua de São Domingos à Lapa 37

  consulate: (Map 5; ☎ 395 40 82), Rua da Estrela 4
USA
  embassy & consulate: (Map 1; embassy ☎ 726 66 00, consulate ☎ 726 55 62), Avenida das Forças Armadas

There are no embassies for Australia or New Zealand in Lisbon, but both countries have honorary consuls. Australian citizens can call ☎ 353 07 50 on weekdays between 1 and 2 pm; the nearest Australian embassy is in Madrid. New Zealand citizens should call ☎ 357 41 34 during business hours; the nearest New Zealand embassy is in Rome.

CUSTOMS

There's no limit on the amount of foreign currency you can bring into Portugal. Customs regulations say those visitors who need a visa must bring in a minimum of 10,000$00 plus 2000$00 per day of their stay, but this isn't stringently enforced. If you leave with more than 100,000$00 in *escudos* or 500,000$00 in foreign currency you may have to prove that you brought in at least this much.

Travellers over 17 years of age from non-EU countries can bring in, duty-free, 200 cigarettes (or 100 cigarillos or 50 cigars or 250g of tobacco); 1L of alcohol which is over 22% alcohol by volume, or 2L of wine or beer. EU citizens can stagger in with considerably more, including up to 800 cigarettes (400 cigarillos, 200 cigars or 1kg of tobacco) and either 10L of spirits, 20L of fortified wine, 60L of sparkling wine or a mind-boggling 90L of still wine or 110L of beer!

You can bring in enough coffee, tea etc for personal use. You cannot bring fresh meat into the country.

MONEY
Cash

Although major credit cards are widely accepted, you'll still need cash to pay for goods in small shops, cafés and restaurants, most pensões and small hotels, and at open-air markets.

It's a good idea to tuck away in your bags

a stash of about US$50 for emergency use in case your credit cards or travellers cheques are stolen.

Travellers Cheques & Eurocheques

Although travellers cheques are easily exchanged, and at rates about 1% better than for cash, they are very poor value because additional fees are so high. A bank may charge 2000$00 or more (in addition to government taxes of about 140$00) for each cheque or transaction of any size. Far better deals are available at the private exchange bureaux which charge a flat fee of about 500$00 for changing cash and 950$00 for travellers cheques.

American Express travellers cheques can be exchanged commission-free at Top Tours, Portugal's American Express representative (see Travel Agents in the Getting There & Away chapter). You can also use your Amex card here for cash advances at back-home rates.

Eurocheques draw low fees, around 500$00 to 800$00 per transaction, though for these and the accompanying card you also pay an annual subscription fee of about US$15.

ATMs

Cards such as Amex, Visa and Access/MasterCard are the most convenient way to get money thanks to the 24-hour automatic-teller machines (ATMs), widely known as 'Multibanco' (Maps 9 & 11), which are found everywhere in Lisbon (and most other towns). All you need to get a cash advance in escudos is your personal identification number (PIN). There is a handling charge of about 1.5% per transaction, and exchange rates are reasonable.

There are also several 24-hour exchange machines at which you can exchange foreign banknotes (for higher commissions). The most convenient are those opposite Rossio train station at Rua 1 de Dezembro 118-A, and near Praça do Comércio at Rua Augusta 24. There are also others at the airport and at Santa Apolónia station.

Credit Cards

The major international cards are accepted at many of the larger shops, upper-end hotels and a small but increasing number of pensões and restaurants. Especially popular is Visa.

To report lost or stolen cards call the following relevant office and/or the emergency number in your home country.

American Express	☎ 315 5371
Diners' Club	the closest number is in Madrid, ☎ 341-5474 000
MasterCard	☎ 0501 11272
Visa	☎ 0501 1107

International Transfers

To transfer money to Lisbon simply request your home bank to send the funds by Swift telegraphic transfer, giving the full address of the Lisbon bank (preferably a head office) and requesting the money be paid to you 'on application and identification' (ie on presentation of your passport). Although special express transfers should be possible within a couple of days, the catch is that your home bank will probably only follow your written instructions (not fax), which means a postal delay of several more days. The only way to avoid this is by previously authorising someone at home to access your account.

Most UK banks charge around £15 to £20 for the service and there may be similar charges at the Portuguese end. To open an account in a Portuguese bank requires an initial deposit of around 50,000$00.

Currency

The unit of Portuguese currency is the escudo, further divided into 100 centavos. Prices are usually denoted with a $ sign between escudos and centavos, eg 25 escudos 50 centavos is written 25$50.

Portuguese notes currently in circulation are 10,000$00, 5000$00, 2000$00, 1000$00 and 500$00. There are 200$00, 100$00, 50$00, 20$00, 10$00, 5$00, 2$50 and 1$00 coins, though coins smaller than 5$00 are rarely used. Nowadays market prices tend to be rounded to the nearest 10$00.

Portuguese frequently refer to 1000$00 as *um conto*.

Currency Exchange

Following are approximate cash exchange rates in effect at the time of going to press.

Australia	A$1	=	119$40
Canada	C$1	=	127$70
France	1FF	=	30$45
Germany	DM1	=	101$98
Ireland	I£	=	265$50
Japan	Y100	=	139$15
Spain	100 ptas	=	120$90
United Kingdom	UK£1	=	299$30
United States	US$1	=	180$95

Changing Money

General banking hours are roughly 8.30 am to 3 pm on weekdays only, although the Banco Borges e Irmão (Map 8; ☎ 342 10 68) at Avenida da Liberdade 9-A exchanges money until 7.30 pm on weekdays and alternate Saturdays.

Banks and private exchange bureaux accept most foreign currencies, but they're free to set their own fees and exchange rates. Thus an exchange bureau's low commission may be more than offset by an unfavourable exchange rate. If you need to watch every penny, you'll have to shop around, calculator in hand.

Among French banks in Lisbon are the Banque Nationale de Paris (Map 8; ☎ 343 08 04) at Avenida Liberdade 16; Crédit Lyonnais (Map 11; ☎ 347 58 00) at Rua da Conceição 92 in the Baixa; and Société Générale (☎ 383 34 73) at Avenida Engenheiro Duarte Pacheco. The British Barclays Bank is well represented, with its headquarters (☎ 791 11 00) at Avenida da República 50 and many other branches including at Rua Augusta 119 (☎ 347 86 46).

The most convenient private exchange bureaux are Gabriel de Carvalho (Map 9) at Rossio 41, which is open Monday to Saturday from 9 am to 10 pm and Sunday from 1 to 10 pm; and Cota Câmbios at Rua Áurea 283 (Map 9; also known as Rua do Ouro), open weekdays from 9 am to 8 pm and Saturday from 9 am to 6 pm; this bureau even buys foreign coins from 3 to 5 pm on weekdays.

Costs

Although costs are beginning to rise as Lisbon falls into fiscal step with the EU, this is still one of the cheapest cities in Europe. On a rock-bottom budget – using hostels or camping grounds, and mostly self-catering – you could squeeze by on about 3500$00 (US$19) a day per person in the high season. With bottom-end accommodation (especially if you're with someone else as double rooms are cheaper per person than singles) and the occasional inexpensive restaurant meal, daily costs would hover around 4700$00 (US$26). Timing your trip to take advantage of off-season discounts, you could eat and sleep in relative style for about 12,000$00 (US$65) for two.

Tipping & Bargaining

If you're not unhappy with the service, a reasonable restaurant tip is about 10%. For a snack at a *cervejaria*, *pastelaria* or café, a bit of loose change is enough. Taxi drivers appreciate about 10% of the fare, and petrol station attendants 50$00 or so.

Good-humoured bargaining is acceptable in markets but you'll find the Portuguese tough opponents! Off season, you can sometimes even bargain down the price of accommodation.

Discounts

Numerous discounts are available to full-time students and to travellers under 26 years of age or over 60.

The international student identity card (ISIC) is specifically aimed at travel-related costs (reductions on air fares, cheap or free admission to museums etc). Good for a year, it's available from youth-oriented travel agencies such as Campus Travel or STA Travel, from the Portuguese youth-travel agencies Tagus Travel (Map 3) and Jumbo Expresso (Map 1), and directly from ISIC Mail Order, Bleaklow House, Howard Town Mills, Mill St, Glossop SK13 8PT, UK.

Various 'under-26' and other youth-card schemes (including Euro<26, Go 25 and Portugal's own Cartão Jovem) provide more general discounts, such as in theatres and shops, but fewer specific travel benefits. Also valid for a year, these are available for about UK£6 from most youth-travel agencies, or directly from Under 26 Mail Order, 52 Grosvenor Gardens, London SW1W 0AG, UK. More information about the ISIC and Go 25, and application forms, can be sourced at www.ciee.org/idcards.htm.

Only residents of Portugal are eligible to buy the widely used Portuguese under-26 card, Cartão Jovem eg at Movijovem (Map 3), the Portugal youth hostel booking centre in Lisbon, for 1100$00.

Many of the same kinds of discounts are available in Portugal to travellers over 60 too. The Rail Europ Senior (RES) Card gives you about 30% discount for international journeys or internal journeys connecting with an international service, such as Eurostar or Trenhotel. In order to be eligible for an RES Card you must have a local senior citizens' railcard; availability of these to visitors varies between participating countries. In Britain, visitors can purchase a Senior Card (£16) and an RES Card (£5) from accredited British Rail International travel agencies and from main-line stations.

Children under the age of eight are entitled to a discount of 50% in hotels, if they share their parents' room. Children from four to 12 years old get 50% off on Portuguese Railways, and those under four travel for free.

Taxes & Refunds

A 17% sales tax, called IVA (Imposto sobre Valor Acrescentado, 'value added tax'), is levied on hotel and other accommodation, restaurant, car rental and some other bills. If you are a tourist who resides outside the EU, you can claim an IVA refund on goods from shops that are members of the Europe Tax-Free Shopping Portugal scheme.

At the time of research the minimum purchase eligible for a refund was 11,700$00 in any one shop. The shop assistant fills in a cheque for the amount of the refund (minus an administration fee). When you leave Portugal you present the goods, the cheque and your passport at the Tax-Free Shopping refund counter at customs for cash or a postal-note or credit-card refund.

At present this service is available only at Lisbon (and Porto and Faro) airports and Lisbon harbour. If you leave overland, talk to customs at your final EU border point. Further information, including a list of participating shops, is available from Europe Tax-Free Shopping Portugal (☎ 840 88 13) in the international departures concourse of Lisbon airport, open from 7 am to 1.30 am daily.

Items *not* covered by this refund scheme include food, books, prescription lenses, hotel costs and car rental. Don't confuse this with the totally unrelated Duty-Free Shoppers shops at these airports!

DOING BUSINESS

Portugal is one of Europe's most attractive investment opportunities thanks to its political and social stability, a business-friendly government offering EU-backed incentives and generous tax rates (the second lowest in the EU), and a cost-competitive and productive labour force. Inward foreign direct investment from 1990 to 1995 totalled over US$21 billion. The EU (notably France, Spain, Germany and the UK) represented the main source, with the manufacturing industry attracting over 60% of the investment.

Useful Contacts Abroad

First contact your nearest branch of ICEP, the state's umbrella organisation for investment, commerce and tourism (see Tourist Offices earlier in this chapter for addresses; or check the ICEP Web site at www.portugal.org). ICEP can provide detailed information about the Portuguese economy, its laws and regulations, investment areas and incentive schemes and identify suppliers of specific goods and services in Portugal. On request, it can also select contacts and prepare meetings with the Portuguese business community or financial institutions and coordinate negotiations with officials for major investment projects.

Other useful Portuguese Chambers of Commerce or trade commissions include the following:

Chambre de Commerce Franco-Portugaise
(☎ 01 42 22 54 59; fax 01 42 22 87 60), 219 Boulevard Saint-Germain, 75007 Paris
Camara Hispano-Portuguesa de Comercio e Industria en Espana
(☎ 1 442 2300; fax 1 442 2290), Zurbana 67-5B, 28010 Madrid
Portugal-US Chamber of Commerce Inc
(☎ 212-354 4627; fax 212-575 4737), 590 Fifth Ave, 3rd floor, New York
Portuguese UK Chamber of Commerce
(☎ 0171-494 1844; fax 0171-494 1822; marina@pukc.demon.co.uk); the foremost organisation promoting two-way trade and investment between the UK and Portugal, and offering a wide range of support services
UK Department of Trade & Industry Portugal Desk
(☎ 0171-215 4910; fax 0171-215 4711)

Useful Contacts in Lisbon

The trade office of your embassy can provide tips and contacts. Other useful organisations include:

Câmara do Comércio e Indústria Portuguesa (Portuguese Chamber of Commerce & Industry, Map 9; ☎ 342 71 79; fax 342 43 04; port.chamber. ci@mail.telepac.pt), Palácio do Comércio, Rua Portas de Santo Antão 89
Câmara de Comércio Luso-Britanica (British-Portuguese Chamber of Commerce; ☎ 396 1586 contact Mady Kemp), Rua da Estrela 8
Câmara de Comércio Americano (American Chamber of Commerce, ☎ 572 561; fax 357 2508), Rua D Estefania 155

Office Rental

The Lisboa Business Centre (Map 3; ☎ 357 56 57; fax 357 56 58),. at Rua Alexandre Herculano 5, has 40 fully furnished offices for rent from 60,000$00 a month. Secretarial services such as typing (2500$00 per hour), translation (2500$00 per page) and mail, fax and reception facilities are available for 20,000$00 per month. Meeting rooms for up to 16 people can be rented for 2000$00 per hour or 50,000$00 per day. English, French, Spanish and some Italian are spoken by the staff. The Centre is open 24 hours, Monday to Friday, and closed Saturday afternoon and all day Sunday.

The posh Regus business centre (☎ 340 45 00; fax 340 45 75) is part of an international chain (check its Web site at www.regus.com) and has two bases in Lisbon: Lisbon Liberdade at Avenida da Liberdade 114 (Map 6) and Lisbon Torres de Lisboa at Rua Tomâs da Fonseca (near Benfica). Regus offers fully serviced office accommodation for any period of time as well as a work-station with computer for rent by the hour (5000$00). Furnished offices cost around 150,000$00 a month which includes the use of a conference room for four hours a month. Word processing, PA duties and secretarial administration cost 5150$00 per hour. There are conference rooms (with full audiovisual facilities) for up to 12 people. For companies who simply need a prestigious address, Regus can also offer its 'Link' service, providing a dedicated phone number, with calls answered in your company name or forwarded as required.

Computer Rental & Other Services

If you just want to use a PC or Mac Apple computer for an hour or so, Fercopi (Map 11; ☎ 343 14 68; fax 346 50 13), at Rua da Vitória 91, is the place to go (or its branch, ☎ 388 21 31, at Largo do Rato, 13-A). A minimum of 10 minutes on the computer costs 200$00, an hour, 1200$00. The shop also has excellent photocopying, fax and laser copying facilities. There's a 10% discount for students (for purchases over 500$00). Opening hours are Monday to Friday, 9 am to 7 pm (the Largo do Rato branch is open Saturdays, too, from 9 am to 1 pm).

Another place you can use computers (including Internet and email facilities) and get photocopying done at discount prices is the Espaço Ágora student complex (Map 10) near Cais do Sodré (see Campuses in this chapter). Both the self-service computer room (☎ 342 91 17) and the photocopy shop (☎ 347 03 64) here are open daily, 24 hours, in term-time. During July and August, the computer room is open daily, usually from 10 am to midnight while the photocopy shop opens Monday to Friday, 9 am to 6 pm.

Business Protocol

Although Portugal's rapid economic growth over the last decade has produced a new breed of enthusiastic entrepreneurial managers, who are just as competitive and aggressive as their counterparts in other EU countries, many traditional ways of doing business are still valued. Trust, loyalty and personal contacts are regarded as the most crucial elements in a business relationship. It's who you know that matters, so time and care are needed to select the right local associate with the appropriate contacts with whom you can maintain regular working exchanges. Be aware, too, that bargaining is part of the culture: allow room to be flexible when trying to clinch a deal so that both parties feel they have won. Credit terms are also very important: most Portuguese business people expect to work on 90-day terms.

POST & COMMUNICATIONS
Post

The most convenient post office (☎ 347 11 22) around Rossio is in the pink building opposite the turismo on Praça dos Restauradores. It's open weekdays from 8 am to 10 pm and on weekends and holidays from 9 am to 6 pm.

The not-so-central central post office on Praça do Comércio, is open weekdays only from 8.30 am to 6.30 pm. There is also a 24-hour post office at the airport.

Sending Mail *Correio normal* (posted in red letter boxes) refers to ordinary post, including air mail, while *correio azul* ('blue mail', in the blue letter boxes) refers to priority or express post. Ordinary postcards and letters up to 20g cost 140$00 to destinations outside Europe, 100$00 to non-EU European destinations and 80$00 to EU destinations (except within Portugal: 49$00). International correio azul costs a minimum of 350$00 for a 20g letter.

Stamps are sold not only at post offices but at numerous kiosks and shops with a red *Correios – selos* sign, as well as from coin-operated vending machines. 'By airmail' is *por avião* in Portuguese and 'by surface mail' is *via superfície*. For delivery to the USA or Australia, allow eight to 10 days; delivery times for Europe are four to six days.

A 4 to 5kg parcel sent surface mail to the UK would cost 4650$00 (about US$30). 'Economy air' (or surface airlift, SAL) costs about a third less than ordinary air mail, but usually arrives a week or so later. Printed matter is cheapest (and simplest) to send in batches of under 2kg.

Receiving Mail Lisbon's *posta restante* service is at the central post office (Map 11) on Praça do Comércio (officially known as Terreiro do Paço). Letters should be addressed with the family name first, capitalised and underlined, c/o Posta Restante, Central Correios, Terreiro do Paço, 1100 Lisboa. To collect poste restante mail (usually from counter 13 or 14), you must show your passport. A charge of 60$00 is levied for each item of mail collected. Unclaimed letters are normally returned after a month.

American Express credit card and travellers cheque holders can have mail sent to the American Express representative, Top Tours (see Travel Agents in the Getting There & Away chapter).

Addresses Addresses in Portugal are written with the street name followed by the building number. An alphabetical tag on the number, eg 2-A, indicates an adjacent entrance or building. Floor numbers may be included, with a degree symbol, eg 15-3° means entrance No 15, 3rd floor. The further abbreviations D, dir or Dta (for *direita*, right), or E, esq or Esqa (for *esquerda*, left), tell you which door to go to. Floor numbering is by European convention, ie the 1st floor is one flight up from the ground floor. R/C (*rés do chão*) means ground floor. ·

Telephone

Coin operated telephones are gradually being outnumbered by those accepting only *cartões telefónicos* (phonecards). These are widely available from newsagents, tobacconists and telephone offices (ask for a *telecard* or *cartão*). They're sold in 875$00 (50 unit) and 2100$00 (120 unit) denominations (a youth or student card should get you a 10% discount). Lisbon (together with Porto) has its own TLP (Telefones de Lisboa e Porto) phonecard system, but you may also come across phones accepting only the nationwide Portugal Telecom 'Credifone' system's phonecards (neither card works in the other system though they cost the same).

At the front of the *Páginas Amarelas* (Yellow Pages) in the telephone directory is a list of headings, in English and other languages, useful to visitors. There is also a privately operated 'talking yellow pages' at ☎ 795 22 22.

Local Calls Coin calls are charged at the rate of 20$00 per 'unit' or 'beep' *(impulso)*, card calls at 17$50 per unit. For local calls a unit varies from three minutes at peak times (10 am to 1 pm and 2 to 6 pm) to 12 minutes between 10 pm and 8 am. Cafés often allow customers to use their phones if there isn't a public one nearby, but charge 30$00 to 40$00 per unit.

Long-Distance & International Calls The largest coin accepted by standard coin telephones is 100$00, making them impractical for long-distance and international calls: it's far more convenient to use a phonecard.

The best place for long-distance calls is the Portugal Telecom office at Rossio 68 (Map 9), open daily from 8 am to 11 pm, with around a dozen phones available. Calls can also be made from public telephones as well as booths in Portugal Telecom offices and post offices. International calls to Europe average about 300$00 per minute; to Australia and the USA, they're about 600$00 per minute at peak times and 450$00 off-peak. Calls from private telephones cost about a third less than those from public ones. It's

cheapest if you phone between 9 pm and 8 am, and on weekends and public holidays.

Portugal's international enquiries number is ☎ 118. From Portugal, the international access code is ☎ 00. For operator assistance or to make a reverse-charges (collect) call *(pago no destino)*, dial ☎ 099 (for Europe, Algeria, Morocco and Tunisia) or ☎ 098 (for other overseas destinations).

Hotel Calls Calls from hotels are almost double the standard rate. Any hotel or pensão with a telephone in the room is likely to have a gizmo somewhere that either prints out the number of units in each call or displays a cumulative total. If in doubt about your hotel telephone bill, ask to see the print-out.

Calls to Portugal To call Portugal from abroad, dial the international access code ☎ 351 (Portugal's country code), the telephone or area code (minus its initial zero) and the number. Lisbon's area code is 01.

Mobile Phone Rental You can rent a mobile phone from Telecel at its airport shop, Loja 3 (☎ 846 40 33; fax 846 40 34), opposite the Portúgalia check-in desk. The minimum

---

Longer Lisbon Numbers

In recent years Lisbon has changed most of its six-digit telephone and fax numbers to seven digits. If you can't get a local six-digit number to work, you may have to update it yourself, by replacing the first two digits with a new combination of three digits, as follows:

Replace this...	with this
32	342
34	347
36	346
52	314
53	353
54	354
57	357
60	390
65	385
69	383
80	840
86	886
87	887

three-day charge is 4773$00; one week costs 11,325$00 and two weeks 21,235$00 (all prices include IVA). The shop is open daily from 7.30 am to 11 pm. Nova Rent (☎ 387 08 08; fax 387 31 30) also rents phones for 1404$00 a day (including IVA). Both charge 134$00 per minute for national calls and 262$00 per minute for European calls.

Fax
Post offices operate a domestic and international fax service called Corfax, costing an unconscionable 1330$00 for the first page to Europe, North America or Australia, and more to some other points. On top of that, only half the post office form is available for your message. And to *collect* a fax at the post office you pay 250$00 per page. A friendly private travel agency or guesthouse with a fax is almost certain to be cheaper.

Email
Telepac, Portugal's biggest Internet provider, has a public users' centre called Quiosque Internet (Map 3; ☎ 352 22 92; fax 352 71 90; email@telepac.pt) on the ground floor of the giant Forum Telecom building, at Avenida Fontes Pereira de Melo 38, beside Picoas metro station (take the north-west exit from the metro). You can plug into the web or send email (but not receive it), for 180$00 per half-hour. Some instruction is available, including in English. It's open weekdays from 9 am to 5 pm. For more information (including how to open a local account) check the Telepac's Web site at www.telepac.pt.

The Centro Nacional de Cultura (☎ 346 67 22; fax 342 82 50; info@cnc.pt) has an Internet centre in an annexe of its library, accessed through the Café No Chiado (Map 10) at Largo do Picadeiro 12. Closed for refurbishment at the time of research, its charges for accessing the Net or sending email are 300$00 per quarter-hour or 900$00 per hour. It should be open Monday to Friday from 11 am to 1 am and Saturday from 7 pm to 1 am.

The Espaço Ágora (see Campuses in this chapter) is a student-oriented complex which has an Internet room (☎ 346 03 64) open practically 24 hours during term-time (and from 3 pm to 2 am daily at other times), where you can send (but not receive) emails. The charge is 300$00 per half-hour.

BOOKS
Lonely Planet
If you're planning a wider journey than just Lisbon, consider taking LP's *Portugal* or one of LP's comprehensive 'on a shoestring' guides that include Portugal: *Western Europe* or *Mediterranean Europe*. Is your Portuguese not what it could be? LP can help there too, with its *Western Europe phrasebook*.

Guidebooks
There's a relatively small selection of Lisbon-only guidebooks (see the Shopping chapter for where to find them).

The Andersons' small-format *Landscapes of Portugal* series includes one on Sintra, Cascais and Estoril which will suit drivers and walkers interested in short tours of these areas. *The Real Lisbon* is a slightly outdated English translation of a popular Portuguese guide to Lisbon's food, entertainment, shops etc; it's available from city bookshops and at the turismo on Praça dos Restauradores. ANA (Aeroportos e Navegação Aérea), the airport authority, publishes and regularly updates the free *Your Guide: Lisboa*, which has a slightly muddled walking tour and lists of food, upper-end hotels and nightlife; pick one up at the ANA counter at airport arrivals or at the airport turismo.

History & Politics
David Birmingham's *A Concise History of Portugal*, modestly illustrated, academic but very readable, comes to grips with Lisbon's role in the history of Portugal, covering events up to its 1993 publication. Particularly useful in understanding all the brouhaha over the 1998 celebrations in Lisbon (including EXPO '98), commemorating Vasco da Gama's discovery of a sea route to India, are *Prince Henry the Navigator* by John Ure, and CR Boxer's *The*

Portuguese Seaborne Empire, 1415-1825. For insights into the Salazar years, have a look at António de Figueiredo's *Portugal: Fifty Years of Dictatorship.*

Food & Drink

If you enjoy Lisbon's many excellent restaurants you'll be happy to discover Edite Vieira's *The Taste of Portugal.* More than just a cookbook, its selected recipes from all of Portugal's regions are spiced with cultural background information and lively anecdotes. There is also a section on wines, and an appendix on the sort of vegetarian dishes you wish you could find in Portuguese restaurants.

Richard Mayson's brisk, readable *Portugal's Wines & Wine-Makers: Port, Madeira & Regional Wines* is a good introduction to the country's favourite product, and includes a history of Portuguese wine-making over the centuries.

General

One of the best all-round books about Portugal and the Portuguese is Marion Kaplan's perceptive *The Portuguese: The Land & Its People*, published in 1991. Ranging knowledgeably all over the landscape, from Lisbon to literature, agriculture to *emigrantes*, its generous feminine perspective seems most appropriate for a country whose men so often seem to be abroad.

NEWSPAPERS & MAGAZINES
Portuguese-Language Press

Major Portuguese-language daily newspapers include *Diário de Notícias*, *Público*, *Jornal de Notícias* and the gossip tabloid *Correio da Manhã*, which licks all the others for circulation. Popular weeklies include the *O Independente* newspaper and *Expresso* magazine. On the Web you can find *Público* at www.publico.pt and *Jornal de Notícias* at www.dn.pt.

Newsstands groan under numerous sports-only newspapers. For entertainment listings, check the local dailies. *Público's* Lisbon edition has classified sections with big what's-on listings.

JULIA WILKINSON

Newspaper stand in a city street

Foreign-Language Press

Several English-language newspapers are published in Portugal by and for its expatriate population. These can be good sources of information on long-term accommodation, regional events, cheap flights, language and other courses, and even work. Best known are *APN* (Anglo-Portuguese News), published every Thursday, and the *News*, published fortnightly in regional editions.

At city centre newsstands and newsagents it's easy to find transnational papers, including the *European*, the *International Herald Tribune* and *USA Today* and national papers from all over Europe, such as *Le Monde*, *Le Figaro*, *The Guardian* and *The Times* for the equivalent of US$1.50 to US$3. Most are a day or two old. At well-stocked newsagents, such as Tabacaria Mónaco (Map 9), at Rossio 21, and Tabacaria Adamastor (Map 9), at Rua 1 de Dezembro 2, you can also pick up magazines such as *Paris-Match*, *Le Point*, *l'Express*, *Der Spiegel*, *Bünte*, *The Spectator* and *The Economist*.

RADIO

Portuguese domestic radio is represented by the state-owned stations Antena 1 on MW and FM, and on Antena 2 and 3 on FM, the private Rádio Renascença (RR) and a clutch of local stations.

Rádio Difusão Portuguesa (RDP) transmits daily programmes of national and international news and other information of interest to visitors in English, French and German during the summer. Look for it at MW 666 kHz, FM 99.4 MHz or FM 95.7 MHz. English-language broadcasts of the BBC World Service, Voice of America (voaeurope@voa.gov) and Radio Australia (www.abc.net.au/ra) can be picked up on various short-wave frequencies.

TV

Portuguese TV consists of channels from the state-run Telivisão Portuguesa, Canal 1 (on VHF) and TV2 (on UHF), plus two private channels, Sociedade Independente de Communicação (SIC) and TV Independente (TVI). The country also has at least 14 cable-TV companies. Portuguese and Brazilian soap operas *(telenovelas)* appear to take up the bulk of TV airtime. There are also lots of subtitled foreign movies.

At least a dozen international channels, heavy on sports, music and movies, also come in via satellite. including CNN.

PHOTOGRAPHY & VIDEO

It's best to take film and camera equipment with you, especially if you hanker after Kodachrome, which is generally either unavailable or very expensive. Other brands of E6-process slide film, such as Ektachrome and Fujichrome, as well as print film and 8mm video cassettes, are widely available at franchise photo shops. Prices are around 870$00 (US$5.50) for 36 frames of Kodak Gold 100 and 1000$00 (US$6.50) for a 90-minute TDK 8mm video cassette.

Print film processing is as fast and cheap as anywhere in Europe. Slide and video processing are rare. Imported 'quick-shoot' cameras are also available in franchise shops and elsewhere, though at significantly marked up prices.

Portugal uses the PAL video system, which is incompatible with the French SECAM system, and the North American and Japanese NTSC system. Australia and most of Europe use PAL.

There are no significant restrictions on what you can shoot in Lisbon, though some museums and galleries forbid flash photography. Few Portuguese will object to being photographed, especially if their children are the focus of the attention. Nevertheless, the courtesy of asking beforehand is always appreciated. 'May I take a photograph' is *Posse tirar uma fotografia, por favor?*

TIME

Portugal is on 'British' time, ie at GMT/UTC in winter and GMT/UTC plus one hour in summer. This puts it an hour later than Spain all year round. Clocks are set forward by an hour on the last Sunday in March and back an hour on the last Sunday in October.

ELECTRICITY

Electricity is 220V, 50Hz. Plugs are normally of the two-round-pin variety.

WEIGHTS & MEASURES

Portugal uses the metric system. Decimals are indicated with commas, and thousands with points. See the conversion table at the back of the book.

LAUNDRY

Lave Neve laundry (☎ 346 61 05) is centrally located at Rua da Alegria 37. A 5kg load costs 800$00 (wash only) and 10kg 1100$00. Tumble dry costs an additional 500$00. For 2400$00 you can get a 5kg load washed, dried and ironed. 'Wash and dry' in Portuguese is *limpeza e seco*.

Lavandaria Sous'ana (Map 7; ☎ 888 08 20), in shop No 423 of the Centro Comércial da Mouraria, Largo Martim Moniz (metro: Socorro), is self-service but they'll do your wash for you in a few hours for the same price (4.5kg for 1000$00). It's open Monday to Saturday from 9.30 am to 8.30 pm.

TOILETS

Public toilets *(sanitários* or *casas de banho)* are scarce. Those that you find tend to be sit-down style, generally clean and usually free. Most people, though, go to the nearest café for a drink or pastry and take advantage of the facilities there (the sign 'H' means *homens*, men, and 'S' *senhoras*, women).

HEALTH

Lisbon, like other European cities, presents no serious health problems to the sensible traveller. Your main risks are likely to be an upset stomach from enjoying too much food and wine, or sunburn from the nearby beaches. No vaccinations are required for entry into Portugal unless you're coming from an infected area and are destined for the Azores and Madeira, in which case you may be asked for proof of vaccination against yellow fever. There are a few routine vaccinations that are recommended whether you're travelling or not, including up-to-date tetanus, polio and diptheria.

Although one reader reports falling sick apparently from drinking tap water in Portugal, you shouldn't have any problems with Lisbon's supply: bottled water is widely available if you prefer. Salads and fruit are safe and ice cream usually OK, though beware of ice cream that has melted and been refrozen. Take care with shellfish (eg cooked mussels that haven't opened properly can be dangerous) and avoid undercooked meat.

If you're spending lots of time at the beaches, make sure you drink enough and use a sunscreen: you can get sunburnt here surprisingly quickly, even through cloud. Good-quality sunglasses are invaluable not only for beach excursions but also for shielding your eyes from Lisbon's dust.

Condoms *(preservativos)* are the most widely available form of contraception, found in supermarkets or pharmacies. If you're taking the contraceptive pill, though, it's safest to bring a supply from home. Also worth bringing, if you wear glasses, is a spare pair and your prescription.

EU residents are covered for emergency medical treatment in Lisbon, as elsewhere in the EU (see Documents earlier in this chapter for information on the required E111 form).

Medical Services

Farmácias (pharmacies) are plentiful in Lisbon. They often have English-speaking staff who can advise on suitable medicines for minor problems. They are typically open weekdays from 9 am to 6 or 7 pm, except at lunch time, and Saturdays from 9 am to 1 pm. The closed ones usually post a list of others that are open. Operators at the general telephone enquiries number (☎ 118) can tell you where to find an open farmácia at any hour of the day or night, or check the listing in the daily *Público* newspaper. Near the city centre, at Rossio 62, is the competent Farmácia Estácio (Map 9), and for homeopathic remedies, you could try Farmácia Homeopática Santa Justa (Map 9), at Rua Santa Justa 6.

Lisbon has half-a-dozen *centros de saúde* (state-administered medical centres), typically open from 8 am to 8 pm, though you're less likely to find any English speakers.

For more serious problems, the Hospital Británico (Map 5; ☎ 395 50 67, ☎ 397 63 29 after hours), at Rua Saraiva de Carvalho 49, has English-speaking staff and doctors. Other large hospitals include São José (Map 9; ☎ 886 01 31), on Rua José António Serrano, and Santa Maria Hospital School (Map 1; ☎ 352 94 40, ☎ 797 51 71) on Avenida Professor Egas Moniz. There are also numerous – and pricier – private clinics and physicians and several private hospitals: ask at the turismo.

WOMEN TRAVELLERS

Despite the official reversal of many traditional attitudes towards women after the 1974 revolution, Portugal remains, at least on the face of it, a man's world. While well over half of Portuguese university graduates are women, and women are increasing their representation in universities, business, science, government and the professions, there are still few women in positions of public trust. Inevitably, there's greater freedom and sense of equality in Lisbon, but it's not representative of the rest of the country.

An official organisation called the Comissão para a Igualdade e para os Direitos das Mulheres (the Commission for the Equality & Rights of Women; other sources refer to the Comissão da Condição Feminina or Commission on the Status of Women) was founded in 1976 to alter public perceptions on women's social status and is a leading advocate of women's rights. Its office is at Avenida da República 32.

According to women's groups in Portugal (and to a 1994 report by the US State Department, *Portugal Human Rights Practises*), domestic violence against women is a persistent problem. There are no centres for battered women or rape victims, nor are there reliable statistics on either. Sexual harassment in the workplace is fairly common.

But women travelling on their own in Lisbon report few serious hassles. Portuguese machismo, when it manifests at all, is irritating rather than dangerous, mainly taking the form of hissing or whistling by clusters of post-adolescent men.

Nevertheless, Lisbon is still a big city, and women should therefore be cautious about where they go alone after dark, in particular the Alfama and Cais do Sodré areas and the Bairro Alto late at night, and on the metro. Hitching is not recommended for solo women anywhere in the city or elsewhere.

GAY & LESBIAN TRAVELLERS

Attitudes towards gay lifestyles in Lisbon have changed dramatically in the last two years. Thanks to steady political lobbying by ILGA-Portugal (the country's first official gay and lesbian organisation), and a more liberal environment generally, the homosexual movement has rapidly developed.

The year 1997 was a watershed for both legal reform and public awareness: city authorities backed the first Gay Pride Festival and Gay & Lesbian Film Festival (see the following boxed aside) and the opening of the first Gay & Lesbian Community Centre (Centro Comunitário Gay e Lésbico de Lisboa, Map 6). The Centre, at Rua de São

---

Gay Festivals

On 28 June 1997, during the Festa de Santo António, gay history was made in Portugal when some 3000 people participated in Lisbon's first Gay Pride Festival, organised by ILGA-Portugal (the country's branch of the International Lesbian & Gay Association) and supported by the Lisbon City Council. Several gay and lesbian establishments joined in the celebration in the Praça Principe Real which included a drag-queen show and fireworks.

In September, ILGA-Portugal launched another first: with the support of local authorities and the Cinemateca Portuguesa (Cinema Museum), the 1st Gay & Lesbian Film Festival was held in the city, featuring 66 films including the famous gay movie *Celluloid Closet*.

Both events attracted widespread support and media coverage and are expected to be repeated annually. ■

Lazaro 88 (near Socorro metro station), has one-on-one legal, medical and psychological support and counselling facilities; a coffeeshop, library, bookshop and an Internet access point.

Gay-owned and gay-friendly businesses are now steadily increasing. Indeed, Lisbon is the only city in Portugal with a substantial range of places for gay/lesbian socialising – restaurants, bars, discos, saunas, beaches and cruising areas (but parks after dark are not a good idea).

The trend has yet to reach to the rest of Portugal, however, especially to rural areas where gay lifestyles are generally a source of bafflement and lesbians appear to be more or less ignored. There are many public figures, too, who, though closeted, are generally known to be homosexual. In overwhelmingly Catholic Portugal, there is still little understanding of homosexuality and negligible tolerance of it within families.

Legal Situation

Homosexuality is not illegal in Portugal. In January 1997, the government approved the new penal code recognising the same age of consent (16) between homosexual and heterosexual partners. Further legal reforms may be on the way. At the time of writing, a Socialist Party Parnership Bill was about to be presented to parliament. If passed, the bill would represent a huge step forward for recognition of gay and lesbian couples, allowing those who have lived together for at least two years the same civil rights (excluding adoption) as married couples. Foreigners will also be allowed to stay in the country without the usual bureaucracy if they can prove they have been in a relationship with a Portuguese national for at least two years.

Organisations

Founded in 1995 and only registered in Portugal in April 1996, ILGA-Portugal is now widely recognised as the nation's official gay voice. You can contact it at Apartado 21281, 1131 Lisboa Codex, Portugal (ilga-portugal @ilga.org). Its good web site, including pages on Portuguese gay news, organisations, gay life, and a big bar guide, is at www.ilga-portugal.org.

A small discussion group called GTH (Grupo de Trabalho Homossexual, or Homosexual Work Group; ☎ 888 27 36) at Rua da Palma 268 is connected with the Revolutionary Socialist Party. A bimonthly gay newspaper, *Trivia*, was launched in January 1996; it's at Apartado 21221, 1131 Lisboa Codex (☎ 362 63 16). *Lilas* is a new lesbian-oriented periodical at Apartado 6104, 2700 Amadora.

DISABLED TRAVELLERS

Portuguese law requires public offices and agencies to provide access and facilities for disabled people. But it does not cover private businesses, and relatively few places even in Lisbon have special facilities for disabled travellers. Lisbon airport is wheelchair-accessible, and most major train stations (eg Santa Apolónia) have wheelchair-accessible toilets. Carris, Lisbon's public transport agency, offers a 7 am to midnight minibus 'dial-a-ride' service (☎ 758 56 76) for disabled people, at a cost roughly comparable to taxis. It usually needs two days notice. It

also has some adapted coaches for hire; call ☎ 363 92 26.

The UK's 'Orange Badge' scheme entitles people with severe walking difficulties to certain on-street parking concessions, and there are reciprocal arrangements with other EU countries. But there seem to be very few 'disabled' parking spaces around Lisbon. The Royal Association for Disability & Rehabilitation (RADAR) publishes a guidebook, updated every two years or so, called *European Holidays & Travel Abroad: A Guide for Disabled People*. Its Portugal section includes transport help and selected accommodation, although mostly in the Algarve. RADAR is at 12 City Forum, 250 City Rd, London EC1V 8AF, UK (☎ 0171-250 3222; fax 0171-250 0212).

ICEP offices abroad can also furnish some information on barrier-free accommodation in Lisbon; for ICEP addresses see Tourist Offices earlier in this chapter. It's mainly the upper-end hotels that have the capital to spend modifying their doors, toilets and other facilities. For local barrier-free hotels, camping grounds and other facilities, ask at the local turismo.

A relevant Web site worth checking out is www.access-able.com, a Web page for travellers with disabilities.

Organisations

The Secretariado Nacional de Rehabilitação (National Rehabilitation Secretariat; ☎ 793 65 17; fax 796 51 82), Avenida Conde de Valbom 63, publishes a guide in Portuguese, *Guia de Turismo para Pessoas com Deficiências* (Tourist Guide for Disabled People), updated every few years, with sections on barrier-free accommodation (including camping), transport, general information (including shops, restaurants and sights), and help numbers throughout Portugal. It's only available at its (barrier-free) offices, open weekdays from 10 am to noon and 2 to 7 pm.

A private agency that keeps a more up-to-date eye on developments and arranges holidays for disabled travellers is Turintegra (☎ & fax 859 53 32, contact Ms Luisa Diogo),

Praça Dr Fernando Amado, Lote 566-E. This is also known as APTTO (Associação Portuguesa de Turismo Para Todos, or Portuguese Association for Tourism for All).

LISBON FOR CHILDREN

Portugal is a splendidly child-friendly place. As Marion Kaplan observes in *The Portuguese: The Land & Its People*, 'To the Portuguese, small children, no matter how noisy and ill-behaved, are angels to be adored and worshipped, overdressed and underdisciplined'. Shopkeepers pass sweets over the counter. Waiters (or waiters' kids) scoop up your bundle of joy to play behind the counter. Even teenage boys seem to have a soft spot for toddlers.

Following are some tips for making a trip to Lisbon with kids easier. For more detailed and wide-ranging suggestions (not all of them necessary in Portugal), pick up the current edition of Lonely Planet's *Travel with Children*.

Supplies

Most *minimercados* (groceries) have at least one or two brands of disposable nappies. Pharmacies are a handy sourcese of baby supplies of all kinds, from bottles and nappies to food supplements. The big chain *supermercados* stock toys and children's clothes as well. For more tastefully ethnic toys, check out the handicraft shops listed in the Shopping chapter.

Health & Hazards

Lisbon presents no significant health risks for kids other than the usual city hazards of traffic and pollution and too much sun at the nearby beaches (beware, too, of the Atlantic Ocean's strong undertow). Restaurant food is quite safe except at obviously grotty places.

Accommodation

The best bets are self-catering flats (see the Places to Stay chapter) or simple pensões, which are accustomed to families with young children and are casual enough to actually enjoy them. Try and get a room away from the street to avoid night-time noise. Lisbon's nearby camping grounds are excellent places to meet other children from all over the world, and its youth hostel (which has private rooms as well as dormitories) is good for meeting older kids. Most hotels and pensões can come up with a baby cot, especially if you request it when you book the room.

Children under the age of eight are entitled to a 50% discount in hotels and pensões if they share their parents' room. Lower-end places may charge nothing extra at all.

Food

Most minimercados, and many farmácia, have various Portuguese and imported brands of tinned baby food, and markets abound in fresh fruit and vegetables.

All but the stuffiest restaurants tolerate kids well and can provide child-sized portions. But a constant problem with eating out is the late hour at which restaurants open for the evening meal – 7 pm at the earliest. Some restaurants may let you in before regular hours and cook up something simple for a child. Lucky you if your child likes soup: there is often a pot of it ready to be served as soon as you walk in the door. Places to dine out or picnic where there's traffic-free space for kids to run around include the Castelo de São Jorge, Largo do Carmo, or the open-air restaurants at the new Doca de Santo Amaro riverside development (see the Places to Eat chapter).

Entertainment

Lisbon may look like a pretty stuffy place to a child. But its *elevadores* and trams are great fun (especially the ones to Belém and the Alfama); several of its museums, especially the Museu da Marioneta (Puppet Museum, Map 12) and Belém's Museu de Marinha (Naval Museum, Map 13) are very appealing; and there are plenty of day-trip attractions including the palaces and castle at Sintra and the beaches of Estoril, Cascais and Praia Grande (see the Excursions chapter). Even feeding the pigeons in Praça da Figueira can keep toddlers happy for hours (and at 100$00 for a bag of seed it's one of Lisbon's cheapest thrills).

As elsewhere in Portugal, however, Lisbon has many playgrounds so bashed up and rusty as to be dangerous. The best city-centre *parque infantil*, approved by my three-year-old, was the new adventure-style one in Praça do Principe Real (Map 6) – decent toilets are nearby, too. The superb Castelo de Brincar playground inside the Castelo São Jorge (Map 12) used to be one of the best in the country, but on our latest visit we found an archaeological dig in progress on the site, possibly in preparation for an underground car park.

Keep an eye out for festivals which often come complete with parades, fireworks, music and dancing. For older children interested in windsurfing, hiking or horse-riding, see the Excursions chapter. Other suggestions for keeping the kids entertained include the following:

Aquaparque (Map 1; ☎ 301 50 17), a water park in Caselas, north of Belém (take bus No 43 from Belém or directly from Praça da Figueira)

Centro Artístico Infantil (Map 3; ☎ 793 51 31), at the Museu Calouste Gulbenkian; free art workshops *(ateliers)* for children over four years old on Saturdays and Sundays at 3 pm

Centro de Pedagogia e Animação (☎ 361 28 99), in the Centro Cultural de Belém; weekend programme of performances for children (even babies) during term time

Centro Nacional de Cultura (Map 10; ☎ 346 67 22), Rua António Maria Cardoso 68; Saturday morning sessions (during term-time only) of traditional Portuguese music and dance; geared for children aged four to 10, the classes are officially open only to those who have registered in September, but you may be able to attend a class if you call ahead

Chapitô (Map 12; ☎ 887 82 25), a school of circus arts (see the boxed aside in the Entertainment chapter) with regular performances (except during August) which will enthral parents as well as kids

Feira Popular (☎ 793 44 35), Avenida da República, Entre-Campos (right by the metro); a run-down, old-fashioned fairground with roller-coasters, big wheels and all kinds of stalls; open Monday to Friday from 4 pm to midnight and from 3 pm to midnight on weekends and holidays; 200$00 admission (free for children up to 11)

Jardim Zoológico de Lisboa (Map 1; ☎ 726 93 49), Estrada de Benfica 158 (near the Sete Rios station or by bus Nos 16, 31, 41, 46, 54, 55, 58, 63, 68); fairly depressing, with most of the animals in small, unimaginative cages. Its best attraction is its dolphin shows (at 11 am, 3 and 5 pm). The all-inclusive admission charge is 1650$00 for adults; 1250$00 for children aged three to 11 (under three-year-olds free) or senior visitors over 65; 1450$00 for students with a card; open daily from 10 am to 8 pm (6 pm in winter).

Parque Infantil da Serafina (☎ 774 30 21, also known as the Parque dos Indios); children's playground in the Parque Florestal de Monsanto (bus No 2 from Praça dos Restauradores or 13 from Praça do Comércio to Serafina, then a 15 minute walk); Indian-style wigwams as well as slides, swings and other traditional activities; open daily from 9 am to 8 pm

Planetário Calouste Gulbenkian (Map 13; see Belém in the Things to See & Do chapter); a special children's session (for over-six-year-olds) every Sunday at 11 am (free admission)

Museu da Marioneta (Map 12; ☎ 886 33 04), Largo Rodrigues de Freitas 13 (see the Things to See & Do chapter); puppet curiosities and weekend puppet shows

Museu das Crianças (Children's Museum, Map13; ☎ 362 28 28), 1st floor of Belém's Museu de Marinha; mainly for Portuguese school children aged four to 12, with simple, interactive exhibitions (in Portuguese only) which change every year or so; open weekdays during term time to school groups only and to the public on weekends from 10 am to 6 pm; it's open to the public from August to mid-September, daily except Monday, from 10 am to 6 pm; the over-priced 750$00 adult entry fee (450$00 for children) includes admission to the Museu de Marinha

Teatro Infantil de Lisboa, at the Teatro Maria Matos (☎ 849 70 07), Avenida Frei Miguel Contreras 52 (near Roma metro station); special performances for children during term time

Childcare

Babysitters Of course you're going there to travel with the kids, but you may long for the occasional few hours on your own. Babysitting services are advertised in the classified pages of *Público* and the free monthly *Lisboa em...* guide, available at the turismo. For example, Clube dos Traquinas (☎ 793 35 71 or mobile ☎ 0936 672593; ask for Dona Vitoria) advertises a babysitting service at hotel or home for around 1100$00 an hour. Upper-end hotels, resorts or self-catering apartment complexes sometimes have their own childcare facilities staffed by trained nursery nurses.

Kindergartens Ludoteca can be found all over Lisbon (and the rest of the country). These privately funded play areas for four to 12-year-olds are staffed by professional kindergarten teachers and equipped with good-quality games, toys, art supplies etc. Established primarily for Portuguese kids (the staff usually speak little English), they're open to visiting children too. The most convenient ones are at the Calouste Gulbenkian's Centro Artístico Infantil (open from 15 July to 2 September, Monday to Friday from 10 am to 12.30 pm and 2.30 to 5 pm) and at Chapitô's Collectividade Cultural, Costa do Castelo 7 (similar hours but closed during school holidays in July, August, Christmas and Easter time).

Teddy Traumas
Is your child throwing a fit because her teddy's lost its eye or its leg has been wrenched off and lost forever? Help is at hand, thanks to the unique Hospital das Bonecas (Dolls' Hospital), founded in 1830 and still going strong. Now run by Senhoras Júlia Valentim and Manuela Cutileiro, the 'hospital' (Map 9; ☎ 342 85 74) is actually a small workshop which can repair and replace everything from dolls' eyes, limbs and hair to wigs, hats and clothes. Emergency repairs can be undertaken within hours if necessary. New supplies are also on sale at the 'hospital' entrance at Praça da Figueira 7. Opening hours are Monday to Friday from 10 am to 7 pm, Saturday from 10 am to 1 pm. ■

LIBRARIES
Among Lisbon's best *bibliotecas* are the General Arts Library of the Fundação Calouste Gulbenkian (☎ 793 51 31; fax 793 51 39; apg@gulbenkian.puug.pt) at Avenida de Berna 56 (metro: Pahlavã); and the

Biblioteca Nacional (Map 1; ☎ 795 01 30, ☎ 797 47 41) at Campo Grande 83 (metro: Entre Campos). The central municipal library (☎ 797 13 26) is in the Palácio das Galveias (metro: Campo Pequeno).

CAMPUSES
The vast Universidade de Lisboa campus, 5km north-west of Rossio, has its own metro station, Cidade Universitária. The most prestigious university in Lisbon is the Universidade Católica, near Sete Rios. There are nearly a dozen other private universities as well.

A good central place to meet students is the new Espaço Ágora (Map 10; ☎ 342 47 01; fax 342 47 04) run by the Associação Academica de Lisboa. This warren of rooms in a prefab building at Avenida da Ribeira das Naus, Pavilhão 2, right on the riverfront near the Cais do Sodré car ferry terminal, has a café (with discount prices for students), a cheap photocopying service, self-service computer and Internet rooms and 10 study rooms. During term time, it's all open 24 hours. Message boards here are useful sources of information for renting flats or buying and selling anything from motorbikes to computers.

CULTURAL CENTRES
The reading room of the USA's Abraham Lincoln Center (Map 3; ☎ 357 01 02), Avenida Duque de Loulé 22-B (two blocks from Picoas metro), has a massive stock of American books and magazines and opens weekdays from 2 to 5.30 pm.

The British Council (Map 6; ☎ 347 61 41; ☎ 347 95 18), at Rua de São Marçal 174, also has a good reading room. It's open Tuesday through Friday from noon to 6 pm. Take bus No 15 or 58 from Rua da Misericórdia.

At Avenida Luís Bívar 91 (Map 3) are the the Alliance Française (☎ 315 88 06) and Institut Franco-Portugais de Lisbonne (☎ 311 14 00) . There is also a reading room (☎ 352 01 49) at the German Embassy, at Campo dos Mártires da Pátria 37.

DANGERS & ANNOYANCES

Crime

Lisbon has a low crime rate by European standards, but it's on the rise. Though the occasional armed robbery has been reported, crime against foreigners usually involves pickpocketing or purse-snatching, break-ins and theft from cars (especially rental cars), and pilfering from camping grounds. Try to avoid wandering after dark in the back streets around Alfama and Cais do Sodré. The Bairro Alto is fairly safe, and is in fact the place to be for nightlife and good food though late-night revelries, especially at weekends, can get a bit wild. Use a money belt, and keep cameras and other tourist indicators out of sight when not in use. For peace of mind, take out travel insurance. And if you *are* robbed, do not under any circumstances put up a fight!

Traffic

Among Lisbon's other dangers, the most serious is probably the traffic – especially if you're behind a wheel yourself. Normally gentle, peace-loving Portuguese men and women can become irascible, deranged speed-freaks on the road, especially when they hit motorways: tailgating at 120 km/h and passing on blind curves are the norm. Solid lines between streams of opposing traffic seem to have little meaning. Not surprisingly, Portugal has one of the highest per capita road-accident rates in Europe: one of the most dangerous highways is the A5 westwards to Estoril.

Air Pollution

Air pollution can be a worry, too: thanks to Lisbon's flurry of pre-EXPO '98 development and increasing car use, air pollution has noticeably worsened in recent years. Taking a lunchtime break may not help: three-quarters of the Portuguese population seems to smoke, and few restaurants have no-smoking areas.

Beaches

If you escape to the beaches, beware of the strong Atlantic Ocean currents and waves,

---

Help!

If you've had anything robbed or stolen, you should visit the local police – not necessarily for help in solving the crime, but for a police report, which you'll need if you hope to make an insurance claim. There is a 24-hour, English-speaking, tourist-oriented police subsection (Map 10; Subsecção de Turismo) inside the courtyard at the Polícia de Segurança Pública (PSP) section office at Rua Capelo 13 in Chiado. Call ☎ 346 61 41, ext 279, or the country-wide emergency number (☎ 112). ∎

---

especially at popular surfing spots like Praia do Guincho near Cascais.

LEGAL MATTERS

Foreigners here, as elsewhere, are subject to the laws of the host country. Penalties for dealing in, possessing and using illegal drugs are stiff in Portugal, and may include heavy fines or even jail terms. See also Drinking & Driving and Road Rules under Car & Motorcycle in the Getting Around chapter.

BUSINESS HOURS

Don't plan on getting much business or shopping done anywhere between the hours of 1 and 3 pm, when the Portuguese give lunch serious and lingering attention.

Offices normally operate on weekdays only from 9 am to 1 pm and from 3 to 5 pm. Most banks are open on weekdays only, from 8.30 am to 3 pm.

The majority of shops open from 9 or 9.30 am to 1 pm and from 3 to 7 pm; many close at noon. Most are closed on Saturday afternoons and Sundays. Shopping centres are usually open every day of the week, from 10 am to around 10 or 11 pm. Coffee shops, restaurants, newsagents and tourist shops are now allowed to operate any time between 6 am and 2 am daily. Clubs and bars are taking advantage of the more liberal rules to stay open until 4 am (or, unofficially, even later).

Museums are typically open Tuesday to Saturday from 10 am to 12.30 pm and 2 to 5 pm. If the Monday is a holiday, museums are usually closed on the following day as well.

PUBLIC HOLIDAYS & SPECIAL EVENTS

The following are national public holidays, when banks, offices, department stores and some shops close; restaurants, museums and tourist attractions tend to stay open to the public, though public transport services are reduced.

For details about EXPO '98, see the Things to See & Do chapter.

New Year's Day
: 1 January

Carnival
: February/March (variable) Shrove Tuesday, about six weeks before Easter

Good Friday
: March/April (variable)

Liberty Day
: 25 April; celebrating the 1974 revolution

Labour Day
: 1 May

Corpus Christi
: May/June (variable)

Portugal Day, or Camões & the Communities Day
: 10 June

Feast of the Assumption
: 15 August

Woman in festival dress

Republic Day
: 5 October; commemorating the declaration of the Portuguese Republic in 1910

All Saints' Day
: 1 November

Independence Day
: 1 December; commemorating the restoration of independence from Spain in 1640

Feast of the Immaculate Conception
: 8 December

Christmas Day
: 25 December

Like the rest of Portugal, Lisbon also enjoys celebrating various *romarias* (religious pilgrimages), *festas* (festivals) and *feiras* (fairs). At the core of many are religious processions. Following are some of the more important ones in the city and nearby provinces.

Carnival
: February/March (variable); the last few days before the start of Lent (about six weeks before Easter), was traditionally an occasion for people to let off steam and thumb their noses at public decorum. Now it seems to consist mainly of parades, and a lot of weirdly made-up kids out begging for sweets.

Two annual pilgrimages to Fátima (Estremadura)
: 12-13 May and 12-13 October; celebrating the first and last apparitions of the Virgin Mary to three shepherd children here in 1917. These are strictly religious events, with hundreds of thousands of pilgrims from around the world visiting one of the Catholic world's major holy sites.

Feira Nacional da Agricultura
: First week in June; Santarém's (Ribatejo) grand farming and livestock fair also includes bullfighting, folk singing and dancing.

The Festa de Santo António
: 12-13 June (see the St Anthony boxed aside in the Facts about Lisbon chapter.) This event is incorporated into the month-long Festas dos Santos Populares celebration, sometimes referred to as the Festa do Lisboa (Lisbon Festival).

The Festa de São Pedro (St Peter)
: 28-29 June; celebrated with particular gusto across the Rio Tejo at Montijo. Originally a fisherfolk celebration dating from the Middle Ages, there's a blessing of the boats, bullfights and a running of the bulls.

The Feira de São Martinho or National Horse Fair in Golegã (Ribatejo)
: 3-11 November; features horse parades, riding competitions and bullfights, finished off with a feast of roast chestnuts and young wine.

✓ ✓

Festas dos Santos Populares

In June Lisbon lets its hair down with its Festos dos Santos Populares (Festivals of the Popular Saints), Christianised versions of traditional summer solstice celebrations. Lisbon is the birthplace of Santo António (known elsewhere as St Anthony of Padua), and the city's biggest bash of the year is the Festa de Santo António on 12 to 13 June. The Alfama district (and to some extent Mouraria and Bairro Alto) parties through the night of the 12th, with little *tronos* (thrones) for Santo António in every square, plus parades, music, dancing, fireworks and, of course, lots of wine and grilled sardines. On the 13th, a municipal holiday, revellers rest and the devout go to church.

The city then goes on buzzing for the rest of June, with city-sponsored concerts, exhibitions and street theatre. ■

✓ ✓

Music Festivals

The Fundação Gulbenkian (see the boxed aside on Calouste Gulbenkian in the Things to See & Do chapter) organises several annual international music festivals in Lisbon. These include Jornadas de Música Contemporânea (Journeys in Contemporary Music) at venues around the city in May; Jazz em Agosto (Jazz in August) in the Foundation's gardens in early August; and Jornadas de Música Antiga (Journeys in Ancient Music) at various historical sites around Lisbon in October.

The new Lisboa Mexe-me (literally Lisbon Moves Me) festival from mid-July to mid-August is an initiative of the city authorities to liven up some of the older neighbourhoods. Free open-air performances of dance, music and theatre take place in the Alfama, Bairro Alto, Madragoa (Alcântara) and Mouraria districts.

Athletic Events

Lisbon hosts an international marathon, the Maratona de Lisboa (known in English as the Discoveries Marathon), every year in late November, and an annual half-marathon in early March. If this sounds like a nice way to see the city, contact the Federação Portuguesa de Atletismo (☎ 414 60 20), Largo da Lagoa 15-B, 2795 Linda-a-Velha.

WORK

EU nationals can compete for any job in Portugal without a work permit. Non-EU citizens who want to work in Portugal are expected to get a Portuguese work permit before they arrive, with the help of their prospective employer.

Several organisations can help you search for a job in Portugal before you go, and even arrange your work permit. One of the best known is the Work Abroad Program of CIEE, the Council on International Educational Exchange (☎ 212-822 2600; fax 212-822 2699; info@ciee.org; www.ciee. org), 205 East 42nd St, New York, NY 10017-5706. The Directory of Summer Jobs Abroad (☎ 01865-241 978; fax 01865-790 885; www.youthnet.org.uk/), care of Vacation Work Publications, 9 Park End St, Oxford OX1 1HJ, UK, is another possible resource. An index on the Web of library resources on overseas jobs is available at www.lib.calpoly. edu/retriever/current/overseas.html.

The prospects of on-the-spot work in Lisbon are limited unless you have a skill that's scarce or can speak passable Portuguese. Except for work where you're paid in kind or in petty cash, you'll probably have to sign a work contract.

The most realistic option is English teaching, but only if you're prepared to stay for at least a few months. A TEFL certificate is a big help, though you may find work without one. See the *Páginas Amarelas* (Yellow Pages) under Escolas de Línguas for the names of schools.

For other work, check out the classified ads in the local papers (see Newspapers & Magazines in this chapter) or ask around the tourist bars in nearby beach resorts like Cascais.

If you plan to stay more than three months, you'll also need a residence permit, available from the Serviço de Estrangeiros e Fronteiras (Foreigners' Registration Service, Map 3) office (see Visa Extensions under Documents earlier in this chapter). A somewhat dated but comprehensive reference for the long-term job seeker is Sue Tyson-Ward's, *How to Live & Work in Portugal*.

Getting There & Away

Lisbon airport is the city's main international gateway (Portugal's other international airports are at Porto and Faro). All overland connections are through Spain, of course. The two main rail crossings are at Vilar Formoso (the Paris to Lisbon line) and Marvão-Beirã (the Madrid to Lisbon line). Two other important crossings are at Valença do Minho (Vigo in Spain to Porto) and Elvas (Badajoz in Spain to Lisbon).

Of the dozens of highway crossings, the ones with fast, high-capacity roads on both sides are at Valença do Minho, Feces de Abajo (Chaves), Vilar Formoso (Guarda), Elvas, Vila Verde de Ficalho (Serpa) and Vila Real de Santo António. Land border controls between the two countries have virtually disappeared.

AIR

From Lisbon, both TAP (Air Portugal, the country's flagship carrier) and Portugália (Portugal's main domestic airline, which also has some European connections) have multiple flights daily to/from Porto and Faro, year-round. TAP has a daily evening flight to Faro and a morning one back, scheduled to connect with all its international arrivals and departures in Lisbon. For the short distances involved, however, these flights are so expensive they're hardly worth considering – unless you have an under-26 card, which gets you a 50% discount with Portugália.

Over two dozen carriers have scheduled international services to/from Lisbon, including AB Airlines, Aeroflot, Air France, Air Liberté, Alitalia, British Airways (BA), Delta, Iberia, KLM, Lufthansa, Luxair, Portugália, SAS, Swissair, TWA and Varig.

Lisbon airport is 30 minutes from the city centre when there's no traffic, but 45 minutes or more in rush hour; see the Getting Around chapter for airport transport information.

For flight arrival and departure information, call ☎ 840 20 60.

Portugal's departure tax for any international flight is 1950$00. This is included in the price of any ticket from a scheduled carrier, but payable at check-in in the case of a charter flight. Domestic departure tax depends on your destination; eg 780$00 for a Faro-Lisbon flight. This is also included in the ticket price.

Airline Numbers	
You can contact some of the major airlines on the following numbers:	
TAP	☎ 841 69 90
or toll-free	☎ 0808-21 31 41
Portugália	☎ 847 20 92
Air France	☎ 790 02 02
Alitalia	☎ 353 61 41
British Airways toll-free	☎ 0808-21 21 25
AB Airlines	☎ 313 95 60
Iberia	☎ 355 81 19
Delta	☎ 353 76 10
KLM	☎ 847 63 54
Lada	☎ 793 27 01
Lufthansa	☎ 357 38 52
Sabena	☎ 346 55 72
SAS	☎ 347 30 61
SATA Air Açores	☎ 353 95 11
Swissair	☎ 347 11 11
TWA	☎ 314 71 41
Varig	☎ 353 91 53
or toll-free	☎ 0500-1234

Buying Tickets

If you're just looking for a cheap flight, then you need an agency specialising in discounted tickets. Shop around, and start early – some cheap tickets must be purchased months in advance. Check the travel ads in major newspapers. Also ask your travel agent about any special fares on offer (eg if you leave midweek and your stay includes a Saturday or Sunday night).

Some good deals are offered by London's 'bucket shops' but not all of them are straight shooters. Increasingly, however, these outfits are going respectable as 'consolidators' – that

---

Arriving in Lisbon by Air

As you exit from the arrivals concourse at the airport, you'll find a helpful turismo (☎ 849 43 23, 849 36 89), which is open daily from 6 am to 2 am. Further on is a desk maintained by ANA, the city airport authority, with arrivals and departures information, its own handy mini-guidebook to the city called *Your Guide: Lisboa*, and a very useful *Taxi Information* pamphlet to help you avoid getting stung by the less-than-scrupulous drivers who hang out here. ■

---

is, official outlets for the airlines' discounted and last-minute tickets. If you have a preferred airline, this may be your best bet for a cheap ticket. Call and ask the airline who its consolidators are.

Recommended travel agents are the youth-oriented ones, including Trailfinders and Campus Travel (UK), Council Travel (USA), Travel CUTS (Canada) and STA Travel (worldwide), which specialise in finding low air fares. Most offer the best deals to students and under-26s but they are open to all, and they won't play tricks on you. All are members of their national travel-agent associations.

Note that fares tend to be 40 to 50% lower outside of peak season (in North America and Europe, peak season is roughly June to mid-September plus Christmas, and 'shoulder season' is April-May and mid-September to October; peak season is roughly December-January in Australia and New Zealand).

The USA & Canada

The *Los Angeles Times*, *San Francisco Examiner*, *Chicago Tribune*, *New York Times*, and Canada's *Globe & Mail* and *Sun* have big weekly travel sections with lots of travel-agent ads.

Council Travel and STA Travel are reliable sources of cheap tickets in the USA. Each has offices all over the country. Council Travel's toll-free number in the USA and Canada is ☎ 800-223-7402; STA Travel's is ☎ 800-777-0112, and www.statravel.com is its

Internet address. Canada's best bargain-ticket agency is Travel CUTS, with some 50 offices in major cities. The parent office (☎ 416-979-2406) is at 187 College St, Toronto M5T 1P7.

TWA, Delta and TAP have daily direct flights from New York to Lisbon in summer.

The UK

Thanks to Britain's long love affair with Portugal (and London's bucket shop tradition), you can find some great air fare deals here. Check out the travel classified sections of the Saturday *Independent*, *Sunday Times* and London's weekly *Time Out* magazine.

The UK's best known bargain-ticket agencies are Trailfinders (☎ 0171-937 5400) at 42-48 Earl's Court Rd, Kensington, London W8 6EJ; Campus Travel (☎ 0171-730 3402) at 52 Grosvenor Gardens, London SW1W 0AG; and STA Travel (☎ 0171-938 4711) at Priory House, 6 Wrights Lane, London W8 6TA. All have branches throughout London and the UK, and Campus Travel is also in many Hostelling International (HI) shops.

In summer, both TAP (☎ 0171-828 0262, www.TAP-AirPortugal.pt) and BA (☎ 0345 222111; www.British-Airways.com) fly from London (Heathrow), three times a day to Lisbon. Both airlines offer youth and student fares. From London (Gatwick) AB Airlines (☎ 0345 464748) flies to Lisbon twice daily during the week, with limited weekend services. From Manchester, Portugália Airlines (☎ 0161-489 2220; www.pga.pt) flies five times a week via Porto.

There are often cheap package deals including accommodation (see Organised Tours later in this chapter for details) or flight-only arrangements on charter flights, but bear in mind that charter flights have fixed dates and involve high withdrawal penalties. Scheduled flights offer increasingly good deals, too, especially if you fly out midweek and your trip includes a Saturday night (maximum stay one month). Some examples of economy high-season return fares with these restrictions include AB Airlines (£119), TAP (£200), and BA (£290), all plus taxes. Portugália's equivalent Manchester-Lisbon return fare is £189 (cheaper, incidentally, than its standard youth fare).

France
Since France, and Paris in particular, has a huge population of Portuguese immigrants, there are frequent scheduled flights at reasonable prices to/from Paris (from around 1300FF economy return with Air Liberté or 1750FF with Air France). Summer flights from Paris (Orly) to Lisbon include four a day by TAP and one a day each by Air France, Air Liberté and Air Inter Europe; from Paris (de Gaulle), Air France and Air Inter Europe each fly at least two or three times a day.

STA Travel has offices in Paris; the main one is at CTS Voyages (☎ 01 43 25 00 76), 20 Rue des Carmes, 75005 Paris.

Air France is at ☎ 01 44 08 24 24 (or ☎ 01 44 08 22 22 for reservations), and TAP is at ☎ 01 44 86 89 89. Both offer discounted youth/student prices.

The Rest of Europe
A reliable source of bargain tickets within the Netherlands is NBBS Reizen (☎ 071-523 2020; fax 071-522 6475), at Schipholweg 101, 2300 AJ Leiden with over 50 'travelshops' and 'Budgetair' counters in post offices around the country.

There are abundant summer flights to Lisbon from Germany, including several flights daily from Frankfurt and daily connections from Berlin, Dresden, Hamburg and Munich. The major scheduled carriers are Lufthansa, TAP, Portugália and Iberia.

Elsewhere in Europe, there are several flights daily from Amsterdam, Brussels and Madrid and frequent connections from other cities including Barcelona, Bilbao and Hanover. Portúgalia, Iberia, TAP or Sabena are the main carriers.

Economy return fares to Lisbon are around DM1030 from Frankfurt, 30,000 ptas from Madrid, and Bf13,200 from Brussels.

Australia & New Zealand
STA Travel and Flight Centres International are major dealers in cheap air fares, each with dozens of offices. STA Travel's headquarters are at 224 Faraday St, 1st floor, Carlton, Victoria 3053, Australia (☎ 03-9347 6911; fax 03-9347 0608); and 10 High St, PO Box 4156, Auckland, New Zealand (☎ 09-309 9995; fax 09-309 9829). Flight Centre's main offices in Australia are at 19 Bourke St, Melbourne, Victoria 3000 (☎ 03-9650 2899; fax 03-9550 3751), and 82 Elizabeth St, Sydney, NSW 2000 (☎ 02-9235 3522; fax 02-9235 2871).

BUS
National
Express coaches *(expressos)* connect Lisbon with nearly all of Portugal's major towns on a daily basis. Some sample one-way fares are: Porto (around a dozen buses daily, 3½ hours) 1900$00; Coimbra (at least 11 daily) 1350$00; Évora (around 10 daily) 1350$00; Faro (seven daily; just under five hours) 2100$00; Viano do Castelo (one or two daily) 2000$00. An under-26 card should get you a discount of about 25%.

Rede Expressos (☎ 310 31 11 for 24-hour information) and its affiliates, a few other descendants of the now-privatised Rodoviário Nacional (RN) line such as EVA (from the Algarve), and all international coaches, operate from the long-distance bus terminal (☎ 354 54 39) at Avenida Casal Ribeiro 18 (metro: Saldanha). This is the best bet for most destinations within Portugal.

Renex (Map 7; ☎ 887 48 71, ☎ 888 28 29), which includes local lines Resende, Caima and Frota Azul, operates from Rua da Alfandega, a few blocks east of Praça do Comércio. Buses run to Mafra every few hours from the little Mafrense bus company terminal (Map 7) at Rua Fernandos da Fonseca 18 (metro: Socorro), via Avenida Casal Ribeiro.

International
Europe The easiest way to arrange coach travel to/from Lisbon to other destinations in Europe is through Eurolines, a consortium of coach operators with offices all over the region. Eurolines' coaches are reasonably

comfortable, with on-board toilets, reclining seats, and sometimes air-con. They stop frequently for meals, though you'll save a bit by packing your own munchies.

Discounts depend on the route, but children from four to 12 years old typically get 30 to 40% off; youth/student and senior discounts are rare or minimal. Fares given here are adult fares. You can usually get away with booking even long-distance journeys a few days ahead, though earlier booking is advisable in summer.

Lisbon's main Eurolines affiliate is Intercentro (Map 3; ☎ 357 17 45; fax 357 00 39), Rua Actor Taborda 55 (a block from the main bus station in Lisbon).

Among some 200 Eurolines offices in Europe are the following:

Amsterdam
    Eurolines (☎ 020-627 5151; fax 020-627 5167), Rokin 10
Frankfurt
    Deutsche Touring (☎ 069-790 353; fax 069-706 059), Am Romerhof 17
London
    Eurolines (bookings ☎ 0990-143 219, information ☎ 0171-730 8235; fax 0171-730 8721), 52 Grosvenor Gardens, London SW1
Madrid
    SAIA (☎ 91-530 76 00; fax 91-327 13 29), Estación Sur de Autobuses
Paris
    Eurolines (☎ 01 49 72 51 51; fax 01 49 72 51 61), Gare Routière Internationale de Paris, Avenue de Général de Gaulle, Bagnolet

Intercentro/Eurolines has a year-round London-Lisbon service (via Coimbra and Fátima) departing from Victoria Coach Station three times a week. You'd have to be a coach junkie to go for this: the 40 hour trip involves a seven-hour layover and a change of coach in Paris. The adult one-way/return fare is £75/139.

The eight hour service between Madrid and Lisbon runs three times a week (5850/9350 ptas); from April to September this starts at Barcelona. SAIA Eurolines has a Salamanca to Lisbon service twice a week for 4000/7200 ptas. All of these stop at major intermediate towns as well.

Eurolines France runs from Paris to Lisbon five times a week, a 24 hour jaunt for 520/910FF. The private line IASA (☎ 01 43 53 90 82, fax 01 43 53 49 57 in Paris; ☎ 01-793 64 51, fax 01-793 62 76 in Lisbon) runs deluxe coaches five times a week between Paris and Lisbon (via Coimbra) for around 500FF.

From Hamburg and Hanover, the German Eurolines affiliate runs twice a week to Lisbon for DM257/415. Fares from Cologne and Düsseldorf are slightly lower.

TRAIN
National
Travelling on the Caminhos de Ferro Portugueses (CP) domestic rail network is cheaper (if slower) than by bus, thanks in part to state subsidies. There are three main levels of service: *regional* (R), *interregional* (IR), *intercidade* (IC) and *Alfa* (slightly faster than IC). Most trains have both 1st and 2nd class carriages. Long-distance trains all have restaurant cars, and some have bars. Some sample IC/IR 2nd class fares from Lisbon are 2350$00/1900$00 to Porto (four IC, four IR trains a day); 1650$00/1400$00 to Coimbra (six IC, four IR a day); and 1900$00/1650$00 to Faro (three IC, two IR a day). There is also Alfa service to some points, eg four a day to Porto (2950$00) and three a day to Coimbra (2150$00). These Alfa and IC fares include mandatory seat reservation charges.

For information about Lisbon's railway stations, see the Getting Around chapter. Frequent train travellers may want to buy a copy of the *Guia Horário Oficial* with CP's complete domestic and international timetables, available from the *bilheteiras* (ticket windows) at major stations for 360$00.

International
Trains are a popular way to get around Europe but the long ride from the UK to Lisbon isn't really worth considering unless you plan to stop en route or have one of several available rail passes (eg the Inter-Rail pass for under-26-year-olds) which makes it a comparatively cheap option.

Check with a youth-oriented travel agent such as Campus Travel (see the following UK section) about these passes.

There are two standard long-distance train routes to Lisbon. One takes the TGV Atlantique from Paris to Irún in Spain (where you must change trains), then the *Rápido Sud-Expresso* across Spain via Vilar Formoso in Portugal to Pampilhosa and south to Lisbon. The other route runs from Paris to Madrid, where you can catch the Talgo *Lusitânia Express* via Marvão-Beirã in Portugal to Encontramento and on to Lisbon. Another well-used route originating in Spain is Badajoz-Elvas-Lisbon; the crossing is at Caia in Portugal.

Tickets cannot be purchased on the train, only from the departure station or a travel agent. Discounted and other special tickets can be purchased only at certain 'main-line' stations. You can book tickets up to 20 days ahead, though in most cases you'll have little problem booking one for the next or even the same day, even in summer.

The UK The normal cheap route from the UK to Lisbon is from London's Victoria Station, across the Channel to Paris via ferry (usually Dover-Calais, sometimes Newhaven-Dieppe) and train, followed by a change of stations in Paris (from Nord to Austerlitz or Montparnasse), then another change at either the Spanish border (Irún) or in Madrid. The daily 4 pm train from Paris to Irún has a connection to Lisbon arriving at 11.25 am next day.

A 2nd-class adult single/return London-Lisbon fare is £122/205. For under-26 travellers it's £100/184 and £92/176 for seniors. In all cases a sleeper for the Irún-Lisbon sector would cost about £18 extra. Tickets are valid for two months, and you can break the journey en route.

For further information, contact British Rail's international division (☎ 0990 848 848). A good source of under-26 bargains is Eurotrain, a service of Campus Travel (☎ 0171-730 3402), 52 Grosvenor Gardens, London SW1W 0AG.

The Channel Tunnel can shorten a

London-Lisbon rail journey by about six hours, but at present it's very expensive. Current London (Waterloo) to Paris (Nord) Eurostar fares are UK£69 (certain midweek days only) or UK£89 other days (same fare for both single or return); £44/79 return if you're under 26 and £62/99 for seniors. For the additional Paris-Lisbon fares, see the following France section.

For more information contact either Eurostar (☎ 01233-617 575) or the Rail Europe Call Centre (☎ 0990 300 003; fax 0171-633 9900) at 179 Piccadilly, London WI. In Paris, Société Nationale des Chemins de Fer (SNCF, French Railways) is at ☎ 01 45 82 50 50 (it also has a Web site at web.sncf.fr).

France The daily train journey from Paris (Montparnasse) takes about 20 hours to Lisbon. A 2nd-class reserved seat costs about 810FF (704FF for under-26 travellers). Per person prices for a *couchette* in a six-person sleeper are about 880FF; 985FF for a *beliche* in a triple sleeper; and 1240FF for a double berth.

If you book 30 days in advance the section of the journey to the Spanish border at Irún will cost 50% less, and 20% less for eight days advance booking.

Spain The main rail route is from Madrid to Lisbon via Marvão-Beirã. The nightly journey on the Talgo *Lusitânia Express* takes 10½ hours; a 2nd-class seat is around 6700 ptas one way, while a berth in a *turista* (four-person) sleeper is around 9000 ptas.

Connections are tedious on the Badajoz to Lisbon route (two trains a day, mostly slow regional services, with a possible train change at Entroncamento), but the scenery through the Serra de Marvão is grand.

CAR & MOTORCYCLE

Roads cross the Portugal-Spain border in at least 30 places. The easiest crossings (ie the best and biggest roads) are at Valença do Minho, Feces de Abajo (Chaves), Vilar Formoso, Elvas, Vila Verde de Ficalho (Serpa) and Vila Real de Santo António.

Portugal's national auto club, the Automóvel Club de Portugal, says that virtually all cross-border roads are now open 24 hours a day, often with no officials even in sight.

If you're driving your own car into Portugal, in addition to your passport and driving licence you must carry vehicle registration and insurance documents (insurance with at least third-party coverage is compulsory throughout the EU). A 'Green Card' from your home insurer confirms you have comprehensive coverage.

The UK & France

The quickest route to Lisbon from the UK is via ferry to northern Spain – from Plymouth to Santander with Brittany Ferries (☎ 0990-360 360) or from Portsmouth to Bilbao with P&O Ferries (☎ 0990-980 980; www.poef.com)

Both lines do the crossing twice a week in summer, taking about 36 hours. Peak summer fares are about £410 for a car, driver and one passenger, and accommodation in a basic two-berth cabin. From Santander it's roughly 1000km to Lisbon.

An alternative is to take a ferry or the Channel Tunnel to France and motor down the coast via Bordeaux, through Spain (via Burgos and Salamanca). From the channel ports of France it's roughly 1900km to Lisbon. One option to reduce driving time is to use motorail (car transport by rail) for all or part of the trip through France. For information in the UK contact Rail Europe's Motorail division (☎ 0171-203 7000; fax 0171-633 9900). In France the SNCF has a nationwide telephone number (☎ 08 36 35 35 35 in French, ☎ 08 36 35 35 39 in English) for all rail enquiries and reservations.

ᘓ ᘓ ᘓ ᘓ ᘓ ᘓ ᘓ ᘓ ᘓ ᘓ ᘓ ᘓ ᘓ ᘓ ᘓ ᘓ ᘓ ᘓ ᘓ

Returning Rental Cars to Lisbon Airport

If you return a car to the airport, watch for signs directing you into the *rental car* lot. If you go into the regular car park instead, you'll have to pay to get out! ∎

ᘓ ᘓ ᘓ ᘓ ᘓ ᘓ ᘓ ᘓ ᘓ ᘓ ᘓ ᘓ ᘓ ᘓ ᘓ ᘓ ᘓ ᘓ ᘓ

BICYCLE

Lisbon is a ghastly place for cyclists (see the Getting Around chapter), but if you're inseparable from your wheels, be sure to fill your repair kit before you leave home since it's unlikely you'll be able to buy that crucial gizmo for your machine in Lisbon. It's also a good idea to pack some sort of document to show you're the owner, in the unlikely event that the police stop you, and a photograph and written description of your bike, to assist the police in case it's stolen.

Bicycles can travel by air. You *can* take yours to pieces and put it in a bag or box, but it's much easier to simply wheel it to the check-in desk, where it should be treated as baggage – but check this with the airline well in advance. You may have to remove the pedals, turn the handlebars sideways and drop the saddle down so that the bike takes up less space in the aircraft's hold. Don't forget to let much (but not all) of the air out of the tyres to prevent them from bursting in the low-pressure baggage hold.

If you're going to Lisbon by train, your bike may be registered and sent separately to your destination, or it may accompany you, usually for an extra charge. Within Portugal, you can take your bike on any regional (R) or interregional (IR) train as accompanying baggage for around 1200$00, regardless of the distance you're going. Arrange this with the baggage office, preferably a few days in advance. European coach lines are fussier, though within Portugal regional buses might be easier going.

BOAT

The only passenger ships that call at Portuguese ports nowadays are cruise ships. Ferries can be a part of a journey by car from the UK, however; see Car & Motorcycle in this chapter.

TRAVEL AGENTS

The city's youth-oriented travel agencies are Tagus Travel (Map 3) and Jumbo Expresso (Map 1). Tagus (☎ 352 55 09 for air tickets or ☎ 352 59 86 for other services; fax 352

06 00) is at Rua Camilo Castelo Branco 20 (metro: Rotunda) and is open weekdays from 9 am to 6 pm, Saturday from 10 am to 1.30 pm. Another Tagus office (☎ 849 15 31) is at Praça de Londres, near Areeiro metro station. Jumbo Expresso (☎ 793 92 64; fax 793 92 67) is at Avenida da República 97, near Entre Campos metro station. Both Tagus and Jumbo offer budget-minded hotel, bus, train and air bookings. They also sell ISIC and Cartão Jovem cards. Another popular student-geared outfit is Wasteels (Map 3; ☎ 357 96 55) at Avenida António Augusto de Aguiar 88 (metro: Parque).

Movijovem (Map 3; ☎ 355 90 81; fax 352 86 21), Avenida Duque de Ávila 137 (metro: Saldanha) is Portugal's central Hostelling International booking office and has an arrangement with Tagus to sell Inter-Rail passes and airline tickets at Tagus' low rates. It's open on weekdays only, from 9.30 am to 6 pm.

Among competent mainstream travel agencies, the easiest to deal with is Top Tours (Map 3; ☎ 315 58 85; fax 315 58 73), Avenida Duque de Loulé 108 (metro: Rotunda). It is also Lisbon's American Express representative, so holders of American Express cards or travellers cheques can get commission-free currency exchange and cash advances, help with lost cards or cheques, and can have mail and faxes held or forwarded (the Lisbon postcode to use is 1050). It's open weekdays only, from 9.30 am to 1 pm and 2.30 to 6.30 pm.

Rotas do Vento (Map 4; ☎ 364 98 52, ☎ 364 98 59; fax 364 98 43), Rua dos Lusíadas 5, organises weekend guided walks (in Portuguese, with some English) for groups of six to 18, to both nearby and remote corners of Portugal; book two weeks or more ahead. Another able outdoor specialist is just across the Tejo. Lanius (☎ & fax 225 77 76), Rua de 25 Abril 35, Paivas, 2840 Amora, organises specialist nature tours in various regions including the Rio Tejo valley. Turnatur (☎ 207 68 86; fax 207 76 75), at Rua Almirante Reis 60 in Barreiro, organises nature walks, jeep safaris, canoeing and canyoning trips.

ORGANISED TOURS

Following are some reliable tour operators overseas that offer complete packages or can arrange made-to-order tours to Lisbon and nearby areas.

For a rundown of many of the UK's most reliable and interesting specialist tour operators, get hold of the free *AITO Directory of Real Holidays*, an annual index of member companies of the Association of Independent Tour Operators (☎ 0181-744 9280; fax 0181-744 3187). The London office of ICEP, the Portuguese state tourism organisation, publishes its own directory of cooperating travel agencies in the UK, the *Portugal Tour Operators Guide*.

Among reliable Portugal-specialist tour operators in France are Lusitania (☎ 01 44 69 75 06; fax 01 44 69 75 15), and Atout Portugal (call ☎ 01 43 20 78 78 or fax 01 43 22 97 20 for a list of cooperating travel agencies around France).

Lisbon City Breaks

Many UK tour operators offer two to seven-day 'city break' packages to Lisbon, including air fare and accommodation. Some of the best deals are from Mundi Color Holidays (☎ 0171-828 6021; fax 0171-834 5752); Osprey Holidays (☎ 0990-605 605; fax 0990-502020); Cresta (☎ 0161-927 7000; fax 0161-929 1114); Time Off (☎ 0990-846363; fax 0181-218 3636); Kirker Travel (☎ 0171-231 3333; fax 0171-231 4771) and Caravela/TAP Air Portugal Tours (☎ 0171-630 9223; fax 0171-233 9680). The Portuguese-run Abreu Travel Agency (☎ 0171-229 9905; fax 0171-229 0274) often has good flight and accommodation deals.

High season prices (including return air fare) for the city breaks range from around UK£270 for a two-night stay in a two star hotel to around UK£450 for a four night stay in a luxury-class hotel. Special offers at many of the hotels include free accommodation for children under 12 and a 'free' night if you stay more than three or four nights.

Lisbon & Elsewhere

Several UK operators, such as Travelscene (☎ 0181-427 8800; fax 0181-861 3674) offer 'multicentre' packages featuring, for instance, Lisbon and Sintra from around UK£320 for two nights at each place including air fare and car hire. Mundi Color Holidays and Caravela (see the Lisbon City Breaks section) offer comprehensive fly/drive packages to the Estoril Coast.

The Individual Travellers Portugal (☎ 01798-869485; fax 01798-869381), Destination Portugal (☎ 01993-773269; fax 01993-771910) and Simply Portugal (☎ 0181-742 2541; fax 0181 995 5346) specialise in fly-drive arrangements, flexible itineraries and accommodation in manor houses and converted farmhouses.

Special Interest Tours

EXPO '98 At the time of writing, only Destination Portugal (see Lisbon & Elsewhere above) had a special EXPO package (including air fare, hotel and EXPO pass) from around UK£315 for a four night stay in a three-star hotel.

Golf The UK-based Longshot Golf Holidays (☎ 01730-268621; fax 01730-231998) offers three to seven-night packages (including air fare, car hire, accommodation and pre-booked rounds at the six major courses near Lisbon). Special tuition packages are also available. Caravela (see Lisbon City Breaks section) can arrange pre-booked, discounted green-fees when you book a tour.

Bicycle Two US operators have itineraries in the Lisbon area: Easy Rider Tours (☎ 508-463-6955, toll-free 800-488-8332; fax 508-463-6988; ezrider@shore.net; www.cyclery.com/easyrider) offers small-group tours from Sesimbra to Lagos; Progressive Travels (☎ 206-285-1987, toll-free ☎ 800-

245-2229; fax 206-285-1988; progtrav@aol.com) offers a number of guided tours including a Lisbon to Lagos trip for the truly fit.

Walking The UK-based Alternative Travel Group (☎ 01865-513 333; fax 01865-310299; info@alternative-travel.co.uk) offers well-researched five-day walking tours, with deluxe bed and board, from Lisbon.

Gardens Mundi Color Holidays (see the Lisbon City Breaks section) has a one-week fly-drive 'Garden Tour', staying at Queluz and Palmela (within reach of five spectacular gardens) from around UK£640.

WARNING

The information in this chapter is particularly vulnerable to change: prices for international travel are volatile, routes are introduced and cancelled, schedules change, special deals come and go, and rules and visa requirements are amended. Airlines and governments seem to take a perverse pleasure in making price structures and regulations as complicated as possible. You should check directly with the airline or a travel agent to make sure you understand how a fare (and ticket you may buy) works. In addition, the travel industry is highly competitive and there are many lurks and perks.

The upshot of this is that you should get opinions, quotes and advice from as many airlines and travel agents as possible before you part with your hard-earned cash. The details given in this chapter should be regarded as pointers and are not a substitute for your own careful, up-to-date research.

Getting Around

THE AIRPORT

Bus No 91, called the Aero-Bus, is a special service departing from outside the arrivals hall about every 20 minutes from 7 am to 9 pm. It takes 30 to 45 minutes (depending on traffic) between the airport and the city centre, including a stop at Praça dos Restauradores, right outside the turismo. The price is 430$00/1000 for a one day/three day Bilhete Turístico that you can use on all city buses, trams and funiculars. Note that the Passe Turístico (see the Bus, Tram & Funicular section) is for some obscure reason *not* good for this bus. For outbound TAP passengers who show their air tickets, the ride to the airport is free.

Local bus Nos 8, 44, 45 and 83 also run right past the turismo, but you have to walk further at the airport to board them, and they're a nightmare in rush hour if you have baggage.

For a taxi, figure on about 1500$00, plus an extra 300$00 if your luggage needs to go in the boot.

BUS, TRAM & FUNICULAR

Companhia Carris de Ferro de Lisboa (Map 9), or Carris, is the municipal transport service (for all but the metro). Its buses and trams run from about 5 or 6 am to 1 am, with some night bus and tram services. *Lisboêtas* are surprisingly orderly in bus and ticket queues, though they justifiably grumble about the crowded buses and ridiculous lack of ticket kiosks. You can get a transport map, *Planta dos Transportes Públicas da Carris* (including a welcome map of night-time services) from the turismo and sometimes from Carris kiosks, though it's not always reliable. Bus routes are clearly listed at major stops.

Individual tickets are 150$00 on board, or half that if purchased beforehand. Prepaid tickets (called BUC: Bilhete Unico da Carris) are sold at Carris kiosks, open daily from 9 am to 8 pm, at Praça da Figueira, at the foot of the Elevador de Santa Justa, and in front of Cais do Sodré station. From these kiosks you can also get a one-day (430$00) or three-day (1000$00) Bilhete Turístico good for all buses, trams and funiculars. Also available here (and most metro stations) are the four-day (1600$00) or seven-day (2265$00) Passe Turístico, which is good for buses (except the Aero-Bus), trams, funiculars *and* the metro. You must show your passport to get the (non-transferable) Passe Turístico.

But none of these is a particularly great bargain unless you plan to do a lot of riding far from the centre. A better deal is the Lisboa Card (see Tourist Offices in the Facts for the Visitor chapter), which is good for most tourist sights as well as bus, tram, funicular and metro travel.

Buses

Useful bus routes include: Nos 32, 44 and 45 (Praça dos Restauradores, Praça do Comércio, Cais do Sodré); Nos 35 and 107 (Cais do Sodré, Santa Apolónia); Nos 9, 39 and 46 (Praça dos Restauradores, Santa Apolónia); and No 37 (Praça da Figueiro, Castelo do São Jorge).

Trams

The clattering, antediluvian trams (*eléctricos* or *tranvías)* are an endearing component of Lisbon. Don't leave Lisbon without riding tram No 28 through the narrow streets of the Alfama district, and back around to Largo Martim Moniz; the best place to catch it is east-bound on Rua da Conceiçao in the Baixa. West-bound from Rua da Conceição, it clanks through Bairro Alto to Estrela peak.

Two other useful lines are the No 15 from Praça da Figueira and Praça do Comércio, via Alcântara to Belém; and the No 18 from Praça do Comércio via Alcântara to Ajuda. The No 15 line now features huge new space-age articulated trams, which also have machines on board for tickets and one and three-day passes. Tram stops are usually

---

Tram Tips

Don't be alarmed if your tram driver suddenly stops the tram and jumps out. He's probably only *mudar as agulhas*, changing tracks. Or he might be judging whether he can get past a badly parked car. This is a particular hazard along the narrow streets of the No 28 tram's route and one which often causes long delays. You might even be asked to help budge the offending vehicle! ■

---

marked by a small *paragem* sign hanging from a lamp post or the overhead wires.

Funiculars

The city has three funiculars (*elevadors* or *ascensors* in Portuguese), which labour up and down the steepest hills around Praça dos Restauradores, plus the extraordinary Elevador de Santa Justa, a huge wrought-iron lift that raises you from the Baixa straight up to eye level with the Convento do Carmo ruins.

Santa Justa is more popular with tourists, but the most charming ride is on the Elevador da Bica through the Santa Catarina district, at the south-western corner of Bairro Alto. The other two funiculars are the Elevador da Glória, from Restauradores up to the São Pedro de Alcântara viewpoint, and the Elevador do Lavra from Largo de Anunciada, on the eastern side of Restauradores.

The Elevador de Santa Justa operates daily from 7 am to 11.45 pm (on Sundays and holidays from 9 am to 11 pm); the Elevadors da Bica and do Lavra from 7 am to 10.45 pm; and the Elevador da Glória from 7 am to 1 am daily. They're not for anyone in a hurry!

TRAIN

Lisbon has four major train stations. Santa Apolónia is the terminal for trains from northern and central Portugal and for all international services. Cais do Sodré serves trains to Cascais and Estoril, while Rossio serves Sintra and Estremadura. Barreiro, on the other side of the Rio Tejo, is the terminal

for *suburbano* services to Setúbal and all long-distance services to the south of Portugal, including the Algarve; connecting ferries leave frequently from the pier at Terreiro do Paço, by Praça do Comércio. You buy two tickets here: a 170$00 ferry ticket to Barreiro plus your onward train ticket.

Santa Apolónia station has a helpful CP information desk (☎ 888 40 25, ☎ 888 50 92) at door No 8; the desk is open from 8 am to 10 pm, the telephones until 11 pm. The international section at door No 47 includes an international ticket desk and a bank and credit-card ATM. The baggage office is at door No 25. Rossio station also has an information office, open from 9 am to 8 pm. All four stations have luggage lockers.

METRO

The modest *metropolitano* (underground) system, with 19km of track and 25 stations, is useful only for short hops across the centre. But at the time of writing, a huge pre-EXPO '98 expansion was pushing it out in all directions, including to Cais do Sodré, Rato and the EXPO '98 site (Oriente is the name of the new station here). By the year 2000 there will be 37km of track and 47 stations. Rossio is by far the busiest station, with some 63,000 passengers a day.

Individual tickets cost 70$00 and it's 550$00 for a *caderneta* of 10 tickets. Tickets can be purchased from windows or automatic dispensers. Single tickets should be validated in the little machine at the entrance to the trains (there *are* ticket inspectors). A one-day metro pass is 200$00 (620$00 for seven days) and both the Passe Turístico and

---

There's Rossio & Then There's Rossio

Rossio metro station, beneath the square called Rossio (Praça Dom Pedro V), is *not* the closest one to Rossio train station. For the train station you need to get off at Restauradores metro station. ■

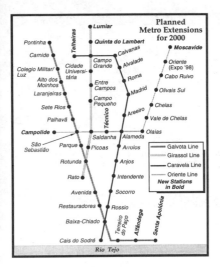

the Lisboa Card are good for free travel on the metro.

The system operates from 6.30 am to 1 am. Entrances are marked by a big red M. Travel is quite straightforward. Useful signs include *correspondência* (transfer between lines) and *saída* (exit to the street). Pickpockets can be a nuisance in rush-hour crowds.

CAR & MOTORCYCLE

Lisbon isn't much fun for car drivers thanks to heavy traffic, metro roadworks and manic drivers. There are two ring roads, both of which are useful for staying *out* of the centre. On maps the inner one is marked CRIL (Cintura Regional Interna de Lisboa), the outer one CREL (Cintura Regional Externa de Lisboa).

If you do venture into the city centre you'll find that parking spaces are scarce and car parks expensive: all-day rates in underground car parks (eg at Praça Marques de Pombal) are around 1000$00, but hotel car parks are often twice that. Hotels with (free) street car parking are mentioned in the Places to Stay chapter.

The city has a few permit-only spaces for disabled drivers, but so far, visitors have no

special access to them. A pilot project is apparently on the cards for an EU-wide permit, however.

Portugal's national auto club, Automóvel Club de Portugal or ACP (Map 6; ☎ 356 39 31; fax 357 47 32), is at Rua Rosa Araújo 24 (metro: Avenida or Rotunda). It's open weekdays from 9 am to 5.30 pm, with maps, guidebooks and camping information on the ground floor, and a helpful information office on the 2nd floor. For details about car-related documents you'll need in Portugal, see the Car & Motorcycle section of the Getting There & Away chapter.

Rental

The best car rental rate I found was from Solcar (☎ 315 05 26; fax 356 05 04): 5640$00 a day for a week or more (unlimited-mileage), or 3000$00 for one day plus 30$00 per kilometre. Mundirent (☎ 313 93 60; fax 313 93 69) is also competitive: 6000$00 all-inclusive daily rate for two to six days (5700$00 for a week or more). Other home-grown companies with low multi day rates include Rupauto (☎ 793 32 58; fax 793 17 68), Nova Rent (☎ 387 08 08; fax 387 31 30), and AA Castanheira (☎ 357 00 60).

Multinational car rental firms in Lisbon include Avis (☎ 356 11 76, or toll-free ☎ 0500-1002 in Portugal), Hertz (toll-free ☎ 0500-1231), Alamo (☎ 383 03 91; fax 387 33 17), Europcar (☎ 353 51 15; fax 353 67 57) and Tupi (Budget; ☎ 797 13 77). Some of the best deals, however, are often arranged from overseas, either as part of a package deal with your flight (see Organised Tours in the Getting There & Away chapter) or through an international car-rental company.

Drinking & Driving

The maximum legal blood-alcohol level for anyone behind the wheel is a mere 0.05%. If you drink and drive and are caught, you can expect to spend the night in a lock up, and the next morning in a courtroom. ■

Highways & Toll-Roads

Driving out of Lisbon you'll quickly encounter a rapidly expanding network of *estradas* (highways). Top of the line are *auto-estradas* or motorways, all of them *portagens* (toll-roads). The longest of these is the 304km Lisbon-Porto road, the shortest the northbound lanes of the 2km Ponte de Abril 25 over the Tejo at Lisbon. Other stretches include Porto-Braga, Porto-Amarante and Lisbon-Cascais. The present total of 575km of toll-roads charges cars and motorcycles about 9$00 per kilometre (2690$00 for Lisbon-Porto, for example).

Highway nomenclature can be baffling. Motorway numbers prefixed with an E are Europe-wide designations. Portugal's toll-roads are prefixed with an A. Highways in its *rede fundamental* (main network) are prefixed IP, and subsidiary ones in the *rede complementare* IC. Some highways have several designations, and numbers that change in mid-flow eg the Lisbon-Porto road is variously called E80, E01, A1 and IP1.

Numbers for the main two-lane *estradas nacionais* or national roads have no prefix letter on some road maps (eg the one published by the Automóvel Club de Portugal), while they're prefixed N on others (eg the Michelin No 440 map). ∎

You can rent a motorcycle from Gesrent (☎ 385 27 22). High season prices per day for a Yamaha 50 are 3900$00 for up to three days, 3400$00 for up to a week and 2900$00 for more than a week.

Road Rules

You may not believe it after seeing what Portuguese drivers can do, but there are indeed rules. To begin with, as with the rest of continental Europe, driving is on the right. Most signs use international symbols, and lanes are marked with solid and dashed lines according to international conventions (though solid white lines do not deter Portugal's highway maniacs).

Except as marked otherwise, speed limits for cars (without a trailer) and motorcycles are 60km/h in built-up areas, 90km/h outside towns and villages, and 120km/h on motorways. If your driving licence is less than a year old you're restricted to 90 km/h even on motorways, and your car must display a '90' disc, available from any ACP office.

Safety belts must be worn in front and back seats, and children under 12 years old may not travel in the front seat. Motorcyclists and their passengers must wear helmets.

The legal limit for alcohol in the blood is a minuscule 0.05%, so don't even think about drinking and driving. You're not allowed to use your horn in built-up areas after dark except in an emergency.

Police are authorised to impose on-the-spot fines (in escudos), and must issue a receipt. If you prefer to slug it out in a Portuguese courtroom, you must still pay a deposit big enough to cover the maximum possible fine!

Fuel

Petrol is pricey, around 163$00 and up for a litre of 95-octane *sem chumbo* (unleaded petrol) and 115$00 for *gasóleo* (diesel). Unleaded petrol is readily available in most parts of the country. There are plenty of self-service stations, and major credit cards are readily accepted at many, but not all, stations.

TAXI

Compared with the rest of Europe, Lisbon's *táxis* are quick, cheap and plentiful. You can flag one down, or pick one up at a rank – including at Rossio, Praça dos Restauradores, near all train and bus stations, at top-end hotels, and at the intersections of some major roads.

You can also call for one. The city's biggest radio-taxi company is Rádio Táxis de Lisboa (☎ 815 50 61); other reliable ones are Autocoope (☎ 793 27 56) and Teletáxis (☎ 815 20 76, ☎ 815 20 16). One reliable tourist-taxi outfit (for excursions, at fixed

Top: Azulejo façade on a house at Campo de Santa Clara
Bottom: Old and new-style trams in Praça do Comércio

JULIA WILKINSON

BETHUNE CARMICHAEL

Top: Mime artists in Rua Augusta, Baixa district
Bottom: Inside a traditional wine shop, Belém

standard rates) is Unidos de Lisboa (☎ 814 73 53).

The fare on weekdays during daylight hours is 250$00 flag fall, plus a complex formula depending on distance and elapsed time. Outside the city limits, the fare is calculated at 52$00 per kilometre. Any tolls are paid by the customer. A load of luggage incurs an extra 300$00 charge.

All taxis have meters, but rip-offs do happen. In particular, a few of the taxis that haunt the airport take new arrivals the long way round to their destinations. The good *Taxi Information* brochure – including information about rates and complaint telephone numbers – is free for the taking at the exit from the arrivals concourse. If you think you may have been cheated, get a receipt from the driver and make a claim with the tourist subsection of the police (☎ 346 61 41, ext 279).

Transport For Disabled Travellers

For disabled people, Carris operates a 24-hour dial-a-ride service (☎ 363 20 44 or 758 56 76) at a cost comparable to taxis. Try to book your rides a day or two in advance. Carris apparently also has adapted coaches with wheelchair space for hire – call ☎ 363 92 26.

BICYCLE

Lisbon traffic is a horror for cyclists. You're better off stashing your bike with left-luggage at the train station or airport and seeing the city by public transport. Better hotels and *pensões* may have a storage room. See the Getting There & Away chapter for information on putting your machine on a bus or train.

Gesrent (☎ 385 27 22; fax 385 74 36) rents out mountain bicycles as well as motorbikes. Prices are 1500$00 per day for one to three days, 1300$00 per day for four to seven days, or 1100$00 per day for eight or more days.

FERRY

The Transtejo ferry line has several river-front terminals. Two are adjacent to Praça do Comércio: Terreiro do Paço terminal, from where passenger ferries cross the Rio Tejo to Montijo (270$00), Seixal (200$00) every hour or so (fewer at weekends), and Barreiro; and, next to it, Cais da Alfândega terminal, from where passenger ferries go every 10 minutes, all day, to Cacilhas (90$00). Car

---

Street Names

The street names you'll come across in Lisbon crop up time and time again all over Portugal. Most of them are of historical significance or refer to a famous person.

Rua/Avenida

25 de Abril	the date when the 1974 Revolution of the Carnations began
5 de Outubro	the date in 1910 when the monarchy was overthrown and a republic established
1 de Dezembro	the date in 1640 when Portuguese independence was restored after Spanish rule
da Liberdade	referring to the freedom established by the 1974 revolution
dos Restauradores	the restorers of independence after Spanish rule
Afonso de Albuquerque	the viceroy of India who expanded Portugal's empire; he conquered Goa in 1510, Malacca in 1511 and Hormuz in 1515
Pedro Álvares Cabral	the 'discoverer' of Brazil (in 1500)
Manuel Cardoso	a 17th century composer
Luís de Camões	Portugal's most famous 16th century poet
João de Deus	a 19th century lyric poet
Almeida Garrett	a 19th century poet, playwright and novelist
Alexandre Herculano	a 19th century historian
Alexandre Serpa Pinto	a late 19th century African explorer

ferries go to Cacilhas from a pier at Cais do Sodré. The ferry line serving the Barreiro train terminus is called Soflusa.

ORGANISED TOURS
Bus & Tram Tours
Carris (☎ 363 20 21), the municipal transport company, has a 1½-hour Eléctrico das Colinas (Hills Tour) by tram, up to four or five times a day, up and around the hills on both sides of the Baixa, for 2800$00 (1500$00 for children aged four to 10). It also has a 2000$00 (1000$00 children) open-top bus Tagus Tour of the city and Belém, six or seven times a day, arranged so you can get off, explore and pick up the next bus an hour later. Both tours are in English. They depart from Praça do Comércio and there is no need to book ahead.

From offices next door to one another, Gray Line (☎ 352 25 94), Cityrama (☎ 355 85 69) and Portugal Tours (☎ 352 29 02) run more or less identical sightseeing bus tours of Lisbon and the surrounding region, for identical prices. Typical Lisbon offerings include a three-hour city tour for 5000$00; Lisbon by night (four hours), with a restaurant meal, for 12,000$00; and Lisbon plus the Estoril coast or Lisbon plus the Costa Azul (full day) for 12,000$00. All buses depart from a terminal on Avenida Sidónio Pais, a block south of São Sebastião metro station, and pick up passengers at selected hotels. The easiest place to book a seat is through a travel agent or up-market hotel, but if there's a space you can usually hop aboard the daytime trips without a booking.

River Cruises
For a relaxed look at the city from a unique point of view, Gray Line (☎ 882 03 47) runs two-hour, multilingual cruises on the Tejo (Cruzeiros no Tejo; Map 7). They depart daily (at least from April through October) at 3 pm from the eastern end of the Terreiro do Paço ferry terminal by Praça do Comércio. The boats go down as far as Belém, cross the river and return, with no stops. The price is 3000$00 if you buy a ticket at the terminal, more if you book it through a hotel (in which case you get picked up from – but not returned to – the hotel). In summer tickets are also sold from a kiosk at the bottom of Rua do Carmo. For student-card holders, children under six and adults over 65, the price is 1500$00.

City & Regional Coach Tours
Gray Line (☎ 352 25 94; fax 316 04 04), Avenida Praia da Vitória 12-B, organises three to seven-day coach tours to selected regions of Portugal from Lisbon, usually through travel agents or upper-end tourist hotels. Miltours (☎ 352 41 66), Rua Conde de Redondo 21, also has a choice of day trips.

Walking Tours
Walking Around Lisbon (☎ 340 45 39; fax 340 45 75), Avenida da Liberdade 114, organises two theme walks: Medieval Suburbia covers the Chiado, Bairro Alto and Carmo areas (where ancient Lisbon first expanded beyond its walls) on Tuesdays, Thursdays and Saturdays at 9 am, starting from Praça dos Restauradores. The Old Lisbon walk, visiting the Alfama and Castelo areas, runs on Mondays, Wednesdays and Fridays, at 9 am from Casa dos Bicos, Rua dos Bacalheiros. Both walks last three hours (with a rest stop for a drink) and cost 2500$00 per person.

Things to See & Do

Lisbon is the kind of place where you can spend days just sitting at street cafés watching the world go by or meandering through the old neighbourhoods shopping or listening to night-time *fado*. Other attractively lazy options include taking a tram to the end of the line, or watching the sun set from the city's various hilltop *miradouros*.

During EXPO '98 you'll find major attractions from around the world at the EXPO site in the north-east of the city and a cultural programme that has the city buzzing (see later on in this chapter for full details).

There are plenty of other cultural sights. In addition to the architectural masterpieces at Belém (some 6km west of the city centre), Lisbon also has 40 or 50 museums, ranging from obscure house-museums to the world-class Gulbenkian. The city's best are the Museu Calouste Gulbenkian (not to be missed) and its sibling the Centro de Arte Moderna, the Museu Nacional de Arte Antiga, the Museu do Azulejo and the Museu-Escola de Artes Decorativas. Other good ones are the Museu Nacional de Etnológia, Museu da Cidade and Museu da Água.

Museum hours change like quicksilver, so if you're making a long trip to visit one, it's worth calling ahead. Most museums are closed on Mondays. Several have free admission on Sundays and national holidays, at least until 2 pm. Youth and student discounts are available.

THE BAIXA & THE RIVERFRONT

Following the catastrophic earthquake of 1755, one of the few people who kept their heads was the autocratic Marquês de Pombal. He put Lisbon on the road to recovery and took the opportunity to rebuild the city centre as quickly as possible, in a severe and simple, low-cost, easily managed style.

The entire area from the riverside to the Rossio was reborn as a rectangular grid of wide commercial streets, each dedicated to a trade. The memory of these districts lives on in the district's north-south street names – Áurea (formerly Ouro, gold), Sapateiros (shoemakers), Correeiros (saddlers), Prata (silver), Douradores (gilders) and Fanqueiros (cutlers).

This 'lower town' remains the de facto heart of Lisbon. Down the middle runs pedestrianised Rua Augusta, overflowing with cafés, restaurants, shops and banks. A fair fraction of the city's bus and tram lines funnel through Praça do Comércio at the Baixa's riverside end, or Rossio and Praça da Figueira at its upper end.

From Praça do Comércio to Cais do Sodré (Maps 10 & 11)
Before the earthquake, Praça do Comércio was called Terreiro do Paço (Palace Square), after the royal Palácio da Ribeira that overlooked it until the morning of 1 November

---

HIGHLIGHTS
Though it's a pretty subjective call, my pick of Lisbon's highlights is:

- Mosteiro dos Jerónimos at Belém – wander (in daylight) through the Alfama district, following its lanes to the riverside and up to the views from Castelo São Jorge
- a ride on tram No 28 from Rua da Conceição (Baixa), east into the Alfama and west into the Bairro Alto
- bar-hopping through the Bairro Alto, with a stop somewhere for a taste of *vinho tinto* and fado
- the very fine Museu Calouste Gulbenkian, the Museu Nacional de Arte Antiga and the Museu do Azulejo
- the over-the-top Capela de São João Baptista in the Igreja de São Roque
- the grand mansions and lush gardens of Sintra

In addition, EXPO '98 has added its own range of 'must-sees', notably the Lisbon Oceanarium, Europe's largest (called Oceans Pavilion during the exposition). ■

1755. The huge square, open to the river, still feels like the entrance to the city, thanks to Machado de Castro's bronze **equestrian statue** of Dom José I at the centre; the 18th century, arcaded **government ministries** along three sides; and Verissimo da Costa's **Arco da Victória**, the arch opening onto Rua Augusta.

In fact most visitors coming by river or sea in bygone days would have arrived here. It was also from here that Dom João VI and his massive entourage fled to Brazil in 1807.

At the north-western corner of the square, by the central post office, is the spot where Dom Carlos and his eldest son, Luís Filipe, were assassinated in 1908. Just west of here is a smaller square, **Praça do Município**, dominated by Lisbon's town hall, built in 1874, on the eastern side, the former marine arsenal on the southern side and a finely carved, 18th century *pelourinho* (pillory) at the centre.

Continuing west for another 400m along Rua do Arsenal, you arrive at Lisbon's other main riverfront plaza, Praça do Duque da Terceira, better known by its riverfront name, **Cais do Sodré**. Here are more government offices, a few consulates, the Transtejo car ferry and the Cais do Sodré train station (from where electric trains speed off to Cascais and the Estoril coast).

A few short blocks west of the square is the city's kinetic main market, the domed **Mercado da Ribeira** (Map 10) – officially the Mercado Municipal 24 de Julho. Get here early in the morning to see feisty vendors hawking vegetables, fruit, seafood and more.

From here, Avenida 24 de Julho runs for 3km along the river to the Port of Lisbon and the warehouse district of **Alcântara**. This strip is also a major axis of Lisbon's nightlife (see the Entertainment chapter). A pleasant way to return to Praça do Comércio is along the breezy riverfront promenade.

Eastward from Praça do Comércio

About 250m east of the Arco da Victória, on the northern side of Rua da Alfândega, is the **Igreja da Conceição Velha** (Map 7). Its finely carved Manueline façade was rebuilt and reattached to this church after the earthquake. A bit further along, where Rua dos Bacalhoeiros merges with Rua da Alfândega to become Campo das Cebolas, is the startling early 16th century **Casa dos Bicos** (House of Facets; Map 12), with a prickly façade (restored and reconstructed in the early 1980s) that was a folly of Afonso de Albuquerque, a former viceroy of Portuguese India. It's now the headquarters for the Comemorações dos Descobrimentos (Commemoration of the Discoveries – the discovery of the sea route to India by Vasco da Gama in 1498, and other seafaring exploits). You can visit the ground floor's display of bits of the old Moorish city wall and brick street.

From here, various alleys and gloomy staircases climb up from Rua da Alfândega into the Alfama district and the Castelo de São Jorge.

Central Baixa

Under the streets of the Baixa is a series of tunnels, believed to be the remnants of a **Roman spa** and probably dating from the 1st century AD. You can decend into the mouldy depths – by way of the offices of Banco Comércil Portuguesa (Map 11) at Rua Augusta 62-74 – only on regular group tours organised by the Museu da Cidade at 3, 4 and 5 pm every Thursday afternoon in summer.

Alternatively, you can rise above the Baixa at a stately pace. At the eastern end of Rua da Conceição you can catch a clanking **No 28 tram** up past the Sé into the old Alfama and Graça districts. At the other end of the Baixa, the **Elevador de Santa Justa** (Map 9), an incongruously huge, but charming wrought-iron lift designed by one Raul Mésnier (not Gustave Eiffel as some sources insist) and completed in 1902, will hoist you above the café tables of Rua de Santa Justa to a viewing platform at eye level with the Convento do Carmo ruins in the Chiado district. Metro works have currently closed the exit into the Chiado district but once they're finished you can use the lift as a convenient way to reach the area.

Rossio & Praça da Figueira (Maps 8 & 9)
This pair of plazas form the gritty heart of the Baixa, with transport to everywhere, lots of cafés from which to watch a cross-section of Lisbon's multicultural population and thousands of pigeons. You'll also find hustlers and hawkers preying cheerfully on visitors. You're bound to pass through here every day you're in Lisbon, on your way to more interesting neighbourhoods.

In the middle of the Rossio is a **statue**, allegedly of Dom Pedro IV, for whom the square is formally named. The story goes that the statue is actually of Emperor Maximilian of Mexico and was abandoned in Lisbon en route from France to Mexico after news arrived of Maximilian's assassination. On the northern side of the square is the restored 1846 **Teatro Nacional de Dona Maria II** (Map 9), with a façade topped by a statue of 16th century playwright Gil Vicente.

In less orderly times the Rossio was the scene of animal markets, fairs and bullfights. The theatre was built on the site of a palace in which the unholiest excesses of the Portuguese Inquisition took place in the 16th to 19th centuries. Around the corner, just to the north of Praça da Figueira, is the vast **Igreja de São Domingos** (Map 9). In this church's pre-earthquake incarnation the Inquisition's *autos-da-fé*, or judgements, were handed down.

Rolling Motion Square
This was the nickname given to the Rossio by early English visitors because of the undulating mosaic pattern of the pavements here (and elsewhere in the city). The mosaics were first installed by prison labour gangs in the 19th century and are now mostly in evidence around the fountains.

They may make you seasick, but they're more sensible than they look. Hand-cut white limestone and grey basalt cubes are pounded into a bed of sand, making a hard surface which nevertheless lets the rainwater through. In the course of street works such as the Rossio's pre-EXPO '98 disruptions, they're simply dug up and reused. ∎

Across Largo de São Domingos from the church is the **Palácio dos Condes de Almada** (Map 9), also called the Palácio da Independéncia or Palácio da Restauração, where the *restauradores* met for the last time in 1640 before rising against the Spanish occupation.

West of the theatre is Rossio train station (from where trains tunnel out to the Campolide district before zipping on to Sintra), and a bit to the north is the busy Praça dos Restauradores.

CHIADO & BAIRRO ALTO

These two districts, lying above the Baixa to the west, make a perfect pair for day-and-night exploration. The Chiado, a wedge of wide streets roughly between Rua da Misericórdia and Rua do Crucifixo, is the posh place for shopping and for loitering in elegant cafés. The Bairro Alto, a fashionable residential district in the 17th century (and still boasting some fine mansions), is now better known as the raffish heartland of Lisbon's nightlife.

The best way to get your bearings is from the top of the extraordinary Elevador de Santa Justa, a macho wrought-iron lift rising from the junction of Rua de Santa Justa and Rua Áurea in the Baixa, almost to the doorway of the Convento do Carmo. From the Chiado you can gape at the destruction wrought by fire and earthquake: the ruined **Convento do Carmo** (Map 9) stands as a stunning testimony to the 1755 earthquake. Only the Gothic arches, walls and flying buttresses remain of what was once one of Lisbon's largest churches. It was built in 1423 by Dom Nuno Álvares Pereira, Dom João I's military commander, who turned to religion after a life of fighting, and spent the last eight years of his life in complete obscurity in this Carmelite convent.

Now its ruins serve as an atmospheric open-air home for the rambling collection of artefacts called the **Museu Arqueológico do Carmo** (Map 9; ☎ 346 0473). Among the items scattered around the open-air nave are Luso-Romano statuary, a huge carved tomb of Ança limestone containing the bones of

Ferdinand I, and a 3500-year-old Egyptian mummy clasping its knees beside gruesome preserved Peruvian skulls, complete with hair.

Due to metro works, the museum was closed at the time of research, but on re-opening should function Tuesday to Saturday, from 10 am to 6 pm during April through September, and from 10 am to 1 pm and 2 to 5 pm the rest of the year. Admission is 300$00.

In contrast to the convent, the gutted buildings that have pockmarked the Chiado since a massive fire in 1988 are now being rebuilt and restored by architect Álvaro de Siza Vieira, who is largely maintaining the Chiado's old style. The fire caused irreparable damage to many elegant buildings (especially in Rua do Crucifixo), but one survivor is the **Teatro Nacional de São Carlos** (Map 10) in Rua Serpa Pinto. Lisbon's opera house and its largest, most handsome theatre, it was built in the 1790s in imitation of the San Carlos theatre in Naples. It stands opposite the smaller Teatro Municipal de São Luís.

Nearby, in the former Convento de São Francisco at Rua Serpa Pinto 4, is the **Museu do Chiado** (Map 10; ☎ 343 21 48), known until 1994 as the Museu Nacional de Arte Contemporânea. It's a respectable collection of contemporary Portuguese paintings, drawings and sculpture from approximately 1850 to 1950. Among painters represented are Rafael Bordalo Pinheiro, José de Almada Negreiros, Amadeo de Souza Cardoso and Maria Helena Vieira da Silva. The museum is open Tuesday from 2 to 6 pm and Wednesday to Sunday from 10 am to 6 pm. Admission is 400$00 (free on Sunday mornings).

Two more *elevadores* – the funicular **Elevador da Glória** (Map 8) and **Elevador da Bica** (Map 10) – provide stately entrance to the Bairro Alto, and are worth the ride in any case. The Elevador da Glória climbs from near the turismo on Praça dos Restauradores, up to gardens and a superb viewpoint atop one of Lisbon's seven hills, **São Pedro de Alcântara**. Across the road is the **Solar do Vinho do Porto** (Map 8), where you can sample up to 300 different varieties of port in a suitably salubrious setting (see the boxed aside in the Entertainment chapter).

A short walk downhill to Largo Trindade Coelho brings you to the Bairro Alto's most famous cultural asset, the **Igreja de São Roque** (Map 8). The dull façade of this Jesuit church, built in the late 16th century, largely by architect Felipe Terzi, is one of Lisbon's biggest deceptions: inside, the side chapels are crammed with gold and glitter, mosaics of marble and ornate azulejos in Florentine style. The custodian leads visitors from one chapel to the next, switching on the lights and saying proudly, 'Portuguese! Portuguese!' as if he can't believe it himself.

Just when you think you've seen everything, you arrive at the *pièce de résistance*, the **Capela de São João Baptista**, the chapel to the left of the altar. Commissioned in 1742 by Portugal's most extravagant king, Dom João V, it was designed and built in Rome by the Italian architect Luigi Vanvitelli using the most expensive materials possible, including amethyst, alabaster, agate, lapis lazuli and Carrara marble. After its consecration by Pope Benedict XIV it was dismantled and shipped to Lisbon for what was then a staggering £225,000. Check out the intricate marble mosaics, which from a modest distance look just like paintings. It's all completely over the top, of course, but extraordinary nonetheless.

If you still haven't seen enough gilded artwork and liturgical extravaganza, pop into the **Museu de Arte Sacra** (Map 8; ☎ 346 03 61) next door. Also known as the Museu de São Roque, it's housed in the church's former convent. Inside is a mind-boggling array of liturgical accessories – gold-threaded vestments, book stands of carved bronze, gem-encrusted chalices and bejewelled mitres. The museum is open Tuesday to Sunday, from 10 am to 5 pm. Admission is 150$00, but free on Sundays.

From the southern end of the Bairro Alto (at the junction of Rua da Moeda and Rua de São Paulo, walking distance from Cais do Sodré) the Elevador da Bica creeps up to Rua do Loreto, a few blocks west of Praça de Luís Camões. Riding this gives you a chance to explore the unsung neighbourhood of **Santa Catarina**, the south-westerly arm of the Bairro Alto. This compact, maze-like district couldn't be less like the Chiado. It's bright with hanging laundry, and alive with the sound of balcony gossip, chattering kids and caged songbirds. The district's name comes from the 17th century **Igreja de Santa Catarina** (Map 6) in Calçada do Combro, largely rebuilt after the 1755 earthquake but still full of pre-earthquake gilded woodwork and with a gloriously ornate baroque organ. Downhill, at the end of Rua Marechal Saldanha, on another of Lisbon's seven hills, is the **Miradouro de Santa Catarina** (Map 6), with a bird's-eye view of the river and the Ponte 25 de Abril. There's a statue here to the Adamastor, a legendary monster said to have terrorised Portuguese explorers rounding the Cape of Good Hope. The Walking Tours section later in the chapter describes a route through this Bairro Alto area.

Why Black & White?
Lisbon's mosaic pavements aren't coloured black and white simply for aesthetic reasons. The black is said to recall the holy habit of St Vincent (Lisbon's patron saint), and the white the outfits of the crusaders who helped conquer Lisbon from the Moors. ■

ALFAMA, CASTELO & GRAÇA

This area east and north-east of the Baixa, hurtling all the way down to the river's edge, is Lisbon's oldest and most historically interesting district. It's also one of the most rewarding areas for walkers and photographers, thanks to the warren of medieval streets in the Alfama district and the outstanding views from three of Lisbon's seven hills – São Jorge, Graça and Senhora do Monte (see the later Walking Tours section for a suggested route through the Alfama).

The Alfama area was inhabited by the Visigoths as far back as the 5th century. Though remnants of a Visigothic town wall still remain, it was the Moors who gave the district much of its distinctive appearance and atmosphere, as well as its name: the Arabic *alhama* means springs or bath, probably in reference to the hot springs found near Largo das Alcáçarias. In Moorish times the Alfama was an upper-class residential area, but after various earthquakes destroyed most of the fine mansions (and the churches which the Christians later built) it reverted to a working-class quarter inhabited mainly by fisherfolk. It was one of the few districts to be saved from the ravages of the 1755 earthquake, thanks to its steep layers of stone.

Today, its bewildering maze of alleys and lanes (called *becos* and *travessas)* and steep stairways is in sharp contrast to the Baixa's prim, straight streets. Tumbling downhill from the castle to the river, with streets often narrow enough to shake hands across, the Alfama has a village atmosphere – you can quickly feel like an intruder if you take a wrong turn into someone's back yard. At night, it's probably not wise to wander around alone, not only because it's so easy to get lost (maps are little use in this clustered neighbourhood), but also because the area still maintains a somewhat unruly reputation.

By day, the Alfama is a jovial enclave of cafés and tiny grocery stores, sizzling sardine smells and squawking budgies. Early mornings are probably the best time to catch its traditional flavour, with fisherpeople selling fresh fish from their doorways and hanging laundry from their windows to dry. Not so long ago, they would have congregated at the public open-air laundries too, but in recent years many of their houses have been modernised under the Reabilitação Urbana d'Alfama project. This scheme has inevitably led to some gentrification and commercialisation in the main streets, with an increasing number of souvenir shops and touristy restaurants cramming their tables into the alleys. By lunchtime, the Alfama's traditional buzz has ebbed away and you're more likely to bump into tour groups or bewildered backpackers poring over their maps than local Alfama residents. For real rough-and-tumble atmosphere, delve into the narrowest back alleys, or visit during the Festas dos Santos Populares in June (see Public Holidays & Special Events in the Facts for the Visitor chapter) when the whole quarter buzzes.

The Alfama's most important religious monument is the **Sé** (Map 12), on the western edge of the district at Largo da Sé. This Romanesque cathedral was built in 1150, soon after the city had been recaptured from the Moors by Afonso Henriques. He was wary enough of his enemy to want the church built like a fortress (the French architects designed a very similar fortress-cathedral for Coimbra). It's been extensively restored following Lisbon's various earthquakes and is now rather dull. While you're here, though, it's worth checking out the baroque organs and intricate baroque crib by Machado de Castro in a chapel off the north aisle. The Gothic cloister is open Tuesday to Sunday, from 10 am to 5 pm; entry is 100$00 (free on Sunday). The sacristy (same hours, 400$00) contains various religious paraphernalia, including São Vicente relics in a mother-of-pearl casket.

Across the other side of the largo is the **Igreja de Santo António**, built in 1812 on the site of St Anthony's birthplace (see the St Anthony boxed aside in Facts about Lisbon). It has a small museum inside devoted to St Anthony but little else of interest.

From here you can strike uphill for the castle towards Largo das Portas do Sol (which is also the route of tram No 28). Downhill, following Rua de São João da Praça will bring you to the Largo de São Rafael where there's a ruined **Moorish tower**, part of the Moors' original town wall. The old **Jewish quarter** is adjacent, marked by the tiny Rua da Judiaria. At Largo de São Rafael, the road divides into Rua de São Miguel and Rua de São Pedro. All along these two streets, and to the Largo do Chafariz de Dentro (fountain within the walls) at the bottom of Rua de São Pedro you'll find most of the Alfama's busiest

shops, restaurants and cafés; these are especially lively in the mornings and at lunch times.

Heading uphill from the cathedral along Rua Augusto Rosa you'll pass the unmemorable ruins of a **Roman theatre** (apparently consecrated by Nero in 57 BC) off to the left in Rua de São Mamede, before reaching two of the area's most stunning viewpoints: the **Miradouro de Santa Luzia** (Map 12) and, a little further on, the **Largo das Portas do Sol** (the sun gateway, originally one of the seven gates into the Moors' city). Other worthwhile sights here include the **Igreja da Santa Luzia**, with wall panels of azulejos depicting the capture of the castelo from the Moors, and the nearby **Museu-Escola de Artes Decorativas** (Map 12; ☎ 886 21 83), at Largo das Portas do Sol 2.

This Museum-School is owned and operated by the private Fundação Ricardo do Espírito Santo Silva, founded in 1953 to showcase banker Espírito Santo Silva's striking collection of 16th to 19th century furniture and other decorative articles, ranging from a silver picnic set to beautiful Arraiolos rugs. The foundation has also set up educational projects to encourage traditional crafts, and provides workshop space to cabinet-makers, silversmiths, bookbinders and others working with traditional methods.

All of this, plus a book and souvenir shop, coffee shop, restaurant, library and temporary exhibitions, are housed on several floors of an elegant 18th century palace, the Palácio Azurara (which itself sports some fine original azulejos). It's open Wednesday to Monday, from 10 am to 5 pm (to 8 pm on Tuesdays and Thursdays in summer). Admission is 800$00 (free to art students and children up to 12) and half-hour tours can be arranged.

A short, steep climb from the Largo das Portas do Sol (or catch bus No 37 from the Praça da Figueira) brings you to the **Castelo de São Jorge** (Map 12). From its Visigoth beginnings in the 5th century, the castelo has had quite a history: fortified by the Moors in the 9th century, sacked by the Christians in the 12th century (see the Siege of Lisbon boxed aside), used as a royal residence from the 14th to 16th centuries and as a prison in every century, what's left has now been tarted up for tourists. Within its massive battlements you'll find everything from a posh restaurant and open-air café to caged birds and strutting peacocks, buskers and craft hawkers. Best of all, the castelo's 10 towers and shady paths and terraces offer great panoramas over the city and river.

The inner area, which until recently hosted a superb *parque infantil* (children's playground), is now an archaeological dig, prior to the possible construction of an underground car park. Both Roman and Islamic remains are expected to be found: this was once an elite residential neighbourhood for the Moors, whose mosque stood nearby, on the site of the current Igreja de Santa Cruz.

There's little left of the former palace, Paço de Alcáçova, built in the southern corner of the castelo by Dom Dinis on the site of a Moorish palace (it was already in ruins by the 17th century), but the nearby medieval quarter of Bairro de São Jorge still retains some of its original flavour.

North of the castle is the former **Mouraria** quarter, where the Moors lived after the Christian conquest of Lisbon. It's now rather sombre and lifeless, though the Rua da Mouraria, dominated by an ugly modern shopping centre, has been modernised and pedestrianised.

North-east of the castelo lies the **Graça** district. If you follow Rua de São Tomé up from Largo das Portas do Sol, you'll first pass the small Largo de Rodrigues de Freitas where, at No 13, you'll find the intriguing **Museu da Marioneta** (Map 12; ☎ 886 33 04) for puppet aficionados of all ages, not just for kids. It's crammed with every kind of puppet imaginable, from finger puppets to life-size creations. Especially interesting are the traditional Portuguese puppets from the 19th century and an Asian collection (including elephant puppets from Burma). There's also a tiny theatre where performances for children are often held at weekends. The museum is open daily, Tuesday to Sunday,

from 10 am to 1 pm and 2 to 7 pm; admission is 500$00.

Uphill from here you reach Calçada da Graça. The former Augustinian convent at the end of this road now serves as a barracks, but climb up to the left and you'll come to a splendid viewpoint, the **Miradouro da Graça** (Map 7), atop one of Lisbon's seven hills.

Another 700m beyond the convent (turn left off Rua da Graça into Rua Damasceno Monteiro then bear right, up Calçada do Monte) is the third major viewpoint in the area, the **Miradouro da Senhora do Monte** (Map 7). It's the best place in town for views of the castelo, Mouraria district and Lisbon city centre, studded with the cranes of building sites.

A couple of cultural eye-openers lie within walking distance to the east of Largo de Rodrigues de Freitas (tram No 28 also passes close by): the **Igreja de Santa Engrácia** (Map 12) and the **Igreja de São Vicente de Fora**. If you come here any time on a Saturday or on Tuesday morning, you'll also find Lisbon's **Feira da Ladra** flea market in full swing in the nearby Campo de Santa Clara (see the Markets boxed aside in the Shopping chapter). Dominating the scene is the huge dome of the Igreja de Santa Engrácia. When work began on the church in 1682, it was planned to be one of the grandest in Lisbon. After 284 years of neglect and bureaucratic cock-ups (at one point it was even used as a warehouse for artillery), it was finally inaugurated in 1966 as the Panteão Nacional (National Pantheon; Map 12). Its six marble cenotaphs, dedicated to the memory of historic figures including Vasco da Gama and Luís de Camões, and its tombs of former Portuguese presidents and literary figures such as Almeida Garrett, are all very sombre. The best thing about the place is the view from the dome (the guide can usually be persuaded to take visitors to the top in the elevator). It's open daily from 9 am to 1 pm and 3 to 7 pm.

Far more impressive is the nearby Igreja de São Vicente de Fora (*fora* refers to the church being 'outside' the old city wall).

The Siege of Lisbon

The reconquest of Lisbon from the Moors in 1147 is one of the more unsavoury chapters in Portugal's early history. Afonso Henriques, Count of Porto, had already thrashed the Moors at Ourique in 1139 (and started calling himself King of Portugal) and now set his sights on Lisbon. Short of experienced troops, he persuaded a ruffian band of English, Flemish, French and German adventure-crusaders on their way to Palestine to give him a hand. 'Do not be seduced by the desire to press on with your journey,' begged the Bishop of Porto on the king's behalf, 'for the praiseworthy thing is not to have been to Jerusalem, but to have lived a good life while on the way.'

It sounded an attractive idea (they were offered all the enemy's loot if the city were taken) and in June 1147 the siege of the Castelo de São Jorge began. The Moors were at first contemptuous – 'How many times within your memory have you come hither with pilgrims and barbarians to drive us hence?' – and managed to hold out for 17 weeks. But in October the castelo's defences finally gave way and the 'Christian' forces (described more correctly by a contemporary reporter as 'plunderers, drunkards and rapists ... men not seasoned with the honey of piety') showed their true colours by raping and pillaging their way through the city, despite assurances of leniency for the losers from Afonso himself. The only good man among them appears to have been one Gilbert of Hastings, an English priest who later became Bishop of Lisbon. ■

Built by the master of the Italian Renaissance style, Felipe Terzi, between 1582 and 1627, its wide nave and coffered vault are striking in their simplicity. Check out the cloisters, too, for their 18th century azulejo panels on La Fontaine's Fables. The former refectory (open daily from 10 am to 1 pm and 2 to 5 pm; entry is 200$00) is now a mausoleum containing the black marble tombs of the entire Bragança dynasty – everyone from João IV (who died in 1656) to Manuel II (who died in exile in England in 1932). The dark rooms can feel bizarre and spooky, especially with the sounds of the flea market resonating through one wall and Mass through the other.

SANTA APOLÓNIA

There are three main places of interest near the Santa Apolónia station, north-east of the Alfama, all museums – the first-class Museu Nacional do Azulejo; the obscure but intriguing Museu da Água (Water Museum); and the Museu Militar (Military Museum).

The **Museu Nacional do Azulejo** (Map 1; ☎ 814 77 47), at Rua Madre de Deus 4, is perhaps the city's most attractive museum. A splendid array of tiles from as early as the 15th century (plus displays on how they're made) is integrated into the elegant buildings of the former convent of Nossa Senhora da Madre de Deus Church. Among highlights are a 36m-long panel, upstairs in the large cloister, depicting pre-earthquake Lisbon, and a lovely mural, *Our Lady of Life* by Marçal de Matos (dating from about 1580). There are also some charming 20th century azulejos.

The church itself, with its beautiful tiles (and walls and ceiling crowded with paintings depicting the life of St Francis); the Manueline cloister; and the stupendous baroque chapel and adjacent rooms of carved, gilded wood are highlights in their own right. The complex was founded for the Poor Clare order of nuns in 1509 by Dona Leonor, wife of Dom João II.

The museum also boasts an excellent restaurant in a fine garden setting (see the Azulejos for Lunch? aside in the Places to Eat chapter). Take bus No 104 from Praça do Comércio or No 105 from Praça da Figueira. The museum is open Tuesdays from 2 to 6 pm and Wednesday to Sunday from 10 am to 6 pm; give yourself at least an hour. Entry is 350$00. Reproduction tiles, coffee-table books and other items are for sale in the lobby.

For more information about azulejos, see the boxed aside under Visual & Decorative Arts in the Facts about Lisbon chapter.

The **Museu da Água** (Map 7; ☎ 813 55

22), devoted to Lisbon's water supply down the centuries, won the Council of Europe's Museum Prize in 1990. Lisbon only got a dependable water supply in the 18th century. The system, ordered by Dom João V, included the huge Aqueduto dos Águas Livres or Aqueduct of Free Waters (described in the Rato, Saldanha, Campolide & Sete Ríos section later in this chapter) and several reservoirs, including the main Mãe d'Água (Mother of Water) at Praça das Amoreiras, and the smaller Reservatório de Patriarcal at Praça do Principe Real, by the botanical garden.

The museum, in the former Barbadinhos pumping station on Rua do Alviela (built in 1880 to provide water to higher parts of Lisbon), is open Tuesday to Saturday, from 10 am to 12.30 pm and 2 to 5 pm. Admission is 300$00. Take bus No 104 from Praça do Comércio or No 105 from Praça da Figueira, and get off four stops after Santa Apolónia station. Walk up Calçada dos Barbadinhos, turn right into Rua do Alviela and walk to the end. For information on the museum's joint tours of the aqueduct, see the Rato, Saldanha, Campolide & Sete Ríos section.

Just west of Santa Apolónia station you'll come across the **Museu Militar** (Map 12; ☎ 888 21 31). This museum's main claim to fame is its artillery collection, said to be the world's biggest. War freaks can also look at other heavy and light arms, medals and patriotic paintings. The museum opened in 1842 in a palace at the site of a former military arsenal and foundry on Largo do Museu do Artilharia. It's open Tuesday to Sunday, from 10 am to 5 pm. Admission is 300$00. Take bus No 104 from Praça do Comércio or No 105 from Praça da Figueira.

ESTRELA & LAPA (Map 5)

Those with the stamina to go beyond the Bairro Alto can ascend another of Lisbon's seven hills, Estrela, and explore the surrounding district of the same name. The attractions are limited, but the view from the hill is fine.

The easiest way to get there is on westbound tram No 28 from Rua da Conceição

(Baixa), tram No 25 from Cais do Sodré, or bus No 13 from Praça do Comércio. The most interesting way to get there is through Santa Catarina (see the Chiado & Bairro Alto section earlier) – about a 2.5km walk from the Baixa via Largo do Chiado, Calçada do Combro and Calçada da Estrela, up to the Basílica da Estrela.

As you leave Santa Catarina, head north on the arterial Avenida Dom Carlos I to Largo de São Bento and the imposing **Palácio da Assembleia da República** (or Palácio da Assembleia Nacional), Portugal's houses of parliament, the nucleus of which is the 17th century former convent of São Bento. The Assembleia has convened here since 1833. At the rear is a vast public park, and several other buildings including the official residence of the prime minister.

At the top of Calçada da Estrela are the massive dome and belfries of the **Basílica da Estrela**. Completed in 1790 by order of Dona Maria I (whose tomb is here), in gratitude for bearing a male heir, the church is all elegant neoclassicism outside and chilly, echoing baroque inside. Its best feature is the view across Lisbon from the dome, the weight of which was ingeniously spread over three concentric structures by architect Mateus Vicente de Oliveira. Also check out the life-size Christmas manger, with figures carved by Machado de Castro (better known for the statue of Dom José I in Praça do Comércio). The church is open daily from 7.30 am to 7 pm, except at lunch time.

Across the road is a well-tended, big yet cosy public park, the **Jardim da Estrela**. Beyond this lies a patch of heresy in this Catholic land, the Protestant **Cemitério dos Ingleses** (English Cemetery), founded in 1717 under the terms of the Treaty of 1654 with England. Among expatriates at rest here are novelist Henry Fielding (author of *Tom Jones*), who died in the course of a health visit to Lisbon in 1754. At the far corner is all that remains of Lisbon's old Jewish cemetery.

You can lose yourself for a few hours in the **Jardim Botânico**, a welcoming little hillside park with paths diving down past forests of shrubs to clusters of cacti and palms. It's a great place to go for a picnic and is open on weekdays from 9 am to 8 pm (weekends from 10 am, and in winter until 6 pm only); entry is 200$00. The main entrance, on Rua da Escola Politécnica, is also accessible on bus No 100 from Praça da Figueira.

To the south of Estrela is Lapa, Lisbon's diplomatic quarter. The main attractions for visitors are on its river-facing side: the bars and discos of Avenida 24 de Julho and nearby Doca de Santo Amaro (see the Entertainment chapter), and the first-class **Museu Nacional de Arte Antiga** (☎ 397 60 01). Running a close second to the Gulbenkian Museum in importance, this National Museum of Ancient Art is housed in a 17th century palace at Rua das Janelas Verdes 9. Here is the official national collection of works by Portuguese painters, the largest such collection in Portugal. The museum also features other European paintings of the 14th to 20th centuries, including works by Hieronymous Bosch, Piero della Francesca and Albrecht Dürer, as well as an extensive collection of applied art.

The most outstanding item is undoubtedly the *Panels of São Vicente* by Nuno Gonçalves, the most brilliant of the Portuguese school of painters which flourished in the 15th century, influenced by Flemish artists such as Jan van Eyck (who visited Portugal in 1428). These six panels (Gonçalves' only extant work) show a crowd of Lisbon's citizens paying homage to São Vicente, Portugal's patron saint. It's an extraordinarily detailed and revealing work, portraying every class of citizen, from beggars to fishermen, monks to Moorish knights, Jews, priests and nobles (including the Duke of Bragança and his family). The two stunning central panels feature a kneeling Dom Afonso V and Dona Isabel, Prince Henry the Navigator and the young prince João, the future Dom João II. Gonçalves himself is thought to be the figure in the far left corner of the central left panel.

Few contemporary Portuguese works in the rest of the museum come close to this masterpiece, but the *Annunciation* by the Flemish artist-monk, Frei Carlos, is a lovely work of luminous colour. Among the European paintings, the *Temptation of St Anthony* by Bosch is stunningly horrible: in this vision of the Apocalypse, skeletons play harps, men are rats, fish fly and villages burn (and St Anthony piously ignores it all). After this, it's a relief to look at the gentle works by Dürer, Holbein, della Robia and Van Dyck. Also note the delightfully prim and proper family portrait of the Viscount of Santarém by the 18th century Portuguese artist António de Sequeira.

There are several gifts from Calouste Gulbenkian featured in the museum's applied art collection, including an Apollo torso from the 5th century BC, but the most fascinating items in the museum's new wing are the *namban* screens by Japanese artists. Namban (literally 'barbarians from the south') is the name the Japanese gave to the Portuguese when they landed on Tanegaxima island in southern Japan in 1543, and it has come to refer to all the Japanese arts inspired by this encounter. The 16th century screens show the Portuguese arrival in intriguing detail.

Other items from this empire-building era include Indo-Portuguese chests inlaid with mother-of-pearl, and Afro-Portuguese carved tusks. Interesting, too, are the examples of Chinese porcelain shipped to Lisbon, and 18th century Portuguese attempts at copying these imports.

Finally, don't overlook the incredible silverware collection, which includes dozens of masterpieces by the French silversmith Thomas Germain and his son François-Thomas. Made in the late 18th century for the Portuguese court and royal family, they feature fantastic flights of fancy and whimsical flourishes.

The museum is open Tuesday from 2 to 6 pm and Wednesday to Sunday from 10 am to 6 pm. Admission is 500$00. If you're coming from the city centre, take bus No 40 or 60 from Praça da Figueira, or tram No 15 or 18 west from Praça do Comércio. From Estrela, you can hop on tram No 25 from in front of the basilica.

RATO, SALDANHA, CAMPOLIDE & SETE RÍOS (Maps 2 & 3)

These northern and north-western areas of Lisbon have a hotchpotch of attractions ranging from hothouses to high culture. Energetic walkers can reach the nearest of them by following Avenida da Liberdade, but metro and bus connections are also available.

Saldanha's one must-see is the **Fundação Calouste Gulbenkian** (Map 3) museum complex (see boxed asides in this chapter), best reached by metro to Pahlavã station (or take bus No 31, 41 or 46 from Rossio). Meticulously designed and set in a peaceful, landscaped garden at Avenida de Berna 45-A, the **Museu Calouste Gulbenkian** (Map 3; ☎ 793 51 31) is without a doubt Portugal's finest museum and one of Europe's unsung treasures. The collection spans every major epoch of western art and much eastern art, with hardly an unappealing item in it. Spend at least a full day here if you can.

The foundation's adjacent **Centro de Arte Moderna** boasts the country's best collection of 20th century Portuguese art, including works by Amadeo de Souza Cardoso, Almada Negreiros and Maria Helena Vieira da Silva. Also here is

ACARTE (Serviço de Animação, Criação Artística e Educação pela Arte), the Department of Animation, Artistic Creation & Education through Art, which promotes contemporary Portuguese performance and other arts. ACARTE runs the **Centro Artístico Infantil** (Map 3; Children's Art Centre) in the complex; though designed for Portuguese-speaking children, its exhibitions and related activities may also be of interest to visitors (see the Lisbon for Children section in the Facts for the Visitor chapter).

The Museu Calouste Gulbenkian and the Centro de Arte Moderna also host changing exhibitions and an entire programme of live music and other performances. In summer both are open Tuesday, Thursday, Friday and Sunday from 10 am to 5 pm, and Wednesday and Saturday from 2 to 7.30 pm (in winter, Tuesday to Sunday from 10 am to 5 pm). Entry is 500$00 for each museum (but free on Sunday mornings and to students, seniors over 65 and children). If you're looking for food, there is a snack bar in the main museum building and a restaurant in the Centro de Arte Moderna.

When you need a breather, the **Parque Eduardo VII** (Maps 2 & 3) is just down the road (and at the top end of Avenida da

Calouste Gulbenkian

Calouste Sarkis Gulbenkian, born to Armenian parents in Istanbul in 1869, was one of the 20th century's wealthiest men and best known philanthropists, and an astute and generous patron of the arts years before he struck it rich in Iraqi oil. His great artistic coup was the purchase of works from Leningrad's Hermitage in 1928-30, when the young Soviet Union desperately needed hard currency.

In his later years he adopted Portugal as his home and bequeathed to it his entire, stupendous art collection – snubbing Britain (though he had British citizenship) after it foolishly labelled him a 'technical enemy' for working as an economic adviser in Paris at the time of the Vichy government. He lived in Portugal from 1942 until his death in 1955. In 1969 his art collection was moved into its own purpose-built quarters, Lisbon's Museu Calouste Gulbenkian.

Gulbenkian also bestowed on Portugal an extraordinary artistic, educational, scientific and charitable foundation that has become Portugal's main cultural life force. The Fundação Calouste Gulbenkian, with assets now exceeding one billion US dollars and a budget bigger than some Portuguese ministries, funds architectural restoration and the construction of libraries, museums, schools, hospitals, clinics and centres for disabled people all over the country. In Lisbon it runs the Museu Calouste Gulbenkian and has endowed the adjacent Centro de Arte Moderna, built concert halls and galleries, and gathered together its own Orquestra Gulbenkian, Coro (Choir) Gulbenkian and a contemporary dance ensemble called Ballet Gulbenkian.

The foundation's main offices (☎ 793 51 31; fax 793 51 39; apg@gulbenkian.puug.pt) are at Avenida de Berna 45-A, 1067 Lisbon. ∎

Museu Calouste Gulbenkian Highlights

Among the classical and oriental art collections, some of the most memorable items are in the small Egyptian Room: an exquisite 2700-year-old alabaster bowl, small female statuettes (each with a different hairstyle), the extraordinarily modern-looking sculpture of a priest's head, and a superb series of bronze cats. In the adjoining Greek and Roman section, don't miss the outstanding 2400-year-old Attic vase, Roman glassware in magical colours and an absorbing collection of Hellenic coins, etched with finely carved heads and figures. Moving on to Oriental Islamic art, Gulbenkian's eye picked out only the best in 16th and 17th century Persian carpets (note the Portuguese influence in one, illustrating black-hatted Portuguese explorers in their boats), and illuminated Armenian manuscripts and books from the 16th to 18th centuries. Turkish faïence and azulejos from the same era glow with brilliant greens and blues, rust-reds and turquoise feather patterns, while 14th century mosque lamps from Syria have strikingly sensuous shapes. The Chinese and Japanese collection features an inevitably rich display of porcelain, lacquer, jade and celadon – especially lovely are the 19th century Japanese prints of flowers and birds by Sugakudo.

The huge European art section is arranged in chronological order, from medieval ivories and manuscripts to paintings from the 15th to 18th centuries. You'll recognise plenty of big names including Rembrandt (check out his sad *Figure of an Old Man*), Van Dyck (a much spookier version of an old man), Rubens (the painting of his second wife, Hélène Fourment, shows more than his usual passion) and 15th century Ghirlandaio (his *Portrait of a Girl* is perhaps the loveliest portrait of all here). Other delightful artworks from this era include a white marble *Diana* by Houdon and a trio of 16th century Italian tapestries portraying naughty cherubs in a cherry orchard.

Applied art of the 18th century is comprehensively represented with Aubusson tapestries,

Museu Calouste Gulbenkian

1 Entrance
2 Art Nouveau
3 18th & 19th-century European Art
4 Silverware
5 18th-century French Art
6 Middle Ages to 17th Century
7 Renaissance Art
8 Far Eastern Art
9 Oriental Islamic Art
10 Coins
11 Greek & Roman Art
12 Egyptian Art
13 Upstairs to Temporary Exhibits
14 Foyer

fabulous if often fussy furniture (including items from Versailles), silverware and intricate clocks (all in working order, naturally), and Sèvres porcelain. Some of the most outstanding paintings in the collection are Gainsborough's *Mrs Lowndes* (her cute spaniel trotting beside her), two wonderfully atmospheric La Tour portraits, and some typically turbulent Turners. There's a whole room of works by Francesco Guardi and a passionate *Spring Kiss* by Rodin. Finally, Art Nouveau fans will be delighted with a superb collection of magical jewellery by French designer René Lalique, who created fantasies in the form of coronets and hair combs, brooches and necklaces. ■

Liberdade). Although increasingly sacrificed to development, the park – named after Britain's Edward VII who visited Lisbon in 1903 – is still a delightful escape from the city, especially in its so-called **estufas** (greenhouses) in the north-western corner of the park. The estufa *fria* (cool) and estufa *quente* (hot) contain an exotic collection of tropical and subtropical plants, bursting up among palm trees and cacti, ferns and flamingo pools. They're open daily from 9 am to 6 pm; entry is 75$00. Take the metro to Parque or Rotunda, or bus No 31, 41 or 46 from Rossio.

A few metro stops further north, to Sete Ríos, brings you to the **jardim zoológico** (Map 1). You'd think this would be top of the list for kids, but it's better enjoyed as a hilltop garden than a zoo (see the Lisbon for Children section in the Facts for the Visitor chapter). Far more uplifting is the **Palácio dos Marquêses da Fronteira**, also just called the Palácio Fronteira (Map 1; ☎ 778 20 23), at Largo de São Domingos de Benfica 1, a 10 minute walk west of the zoo. This 17th century mansion, which is still inhabited, is known for its fabulous gardens with manicured box trees, and for its abundant azulejos. The *quinta* is open for guided tours, Monday to Saturday, from 10.30 am to noon. Admission is 1000$00 (quinta and gardens) or 300$00 (gardens only).

Aqueduto dos Águas Livres (Map 2)

Once one of Lisbon's major attractions, but curiously overlooked by visitors nowadays, is Lisbon's extraordinary Aqueduct of Free Waters, with 109 grey stone arches that lope south across the hills into Lisbon from Caneças, over 18km away. It was built to bring the city its first clean drinking water, by order of Dom João V, who laid the inaugural stone at Mãe d'Água (Mother of Water), the city's main reservoir at Praça das Amoreiras. Its cost was borne by the citizenry through a tax on meat, olive oil and wine. Most of the work was done between 1728 and 1748, under the gaze of engineer Manuel da Maia and architect Custódio Vieira. Its construction was interrupted by the 1755 earthquake (but apparently little was damaged) and it was not completed until 1835.

For considerably more information about the aqueduct, check out the Museu da Água, described in the preceeding Santa Apolónia

section. In summer, every Thursday and Saturday, the museum and the municipal water company jointly run walking tours (usually in Portuguese only), of the aqueduct, starting at Mãe d'Água (get there on bus No 9 from Rossio) and including a visit to another reservoir, the Reservatório de Patriarcal in Praça do Principe Real. For meeting times, check with the museum.

The aqueduct is at its most impressive at Campolide, where the tallest arch is about 65m high. Take any train from Rossio station to the first stop, or bus No 2 from Rossio, or bus No 15 from Cais do Sodré.

NORTHERN LISBON

Among the few attractions in Lisbon's northern suburbs is its Moorish-style **praça de touros** (bullring; Map 3), across Avenida da República from Campo Pequeno metro station. See Spectator Sport in the Entertainment chapter for information on the action there.

Further out are three museums in 18th century palaces: the interesting Museu da Cidade (City Museum) and the side-by-side Museu Nacional do Traje (National Costume Museum) and Museu Nacional de Teatro (National Theatre Museum). The **Museu da Cidade** (Map 1; ☎ 759 16 17) provides a telescopic view of Lisbon's history. Its highlights include an enormous model of pre-earthquake Lisbon, numerous old maps and prints from before and after the quake, and azulejo panels of city scenes. Almada Negreiros' portrait of the poet Fernando Pessoa is also here, as well as the shoes and shawl of Amália Rodrigues, Portugal's foremost fado singer.

The museum is housed in the fine 18th century Palácio Pimenta (said to have been built by Dom João V for one of his mistresses), at Campo Grande 245. It's open Tuesday to Sunday from 10 am to 1 pm and 2 to 6 pm. Admission is 330$00 (but free on Sunday mornings). Take the metro to Campo Grande station, or bus No 1 or 36 from Rossio.

The **Museu Nacional do Traje** (Map 1; ☎ 759 03 18) and **Museu Nacional de**

Teatro (Map 1; ☎ 757 25 47) both occupy 18th century palaces in the grounds of the lush Parque Monteiro-Mór (take bus No 7 from Praça da Figueira, or bus No 3 from Campo Grande metro station). The Museu Nacional do Traje features changing exhibits of court and common dress from the Middle Ages to the present, and the Museu Nacional do Teatro has theatrical costumes, props, posters and lots of photos of actors. Both have an entry fee of 400$00 and are open Tuesday from 2 to 6 pm and Wednesday to Sunday from 10 am to 6 pm.

BELÉM (Map 13)

The district of Belém, about 6km west of Rossio, was the launch pad for Portugal's Age of Discoveries. Perhaps most famously, it is the place from which Vasco da Gama set sail on 8 July 1497 for the two year voyage in which he discovered a sea route to India, setting in motion a fundamental shift in the world's balance of power.

Upon Vasco da Gama's safe return, Dom Manuel I ordered the construction of a monastery on the site of the riverside chapel (founded by Henry the Navigator) in which da Gama and his officers had kept an all-night vigil before departing on their historic voyage. The monastery, like its predecessor, was dedicated to the Virgin Mary, St Mary of Bethlehem (in Portuguese, Santa Maria de Belém) – hence the district's name.

The monastery, and an offshore watch-tower also commissioned by Manuel I, are essential viewing for every visitor to Lisbon – don't miss them. Jointly designated a UNESCO World Cultural Heritage Site in 1984, they are among the finest remaining examples of the exuberant Portuguese brand of Renaissance-Gothic architecture called Manueline (for more on the Manueline style, see the Arts section in the Facts about Lisbon chapter). They are also among the few structures in Lisbon to have survived the 1755 earthquake undamaged.

This peaceful suburb, which also boasts several other historical monuments and a clutch of worthy museums, makes a good full-day outing from central Lisbon.

In the summer a mobile turismo sets up in the Praça do Império, the huge square in front of the monastery.

Transportation is straightforward, but *don't* go on a Monday, when nearly everything in Belém is closed.

The most interesting way to get there is on tram No 15, which takes about 20 minutes from Praça do Comércio or 25 minutes from Praça da Figueira. Alternatively, take bus No 43 from Praça da Figueira, bus No 32 from Praça dos Restauradores or bus No 28 from Praça do Comércio. Get off at Largo dos Jerónimos, opposite the monastery.

Trains depart from Cais do Sodré station three to five times an hour on weekdays, slightly less frequently on weekends and holidays, and take seven minutes to get to Belém. You can take any train; tickets are 110$00. From Belém station the monastery is a few hundred metres west along the riverfront.

The railway line and the Estoril motorway cut the riverfront off from the rest of Belém, but pedestrian bridges and tunnels cross them in three places.

Mosteiro dos Jerónimos

Manuel I ordered this monastery to be built in memory of Vasco da Gama's discovery of a sea route to India and, while he was at it, arranged that its church be made a pantheon for himself and his royal descendants (many of whom are now entombed in its chancel and side chapels).

Huge sums were funnelled into the project, including so-called 'pepper money', a 5% tax levied on all income from the spice trade with Portugal's expanding African and Asian colonies.

Work began in about 1502, following a Gothic design by architect Diogo de Boitac, considered one of the originators of the Manueline style. After his death in 1517, building resumed with a Renaissance flavour under Spaniard João de Castilho and, later, with classical overtones under Diogo de Torralva and Jérome de Rouen (Jerónimo de Ruão). The monastery was only completed towards the end of the century. The huge neo-Manueline western wing and the domed bell tower, which date from the 19th century, seem out of keeping with the rest.

The monastery was populated by monks of the order of St Jerome, whose spiritual job was to give comfort and guidance to sailors – and, of course, to pray for the king's soul. When the Order was dissolved in 1833, the monastery was used as a school and orphanage until about 1940.

The façade of the **church** is dominated by João de Castilho's fantastic south portal, dense with sculptures in Renaissance style by Nicolas Chanterène. You enter through the west portal, now obscured by a modern connecting passage. In contrast to the extravagant exterior, the interior is sparsely adorned, spacious and lofty beneath an unsupported baroque transept vault, 25m high. Vasco da Gama is interred in the lower chancel, in a place of honour opposite the revered poet Luís de Camões.

The central courtyard of the **cloisters** is an unnervingly peaceful place, even when it's crowded; perhaps it's the fundamental harmony of its proportions that makes many visitors just sit down on the steps or lean against its columns, as soon as they walk in. In the old refectory an azulejo panel depicts the Biblical story of Joseph. The sarcophagus in the echoing chapter house on the north-eastern corner belongs to the 19th century Portuguese historian Alexandre Herculano.

The monastery and church are open daily, Tuesday to Sunday (closed public holidays), from 10 am to 6.30 pm (to 5 pm in winter). Admission to the cloisters is 400$00. There is no charge to see the church, although entry is discouraged when there are weddings (Saturdays around 11 am and 3 pm, and Sundays around 1 and 3 pm) or Mass is being held (weekdays at 8, 9.30 am and 7 pm, and Sundays at 8, 9 and 10.30 am, noon and 7 pm).

Torre de Belém

Ten minutes on foot south-west from the monastery, the Tower of Belém sits obligingly in the river. This hexagonal chesspiece has come to symbolise Lisbon and the Age of Discoveries and is perhaps Portugal's most photographed monument. Manuel I intended it as a fortress to guard the entrance to Lisbon's harbour. Before the shoreline slowly shifted south, the tower sat right out in midstream (and the monastery sat on the riverbank). Designed by Francisco Arruda, the tower is an arresting mixture of early Gothic, Byzantine and Manueline styles. Admission price and opening times are the same as for the monastery, though there's little inside that you can't see from the outside.

Padrão dos Descobrimentos

After admiring the tower, walk upriver to a modern memorial to Portuguese sea power. The huge limestone Discoveries Monument, inaugurated in 1960 on the 500th anniversary of the death of Prince Henry the Navigator, is shaped like a stylised caravel and crowded with important Portuguese figures. At the prow is Henry the Navigator; behind him are explorers Vasco da Gama, Diogo Cão and Fernão de Magalhães, poet Luís de Camões, painter Nuno Gonçalves and 27 others. Opposite the entrance is a wind rose. Inside are exhibition rooms, and a lift and stairs to the top, which offers a bird's-eye view of the

Padrão dos Descobrimentos

monastery and the river. It's open Tuesday to Sunday, from 9.30 am to 6 pm, and admission is 320$00 (half-price for students, and free for kids under 12).

Centro Cultural de Belém

The massive, squat Belém Cultural Centre, on the western side of Praça do Império, opened to the public in 1993, competing visually with the monastery as a moose would with a unicorn. But it's one of Lisbon's main cultural venues, with a full programme of its own. The interior plaza also gets lots of unofficial use as a rollerblade arena and there's a pleasant terrace garden (with cafe) with panoramic views.

Other Attractions in Belém

There are several other worthy museums in and around Belém. The most famous is the **Museu Nacional dos Coches** (National Coach Museum, ☎ 361 08 50), in the former royal riding school on Praça Afonso de Albuquerque. Though its focus is narrow – royal,

aristocratic and church coaches of the 17th to 19th century – the collection is one of the best in the world. The museum was founded in 1905 to preserve the monarchy's many horse-drawn carriages, and subsequently beefed up with more from the patriarchate and various noble families. There are enough gilded, painted and truly over-the-top vehicles to numb the senses and, like the Museu de Arte Sacra, they illustrate the ostentation and staggering wealth of the old Portuguese élite. It's open daily, except Monday, from 10 am to 5.30 pm. Admission is 450$00 (free on Sunday mornings).

Far more fun is the **Museu de Arte Popular** (Folk Art Museum, ☎ 301 12 82), on Avenida de Brasília by the Centro Cultural de Belém. This collection of clothing, fabrics, ceramics, furniture, tools, toys and more from around the country, organised by region, is as good a one-stop look as you can get of Portugal's charming and diverse folk arts. Among items you're unlikely to spot anywhere else are bagpipes from Mirando do

BETHUNE CARMICHAEL

Belém's Museu Nacional dos Coches

Douro, toby jugs from Aveiro and huge spiked dog collars for the beasts of Castelo Branco. The museum is open Tuesday to Sunday, from 10 am to 12.30 pm and 2 to 5 pm. Admission is 300$00.

Archaeology buffs should head for the **Museu Nacional de Arqueologia** (☎ 362 00 00). First opened in 1893, the National Archaeological Museum in the west wing of the Mosteiro dos Jerónimos, includes ceramics, sculpture, tiles, glass and coins from prehistory through to Moorish times. There's also a large collection of antique gold jewellery from the Bronze Age through Roman times. It's open Tuesday from 2 to 6 pm and Wednesday to Sunday from 10 am to 6 pm (closed Monday). Admission is 400$00 (free on Sunday mornings).

Next door is the **Museu de Marinha** (☎ 362 00 10), featuring model ships from the Age of Discoveries to the present, several small boats including an 18th century brigantine, a turn-of-the-century royal cabin from the yacht *Amélia* (complete with fireplace and pianola), the seaplane *Santa Cruz* that made the first crossing of the south Atlantic in 1922, and cases full of astrolabes and navy uniforms.

This place is great fun, though you can drown in the waves of visiting school groups. Admission is free for children under 10, and half-price for those from 10 to 19 years of age; adults pay 300$00. It's open Tuesday to Sunday, from 10 am to 6 pm (to 5 pm in winter). For details about the Museu das Crianças (Children's Museum) on the 1st floor, see the Lisbon for Children section in the Facts for the Visitor chapter.

Tucked at the back of the Praça do Império, next to the Museu de Marinha, is the **Planetário Calouste Gulbenkian** (☎ 362 00 02). The planetarium has a 40 minute show for 400$00 (200$00 for children and 200$00 extra for headphone translations in English or French) at 11 am, 3 and 4.15 pm on Wednesday and Thursday and at 4 and 5 pm on Saturday and Sunday. There's a special children's session on Sunday (see the Lisbon for Children in the Facts for the Visitor chapter).

The often-overlooked **Museu Nacional de Etnológia** (Map 1; National Museum of Ethnology, ☎ 301 52 64/5) mounts excellent temporary exhibitions, changing several times a year, from its collection of some 26,000 items. Exhibits include audio-visual displays (including music) on Portugal's former colonies in Africa and Asia, and a wide-ranging display of traditional textiles and weaving techniques from all over the world, notably Indonesia.

The museum is on Avenida Ilha da Madeira in the Restelo district, a relatively easy walk up from Belém (or take bus No 32 directly from Praça da Figueira). It's open Tuesday from 2 to 6 pm and Wednesday to Sunday from 10 am to 6 pm. Admission is 350$00.

AJUDA

Ajuda is a former royal quarter on a hilltop above Belém. A 10 minute walk (or take bus No 27) up Calçada do Galvão from Largo dos Jerónimos is a little marble basilica, the Igreja da Memória (Map 13). Built by Dom José I on the site of an unsuccessful attempt on his life, it is now the resting place of his chief minister, the formidable Marquês de Pombal.

If you bear right at the church then left up Calçada da Ajuda (or take bus No 14 or 73 directly from Praça Afonso de Albuquerque in Belém or tram No 18 from Praça do Comércio) you'll come to the oversize Palácio da Ajuda. Begun in the late 18th century, left in limbo when the royal family fled to Brazil, used as a royal residence from 1861 to 1905, but never quite finished, it's now the marginally worthwhile **Museu do Palácio Nacional da Ajuda** (Map 1; ☎ 363 7095).

This endless museum of kitsch royal belongings is dominated by the furnishings of Dona Maria II and her husband Dom Ferdinand, whose lack of taste will be familiar to visitors to Sintra's Pena National Palace, their summer retreat. Also on the grounds is the Galeria de Pintura do Rei Dom Luís (Dom Luís Art Gallery), open from Tuesday to Sunday from 10 am to 6 pm, with changing exhibitions. The palace museum is open Thursday to Tuesday, from 10 am to 5 pm, and admission is 400$00.

Not open to the public, the present official Palácio Nacional de Belém (National Palace; Map 13) and Presidência da República (Presidential Palace) are on Calçada da Ajuda just beyond the Museu Nacional dos Coches.

EXPO '98 (Map 14)

EXPO '98, the last major world exposition of the millennium, is being held in Lisbon from 22 May to 30 September 1998. This year is not only the United Nations' International Year of the Oceans; it also marks the 500th anniversary of Vasco da Gama's historic discovery of a sea route to India. The theme of Portugal's big fair – 'The Oceans, A Heritage for the Future' – honours not only these anniversaries but also recognises the oceans' essential value to humanity. A record 130 countries and international organisations are taking part in the event, at which some 8.5 million visitors are expected (half of them foreigners).

As well as being a festive occasion and major international spectacle, there's also an underlying aim: to enhance the international community's knowledge of the oceans and motivate it to preserve our marine ecosystems for future generations. The local organisers also clearly hope that the event will give Lisbon, and Portugal, a higher scientific and cultural profile in Europe and improve its chances to be the home of one or more newly proposed international organisations devoted to marine resources.

The EXPO '98 site covers 60 hectares of land, stretching for 5km along the city's north-eastern riverfront. It was formerly a polluted industrial area which had to be cleared of thousands of rusting containers, heaps of abandoned rubbish, a redundant oil refinery and storage tanks and lakes of oil and gasoline. It's now the focus not only of EXPO '98 but of Lisbon's greatest urban regeneration project – Expo Urbe (see the boxed aside in the Facts about Lisbon chapter) – which will make use of some 70%

of EXPO '98 facilities to create a vibrant new urban area once the exposition is finished. In the run-up to EXPO '98, Lisbon witnessed the biggest shake-up in its infrastructure since the 1755 earthquake. The metro was expanded in every direction, including to the EXPO '98 site; port improvements were extended as far down as Santa Apolónia station, hotel construction was in high gear, and a new 17km bridge, named after Vasco da Gama, was built to cross the Rio Tejo estuary (see the Ponte de Vasco da Gama boxed aside later in this chapter).

As for EXPO '98 itself, the major visual attractions are the six thematic pavilions around the Doca dos Olivais (Olivais Dock), their architecture and contents inspired by the ocean theme. In addition, there are two international areas housing the displays by the participating countries. A continual programme of entertainment takes place at a number of venues around the site until 3 am daily. And a major arts festival runs at other venues throughout the city.

Orientation

There are two main boulevards running north to south, parallel to each other: the Caminho da Água (Water Way) is the section of Alameda Central (Central Blvd) which runs through the EXPO '98 site, connecting the thematic pavilions and international areas. The Caminho da Costa (Coastal Way), running for 2km along the riverfront, is where most of the evening entertainment takes place.

The renovated Doca dos Olivais is at the heart of the site, with the thematic pavilions nearby.

For information on the EXPO's entrances and exits, see the boxed aside later in this section.

Information

Information Offices There are computerised or staffed information offices scattered around the site as well as electronic information boards and multimedia kiosks. For general information call the toll free number ☎ 0800 22 1998. The administrative headquarters is on the expo site, at Edifício Administrativo, Recinto da EXPO '98 (☎ 831 98 98; fax 831 96 52; tele366@ expo98.pt; www.expo98.pt).

Opening Hours The site is open daily from 9 am to 3 am. There are two different periods: EXPO '98 Day (10 am to 8 pm) is when the theme pavilions and international areas are open. EXPO '98 Night (8 pm to 3 am) is when most of the entertainment and cultural events take place.

Tickets A day ticket, which you can purchase any time from 10 am to 3 pm, costs 5000$00 for adults or 2500$00 for children aged five to 14 and seniors over 65. It's valid for the EXPO '98 Night period as well. A night ticket, valid only from 8 pm to 3 am, costs 2000$00. A three day ticket, valid for any three days (not necessarily consecutive), from 9 am to 3 am each day, costs 12,500$00/6250 adults/children and seniors.

Dedicated EXPO '98 fans might fancy a three month day pass, which gives unlimited access during the first three months (22 May to 22 August), from 9 am to 3 am every day, at a cost of 50,000$00/25,000. Equivalent **three-month night passes**, valid from 8 pm to 3 am, cost 25,000$00. None of these tickets is transferable.

Pavilhão de Portugal
(Portuguese National Pavilion)
Created by Portugal's leading architect, Álvaro de Siza Vieira, this stunning pavilion opposite the Olivais Dock highlights the major contribution Portugal has made to the exploration and discovery of the world's maritime routes and how the oceans have been a means of communication and knowledge.

The building, with its striking single-vault roof spanning 65m in length, is linked to the Ceremonial Plaza, where all EXPO's official ceremonies are held (eg the raising of the participating countries' flags on their national days).

Pavilhão dos Oceanos
(Oceans Pavilion)
This is the largest oceanarium in Europe, hosting 25,000 fish, birds and mammals in a giant two-floor aquarium (designed by American Peter Chermayeff) which re-creates the global ocean. There's both a central aquarium (equivalent to four Olympic swimming pools) – symbolising the vital links between the oceans and the land – and four smaller tanks with typical biological species from the world's four oceans.

Pavilhão do Conhecimento dos Mares
(Knowledge of the Seas Pavilion)
This pavilion, linking a vertical two-storey block and a horizontal one to evoke the bridge of a ship, recreates various scenes in six sections including navigation, ships and shipbuilding and scientific research, to show the process which led mankind to discover the oceans.

Pavilhão da Utopia (Utopia Pavilion)
This unusual pavilion is a multimedia venue dedicated to fascination and escape, and specifically to the dreams, myths and legends that the human mind has always associated with the oceans. A major multimedia show, at noon, 3, 6 and 9 pm, presents a variation on the origins of mankind, the gods and the oceans, evoking Ulysses, Moby Dick and other famous mythological and fictional adventurers of the seas.

Pavilhão do Futuro
(Pavilion of the Future)
Built from materials most widely used in shipbuilding (wood, steel, canvas and glass), this striking Portuguese-designed pavilion is intended to raise awareness of the need to conserve the oceans by leading visitors on a 'journey' from the outer limits of the universe to the depths of the ocean. There are six theme areas including an interactive theatre where visitors are acquainted with the current problems the sea has to contend with.

Pavilhão da Realidade Virtual
(Virtual Reality Pavilion)

Total immersion in the underwater world of virtual reality is on offer in this pavilion, sponsored by Portugal Telecom. A 40-minute voyage takes visitors to the ruins of an underwater city, Oceania, inhabited thousands of years ago by beings from an unknown civilisation.

Áreas Internacionais
(International Areas)

The North International Area, on the Tejo riverfront, houses displays from around 70 of the participating countries, including all member states of the EU (except Portugal which has its own pavilion). Displays from around 60 other countries are housed in the South International Area, just south of the Virtual Reality Pavilion.

Nautical Exhibition

At Olivais Dock you can see vessels from all

over the world, ranging from traditional Portuguese fishing boats and sporting craft to submarines and scientific vessels. Many of them are open to the public. Various major nautical events will also start or finish here, including a naval parade and celebration to mark Portuguese National Day (10 June), a Tejo Cruise (27-28 June) and the Vasco da Gama Memorial International Regatta (31 July to 3 August) part of the Cutty Sark Tall Ships Race, when about 120 tall ships are expected to arrive.

Gardens

The Jardins da Água (Water Gardens), along the riverfront between the Oceans Pavilion and the South International Area, feature the various water activities which mankind has developed from ancient times to the present day.

The Jardins Garcia de Orta (Map 14), along the riverfront by the North International Area, display recreations of exotic landscapes to reflect how Portuguese seafarers introduced different plants to the world. The gardens are named after an eminent 16th century Portuguese doctor and botanist who studied and classified numerous Asian plants.

Arts Festivals

EXPO '98 is a unique opportunity to see and hear Portugal's finest performers as well as leading performers from around the world. Two major arts festivals are linked to EXPO '98: the Festival dos Cem Dias (One Hundred Days Festival) which preceded the opening, and the Festival do Mergulho no Futuro (Dive into the Future Festival) which takes place from 1 July to 31 August at the Centro Cultural de Belém, Teatro Nacional D Maria II and other venues in the city. The programme includes contemporary dance, visual arts and concerts of classical and new music. A highlight of the arts programme, and the cultural finale to EXPO '98 itself, is the world premiere of a new opera by Philip Glass, with libretto by Luísa Gomes and staging and costumes by the Grand Théâtre de Génève. *O Corvo Branco* (The White

---

National Days

Every participating country at EXPO has its national day, during which theatrical events, shows and other entertainment are presented by the relevant country. Some of the major national days are as follows:

Austria	5 June
Brazil	9 September
Canada	1 July
China	10 July
Denmark	1–6 June
Egypt	23 July
France	9 June
Germany	1 June
India	6 July
Japan	20 July
The Netherlands	29 May
Norway	26 June
Portugal	10 June
Russia	12 June
Saudi Arabia	23 September
South Africa	3 August
Spain	25 July
Sweden	3 June
Switzerland	19 June
UK	28 June
USA	14 June

Raven) will be performed at the Jules Verne Auditorium from 27 to 29 September.

Places to Stay

At the time of writing, there were two hotels due to open on site: the *Hotel Oriente*, an aparthotel with 100 apartments (reserved for EXPO '98 needs) and the 250-room, four-star *Hotel Asia* (rates not available at the time of writing). Both are near the Oriente Station.

Places to Eat

There are 37 restaurants scattered around the site. Of these, 12 are 'high level' restaurants (four of them floating) serving the world's best cuisine, and 13 are family type restaurants serving Portuguese and international dishes. They're open from noon to midnight. There are also five self-service restaurants and seven take-away restaurants (open 11 am to 2 am). Several foreign delegations also run their own restaurants on site offering their national cuisines.

In addition there are 50 fast-food kiosks, open either during the daytime (9 am to 8 pm) or at night (10 am to 2 am).

If you're watching a video at the Video Stadium you'll find 20 bars nearby, open to 3 am.

Entertainment

There's something happening practically all the time: during the day, look out for the 'sea monsters' – Olharapos, Olharapas and Olhapins (inspired by Portuguese medieval fairy tales) – which walk around the public areas. Or check the following venues for videos, shows and performing arts events. Scattered around the site (mostly along the riverfront) there are also 10 smaller stages, designed like traditional Portuguese bandstands, which host performances such as folk-dancing and fado.

Two major events take place daily: at sunset there's the Peregrinação (Pilgrimage), a parade of a dozen surreal ships through the site, symbolising a pilgrimage and ending at the river. And at 11.30 pm, there's a multi-

---

Ponte de Vasco da Gama

The 18km-long Vasco da Gama bridge across the Rio Tejo from Montijo to Sacavem (just north of the EXPO '98 site) is one of the most impressive construction projects to emerge from the city's many EXPO '98 developments. The second-largest infrastructure project in Europe after the Channel Tunnel (and the longest river crossing in Portugal), the US$1120 million bridge opened in early 1998. It provides not only direct access to the EXPO '98 site but also a new route for vehicles travelling between northern and southern Portugal and Spain, thereby greatly alleviating traffic congestion in the city centre. ∎

---

media show, filling the Olivais Dock with water, fire, laser lights and sound.

Auditório Júlio Verne (Jules Verne Auditorium) EXPO '98's largest auditorium, within the Camões Theatre, seats 1000 people and is the venue for the participating countries' national day shows as well as major arts events such as Philip Glass's new opera (see the preceding Arts Festivals section).

Video-Estádio (Video-Stadium) This huge video stadium has a giant screen on which you can watch major world events such as the 1998 Football World Cup as well as videos, programmes and films related to EXPO '98's marine theme.

Anfiteatro ao Ar Livre (Open Air Amphitheatre) Situated between Olivais Dock and the Utopia Pavilion, this 500-seat amphitheatre has a floating stage where various night-time cultural events are held. This is also a good place to watch the nightly multimedia show.

Getting There & Away

Coming from central Lisbon the easiest way is by metro to the Estação do Oriente (Oriente Station), which puts you at the heart of the site (see the EXPO's Entrances & Exits boxed aside). This multi-station complex ᵈᵈᵈᵈᵈᵈᵈᵈᵈᵈᵈᵈᵈᵈᵈᵈᵈᵈᵈᵈᵈ

EXPO's Entrances & Exits

There are four entrances. The **Porta Fluvial**, or River Entrance, directly east of the Oriente Station, is for visitors arriving by boat. The **Porta Norte**, or North Entrance, is the one closest to the main parking lot.

The **Porta Poente**, or West Entrance, bang in the centre, is opposite Estação do Oriente (Oriente Station). This is where you'll arrive if you've come by train, metro, bus or taxi. The **Porta Sul**, or South Entrance, distinguished by the former GALP refinery tower nearby, is mainly for visitors arriving on tour coaches. ■

ᵈᵈᵈᵈᵈᵈᵈᵈᵈᵈᵈᵈᵈᵈᵈᵈᵈᵈᵈᵈᵈ

serves long-distance and suburban trains as well as the metro. Buses and coaches also arrive here. At the time of writing, details about special direct bus and ferry links were not available, but will be from the EXPO '98 information line or turismo.

If you're coming by car, you'll find the main parques de estacionamento (car park) at the North Area. There are also smaller car parks at the South Area and Oriente Station. Special information panels on the city's highways recommend the least congested routes and parking areas at any given time.

From the airport, it's five minutes by taxi.

Getting Around

A regular bus service runs around the perimeter of the EXPO '98 site, calling at the North and South Entrances and car parks. In addition, a minibus service shuttles to all the places of interest within the site. There's also a cable car service, 20m above ground, running 1.3km along the riverfront. All operate from 10 am to 3 am daily.

WALKING TOURS

As long as you don't mind the occasional muscle-aching steep street, Lisbon is a joy for walkers: it's generally easy to find your way around, small enough to explore over a few days and is visually pleasing almost everywhere. An added bonus is the proliferation of cafés and restaurants where you can stop for refuelling. Even if you're not a walker you should allow a few hours to stroll in the Alfama, one of Lisbon's most rewarding areas. For information about guided walking tours, see Organised Tours in the Getting There & Away and Getting Around chapters.

The Alfama (Map 12)

From the Baixa, it's an easy stroll from Rua da Conceição up to the Alfama's most important religious monument, the Sé (this and other sights are described fully in the earlier Alfama, Castelo & Graça section). From here you can strike uphill for the Castelo de São Jorge or downhill into the guts of the Alfama from the nearby viewpoint of Largo das Portas do Sol.

From Cathedral to Castle Following Rua Augusto Rosa uphill from the cathedral will soon bring you to the Miradouro de Santa Luzia (Map 12) with its pretty garden and pond, and, a little further on, the Largo das Portas do Sol which has a popular café.

Opposite the Miradouro de Santa Luzia, take Travessa de Santa Luzia on your left and stagger up the steep Travessa do Funil into Rua do Chão da Feira which leads to the entrance of the castle. Bus No 37 can take you directly back to Praça da Figueira from here.

From Largo das Portas do Sol to Alfama This is one of the easiest and most picturesque routes to follow through the Alfama's dense network of alleys and stairways, starting with Beco de Santa Helena (turn right just uphill from the largo). When it meets Rua do Castelo, turn left and then right into the pretty Beco das Cruzes, with its azulejo panels and archway. When this meets the main Rua da Regueira, turn right into Rua de São Miguel, where there are lots of little shops and restaurants.

You then have two choices: drop down into Largo do Chafariz de Dentro via Beco do Mexias (a tiny alley with one of the Alfama's last remaining communal laundries), and then back westwards along Rua de São Pedro which joins Rua de São Miguel at the Largo de São Rafael; or continue westwards along Rua de São Miguel itself. The second option gives you the chance to explore some more becos, in particular the Beco da Cardosa with its attractive 16th and 18th century houses.

At Largo de São Rafael continue along Rua de São João da Praça which leads back to the cathedral. Here you can take tram No 28 or continue walking back to the Baixa district.

Chiado & Bairro Alto
Although the Bairro Alto really comes alive at night, this walk can just as enjoyably be done during the day, with a lunchtime stop at one of the Bairro Alto's many restaurants. Funicular fans can enjoy two of the city's best rides at the start and end of the walk. See the earlier Chiado & Bairro Alto section for details about sights en route.

From the Turismo to Avenida 24 de Julho
First take the Elevador da Glória (Map 8), near the turismo, to hoist you up to the São Pedro de Alcântara viewpoint. From here the walk is all downhill. The first cultural stop is at the nearby Igreja de São Roque. Afterwards, head westwards along Travessa da Queimada to enter the heart of the Bairro Alto. There are plenty of good restaurants to choose from here (see the Places to Eat chapter). When you're ready to move on, head down Rua da Atalaia until it meets Rua do Loreto. Turn right to find the Elevador da Bica, at Rua da Bica Duarte Belo.

The funicular stops at Rua de São Paulo, but if you walk downhill a little further, to Avenida 24 de Julho, you can pick up a tram No 15 or bus No 43 to take you back to the central Praça da Figueira.

From the Turismo & Back
Follow the route above until you meet Rua do Loreto. Then turn left, heading for Praca de Luis Camões. The Café A Brasileira at the western end of nearby Rua Garrett (see the Places to Eat chapter) offers a tempting diversion; otherwise, head north up Rua Nova da Trinidade, turning right into Largo do Carmo to see the ruins of the Convento do Carmo. If the Elevador de Santa Justa is operating, you can take this down to the Baixa, or walk down Calçada do Carmo back to the turismo.

ACTIVITIES
The idea of deliberately exerting yourself to get fit has yet to seriously catch on among food-and-wine-loving Portuguese. The most popular physical activity is probably swimming, and golf for those who can afford it. See the Excursions chapter for more places near Lisbon where you can enjoy both activities, and Organised Tours in the Getting There & Away chapter for sports-specific holidays.

Swimming
Many of Lisbon's top hotels have their own swimming pools (or access to ones at adjacent clubs). The following municipal pools are open Monday to Friday from 12.15 to 2.45 pm and from 8.15 to 9.30 pm, and weekends from 10 am to 6.30 pm. Admission is 220$00 for adults; 110$00 for youths up to 25.

Piscina do Alvito (Map 4; ☎ 363 59 40), Estrada da Pimenteira, Parque de Monsanto (bus No 24 from Alcântara); indoor pool at a *parque infantil* (children's park) for three to 14-year-olds only; open July to September

Piscina do Areeiro (Map 1; ☎ 848 67 94), Avenida de Roma 28 (near Areeiro metro); indoor pool

Piscina do Campo Grande (Map 1; ☎ 796 63 05); Campo Grande (near Alvalade metro station); open-air pool for three to 12-year-olds only; open July to September

Piscina dos Olivais (Map 1; ☎ 851 46 30), Rua Dr Francisco Luís Gomes (bus No 21 from Campo Pequeno); indoor pool

Tennis
You need to book ahead at the following courts:

Centro Desportivo Universidade de Lisboa (☎ 796 0017); part of the Lisbon University sports facilities (metro to Cidade Universitária)

Centro de Ténis de Monsanto (Map 4; ☎ 364 87 41), Estrada do Alvito, Parque de Monsanto (bus No 24 from Alcântara); five fast courts (three floodlit) and seven slow courts (one floodlit)

Complexo Desportivo do Janor (☎ 419 72 2), Praça da Maratona, Cruz Quebrada; west of the city, en route to Cascais (take the train from Cais do Sodré to Algés then bus No 76 to Cruz Quebrada); large complex with 31 slow courts, six fast courts and two indoor floodlit courts

Golf

Golf players are spoilt for choice. North of the Tejo, near Estoril, there are six major courses (see the Golf on the Estoril Coast boxed aside in the Excursions chapter) as well as the Lisbon Sport Clube. South of the Tejo, within easy reach of Lisbon by car, are several others, included in the following list. Expect to pay around 7000$00 for daily green fees at most of the courses.

Lisbon Sport Clube (☎ 431 00 77), an 18-hole par 69 course set in woodlands at Casal da Carregueira, Belas (just north of Queluz); caddies, trolleys and clubs are for hire and the clubhouse has a children's playroom and swimming pool.

Clube Golf Aroeira (☎ 297 1314), a 6040m par 72 course designed by Frank Pennink on the south bank of the Tejo in an estate of pine woods and lakes; buggies, trolleys and clubs available for hire

Quinta do Peru (☎ 210 4515), an 18-hole par 72 course near Vila Nogueira de Azeitão designed by Rocky Roquemore; clubhouse, bar, shop and on-site accommodation

Clube Golf Montado (☎ 065-706648), an 18-hole par 72 course designed by Duarte de Sottomeyer, in a natural landscape of cork oaks, streams and lakes; clubhouse with restaurant

Tróia Golf (☎ 065-44112), a 6337m par 72 course just across the estuary from Setúbal; bordered by sand and set among pine trees, this Robert Trent Jones course is considered the most difficult in Portugal; golf carts and trolleys available for hire; clubhouse with restaurant

COURSES
Language

The Cambridge School (Map 6; ☎ 352 74 74; fax 353 47 29) at Avenida da Liberdade 173 (and three other branches) offers both private Portuguese lessons and group courses. Private courses range from 20 lessons (50 minutes each) at a cost of 194,000$00 for a 'super-intensive' four week course of nine lessons a day to 1,620,800$00. The intensive four-week

group courses (from three to six people in each group, at nine different levels) cost 79,200$00.

CIAL (Centro de Iniciação e Aperfeiçoamento de Linguas, Centre for Initiation and Improvement of Language, ☎ 794 04 48; fax 796 07 83; cialis@telepac.pt) at Avenida da República 41 offers individual lessons at 5200$00 an hour or group lessons from 44,000$00 for a week to 154,500$00 for a month's 60 hour course (three hours a day). As CIAL aims to provide students with a full cultural experience, daily social activities (visits to museums etc) are included in the course price. Homestay accommodation can also be arranged.

The Centro de Linguas Estrangeiras de Cascais (☎ 486 53 50) at Avenida Marginal, Bloco A, Cascais, runs 40-hour group lessons (two hours daily) for 43,000$00 as well as private lessons in business Portuguese for 3900$00 an hour.

Other Courses

Some other things you can learn in Lisbon include:

* Dancing, singing, juggling, circus techniques, TV acting: evening courses from the Collectividade Cultural e Recreativa de Santa Catarina (☎ 887 82 25), Costa de Castelo 1
* Zen meditation: Centro de Alimentação e Saúde Natural (☎ 315 08 98), Rua Mouzinho da Silveira 25
* Riding Portugal's famous Lusitano horses: Escola de Equitação de Alcainça (☎ 061-966 21 22), Rua de São Miguel, Alcainça (near Mafra)
* Arts and crafts: courses in ceramics, azulejos and Arraiolos carpet-making at the Associação dos Artesãos da Região de Lisboa (☎ 796 24 97), Rua de Entrecampos 66. Each course costs 7000$00 plus a 5500$00 registration fee. Azulejo painting and Portuguese handicraft techniques at CIAL (☎ 794 04 48; fax 796 07 83), Avenida da República 41. CIAL also offer a Portuguese gastronomy course, including cooking lessons. Both eight-hour courses cost 25,000$00.

For information on US universities with exchange programmes in Portugal, check out www.studyabroad.com.

Places to Stay

There's a huge range of places to stay in Lisbon, from camping grounds to former palaces. But during high season (mid-June to September) they're often booked out, so it's imperative to book ahead, especially for middle and upper-range accommodation near the city centre. The main turismo will make enquiries about accommodation for you, but no reservations. Prices soar during high season (and drop dramatically in low season). But top end hotels often have special discounts at weekends, children under 12 usually get free (or half-price) accommodation and many places will, if asked, give discounts for stays of four or more days. In this book we use the following price categories for an establishment's most basic double with toilet and shower or bath: bottom end – up to 4500$00; middle – 4500$00 to 9000$00; top end – over 9000$00. Note that room prices can vary

within an establishment, depending on whether it has a shower or bath or good view. If you want the cheapest option, always ask: *Tem um quarto mais barato?* Do you have a cheaper room?

A room with a double bed is called a *quarto de casal*; with twin beds, it's a *duplo*; and a single room is a *quarto individual*.

TYPES OF ACCOMMODATION
Camping
This is easily the cheapest option – around 600$00 per adult plus 500$00 or so for a car and the same again for a small tent. Consistently the best equipped, biggest (but priciest) camping grounds in the country are run by Orbitur (☎ 815 48 71; fax 814 80 45). These can be prebooked through Orbitur's central booking office in Lisbon.

The *Roteiro Campista* (1500$00), published annually in March and sold in most large Portuguese bookshops, is an excellent multilingual guide with details of nearly every camping ground in the country, plus the regulations for camping outside these sites.

Camping Card International
If you're planning to use a lot of camping grounds in and around Lisbon, it's worth getting the handy Camping Card International (CCI), issued by the Fédération Internationale de Camping et de Caravanning (FICC). Formerly known as a Camping Carnet, the CCI can be presented instead of your passport when you register at FICC-affiliated camping grounds. It provides third-party insurance for any damage you may cause, and is sometimes good for discounts. Certain camping grounds run by local camping clubs may be used by foreigners *only* if they have a CCI.

The CCI is available to members of most national automobile clubs, except in the USA; the RAC in the UK charges £4 for one. It's also issued by FICC-affiliated camping clubs such as the Camping & Caravanning Club (☎ 01203-694995) in the UK and the Federação Portuguesa de Campismo e Caravanismo or FPCC (☎ 812 68 90; fax 812 69 18) at Avenida Coronel Eduardo Galhardo 24-C, 1170 Lisbon. ■

Hostels
Portugal has a network of 20 *pousadas de juventude* or youth hostels, which are part of the Hostelling International (HI) system. Rates vary, being higher for popular hostels such as Lisbon's, but in most of them a dorm bed will cost 1200$00 to 1400$00 in the low season and 1450$00 to 1600$00 in the high season. Most also have at least a few double rooms from 2200$00 to 3700$00 per room. Continental breakfast is included in the price.

The hostel in Lisbon plus four other popular places are open 24 hours a day. The rest have curfews, typically opening only from 8 am to noon and 6 pm to midnight or later, though you can usually stash your bags at any hour and come back at opening time to book in.

Demand is high, so advance reservations are essential. You can book ahead from one hostel to another in Portugal free of charge, or pay 1000$00 per set of bookings (not per hostel) at Movijovem (Map 3; ☎ 355 90 81; fax 352 86 21), Avenida Duque d'Ávila 137, 1000 Lisbon – Portugal's central HI reservations office (where you can also book hostels abroad). You can book some of Portugal's hostels directly from abroad and even have a look at them at Movijovem's Website, www.telepac.pt/cataojovem/movjovem.html.

Age doesn't matter in Portugal: rates are the same for anyone with membership. If you don't already have a card from your national hostelling association, you can get HI membership (valid anywhere except at home) by paying an extra 400$00 (and having a 'guest card' stamped) at each of the first six hostels you stay at.

Pensões & Residenciais

The most common types of guesthouses, the Portuguese equivalent of bed and breakfasts (B&Bs), are the *residencial* (plural, *residenciais*) and the *pensão* (plural, *pensões*). Both are graded from one to three stars, and the top-rated establishments are often cheaper and better run than some hotels clinging to their last star. High-season rates for a double with attached bath in the cheapest pensão start at about 4500$00; expect to

pay slightly more for a residencial, where breakfast is usually included. There are often cheaper rooms with shared bathrooms.

These are probably Lisbon's (and Portugal's) most popular form of tourist accommodation, and they tend to fill up in summer. Try to book at least a week ahead in the high season, even further ahead for good-value places. A step down from the pensãos are boarding houses, called *hospedarias* or *casas de hóspedes*, where prices are lower and showers and toilets are usually shared.

Hotels

Hotels *(hotel*, plural *hotéis)* are graded from one to five stars. For a double in the high season you'll pay about 9000$00 to 12,000$00 at the lower end and between 15,000$00 and 30,000$00 (or more) at the top end. Many Lisbon hotels offer special discounts at weekends.

In the same category, but more like up-market inns, are the *albergarias* and the pricier *estalagens*. In the low season, prices drop spectacularly, with a double in a spiffy four-star hotel for as little as 8000$00. Breakfast is usually included.

Room Service (☎ 0171-439 3949) is a UK hotel booking service that claims to be able to get up to 50% off the price of upper-end hotels and resorts in Lisbon and elsewhere in Portugal.

Oops!
Hotels and pensões often collect your passport when you check in so they can register you, as required of them by the state. But they may not always remember to return it – don't you forget! ∎

Turismo de Habitação & Pousadas de Portugal

Under a private (but government-monitored) scheme called Turismo de Habitação or 'Turihab', and smaller schemes known as Turismo Rural and Agroturismo, you can stay in anything from a farmhouse to a mansion as the guest of the owner. Some also have self-contained cottages, though owners prefer stays of at least three or four days in these. Prices for a double in high season start at around 12,000$00 and drop by as much as 50% in low season. Lisbon itself has only one such place, though there are others nearby (see Sintra in the Excursions chapter).

A hefty book, *Turismo no Espaço Rural*, describing most of them, is available from the Lisbon turismo or directly from the Turismo de Habitação (☎ 058-74 16 72; fax 058-74 14 44) at Praça da República 4990, Ponte de Lima.

Pousadas de Portugal are deluxe, government-run former castles, monasteries or palaces (plus some new establishments), over 60 in all, usually in areas of natural beauty or historical significance. The nearest pousadas to Lisbon are in the Setúbal area (see the Excursions chapter). Pousada prices run from around 15,000$00 to 30,000$00 in

high season. For full details contact your nearest ICEP office or Pousadas de Portugal (☎ 848 1221; fax 840 58 46) at Avenida Santa Joana Princesa 10.

PLACES TO STAY – BOTTOM END
Camping

Six km west of Rossio, on the far side of Parque Florestal de Monsanto, is the big (1400 sites), well-equipped *Campismo de Câmara Municipal de Lisboa* (Map 1; ☎ 760 20 61; fax 760 74 74). It's open year-round. Rates from May through September are 420$00 per person over 10 years old, 275$00 per car, 355$00 to 770$00 per tent or caravan, and 330$00 for water and shower; these drop by 60% or more in low season. Youth-card holders get 50% off in low season. To get there take bus No 14 or 43 from Praça da Figueira.

The next nearest camping ground is a pricey one run by Clube de Campismo de Lisboa, about 20km north-west at Almornos. There are half a dozen more across the Tejo along the Costa de Caparica, and others to the west at Sintra, Praia Grande and Praia do Guincho (see the Excursions chapter).

Hostels

Lisbon's big *pousada de juventude* (Map 3; ☎ 353 26 96) is close to the centre at Rua Andrade Corvo 46, just off Avenida Fontes Pereira de Melo. The closest metro station is Picoas.

You can also take bus No 46 from Santa Apolónia or the Rossio, bus No 44 or 45 from Cais do Sodré, or bus No 44, 45 or the Aero-Bus from the airport. Even if you don't stay, the hostel's bulletin board is a good place for messages, tips and suggestions for places to eat.

The next nearest hostel is the beachside *Pousada de Juventude de Catalazete* (☎ 443 06 38) on Estrada Marginal in Oeiras, 12km west of Lisbon. From Cais do Sodré station, take an Oeiras or Cascais train to Oeiras, a 20 to 25 minute trip; there are four to six departures hourly.

Both these hostels are open 24 hours a day. They are very popular so reservations are

This logo is used to indicate which places to stay have received a certificate of competence

essential – in summer, preferably at least a month ahead. There's also a hostel at Sintra, 45 minutes from Lisbon by train from Rossio station (see the Excursions chapter).

Pensões & Residenciais
Rossio & Praça dos Restauradores
(Maps 8 & 9) *Residencial Campos* (☎ 346 28 64), on the 3rd floor at Rua Jardim do Regedor 24, offers simple, good-value doubles with/without private shower or bath for 5000$00/4000. The same people run *Residencial Estrela do Mondego* (☎ 346 71 09) at Calçada do Carmo 25, up behind Rossio station, where rooms are bigger but rates are the same.

Further up, at No 53 in pedestrian-only Calçada do Duque, *Pensão Duque* (☎ 346 34 44) has good vibes and clean rooms with shared shower for about 2500$00/3800. At the top of the hill at Largo Trindade Coelho 6, the noisier *Pensão Estrela de Ouro* (☎ 346 51 10) has similar prices.

Residencial Nova Avenida (☎ 342 36 89), on quiet Rua de Santo António da Glória 87 near Praça da Alegria, has old but well-kept doubles with/without shower for 4000$00/3500.

Drab but adequate, *Pensão Pérola de Baixa* (☎ 346 28 75), at Rua da Glória 10, has rooms without bath for 2500$00/4500. Near the top of Elevador da Glória, at Rua do Teixeira 37, the pleasant *Pensão Globo* (☎ 346 22 79) has doubles with/without shower from 4500$00/3500.

Good value is *Pensão Residencial Alcobia* (☎ 886 51 71; fax 886 51 74), at Poço do Borratém 15 where singles with/without bath are 4500$00/3500 and doubles 6000$00/4000 (all with breakfast).

Baixa Many cheap places in the Baixa are in old residential flats – chipped and fading, but warm and welcoming. A good one is the bright *Pensão Arco da Bandeira* (Map 9; ☎ 342 34 78), just inside the arch of the same name, at Rua dos Sapateiros 226. It has plain, clean doubles with shared facilities for around 4500$00. If you don't mind climbing four flights of grotty stairs, another cheerful

place with slightly cheaper prices is *Pensão Moderna* (Map 9; ☎ 346 08 18) at Rua dos Correeiros 205; it's surrounded by good, modestly priced eateries. The friendly *Pensão Prata* (Map 11; ☎ 346 89 08) is on the third floor of Rua da Prata 71 and has doubles with/without shower for 4500$00/4000 (5500$00 with bath).

Elsewhere *Pensão Louro* (Map 1; ☎ 813 34 22), at Rua Morais Soares 76, three blocks east of Arroios metro station, is a student hostelry during the school year but in July and August some spartan multibed rooms with showers are available, including doubles for about 3000$00.

Residencial Rocha (Map 12; ☎ 887 06 18) is in a slightly depressing corner of the city, at Rua dos Bacalhoeiros 12, but doubles without bath are cheap at 4000$00.

PLACES TO STAY – MIDDLE
Rossio & Praça dos Restauradores Right opposite the turismo, at Praça dos Restauradores 78, the old but friendly *Pensão Imperial* (Map 9; ☎ 342 01 66) is a popular choice, with singles/doubles from 3500$00/5000 (with shared bath). Be prepared to climb four flights of stairs. Clean rooms in a seedy building can be found at *Pensão Iris* (Map 8; ☎ 342 31 57), Rua da Glória 2-A. Doubles with shower (street-facing ones get the funicular noise) are around 5500$00. At Rua da Glória 21, *Pensão Monumental* (Map 8; ☎ 346 98 07) has functional rooms (noisy on the street side) from 5000$00/6500.

Adequate doubles at *Pensão Estação Central* (Map 9; ☎ 342 33 08), Calçada do Carmo 17, behind Rossio station, are over-priced at 6500$00/5000 with/without shower. Similar prices are found at *Pensão Galicia* (Map 11; ☎ 342 84 30), up several flights of stairs at Rua do Crucifixo 50. Some of the pricier rooms here have a little balcony. Offering better value for money is the well-run *Pensão Residencial Florescente* (Map 9; ☎ 342 50 10) at Rua das Portas de Santo Antão 99 where doubles with shower are 5500$00.

Bairro Alto & Chiado The best value in this neighbourhood and price bracket is the briskly efficient *Pensão Londres* (Map 8; ☎ 346 22 03; fax 346 56 82) at Rua Dom Pedro V 53. Spic-and-span rooms on the upper floors, with fine views across the city (and sometimes elegant stucco decoration on the ceilings) run from 4500$00/6200 with shared shower to 7000$00/9800 with attached bath, all with breakfast; downstairs rooms are a little cheaper. This popular place gets booked out a month ahead in summer. From Praça dos Restauradores, it's easy to reach on the Elevador da Glória.

Good value at the southern end of the Chiado is the *Residencial Nova Silva* (Map 10; ☎ 342 43 71; fax 342 77 70), at Rua Vitor Cordon 11, where plain rooms with toilet, shower and river views are 4500$00/5500.

Elsewhere The *Residencial Lisbonense* (Map 3; ☎ 354 46 28, ☎ 354 48 99), on four upper storeys at Rua Pinheiro Chagas 1 in the Saldanha district (metro: Saldanha), has pleasant, bright rooms with bath, telephone and air-conditioning from 4500$00/7000, with breakfast.

Closer to the centre, the good-value *Pensão Residencial 13 da Sorte* (Map 6; ☎ 353 18 51) at Rua do Salitre 13 quickly gets booked up in summer. Double/triple rooms, all with bath, TV and telephone, are 7500$00/9500.

Lofty in every sense is *Pensão Ninho das Águias* (Map 12; ☎ 886 70 08), just below the Castelo de São Jorge – but a long climb above the street at Costa do Castelo 74. With a flower garden, stunning views over the city and 14 elegant rooms, this place gets booked up a month ahead in summer and reservations are essential. Doubles/triples are about 6000$00/7000 with shared toilet and shower and 7000$00/8000 with private facilities.

PLACES TO STAY – TOP END
Rossio & Praça dos Restauradores
Hotel Suiço-Atlântico (Map 8; ☎ 346 17 13; fax 346 90 13), close to the turismo at Rua da Glória 3, has well-maintained rooms with bath for 7500$00/9500. Nearby, at Travessa

da Glória 22A is the *Residencial Roma* (Map 8; ☎ & fax 346 05 57) where rather gloomily decorated rooms come with bath, TV and breakfast for 6500$00/9500. *Pensão Insulana* (Map 9; ☎ 342 31 31), Rua da Assunção 52, has simple, pleasant rooms with bath and breakfast for 8000$00/9000. A couple wrote in to say their backpack full of valuables disappeared at *Pensão Aljubarrota*, across the road at No 53; give it a miss.

If you prefer aparthotels, there's the *Orion Eden Lisboa* (Map 8; ☎ 321 66 00; fax 321 66 66) at Praça dos Restauradores 24 (next to the turismo). It has both studio apartments for one or two people (14,900$00 a night) and apartments which can sleep up to four (19,900$00). The flats have a small working desk and kitchen facilities, satellite TV and a direct phone line.

A three-star hotel offering the facilities of a four-star is the *Hotel Presidente* (Map 6; ☎ 353 95 01; fax 352 02 72), at Rua Alexandre Herculano 13, where rooms (including TV, air-conditioning, mini-bar and great breakfasts) are 10,000$00/12,000. Nearby, at Rua Barata Salgueiro 5, the modern *Hotel Lisboa* (Map 6; ☎ 355 41 31; fax 355 41 39; reservdep @hlisboa.mailpac.pt) is twice as slick and expensive (21,000$00/25,000 and 35,000$00 for an executive room with office).

Offering a good deal more charm for the money is the recently refurbished *Hotel Britânia* (☎ 315 50 16; fax 315 50 21), dating from the 1940s and designed by one of the great Portuguese modernist architects, Cassiano Branco. Its 30 rooms (17,500$00/ 18,500) are huge, but the overall atmosphere is very intimate.

The *Hotel Lisboa Tejo* (Map 9; ☎ 886 61 82; fax 886 51 63) is a new hotel in a fine old building, at Poço do Borratém 4. Doubles, nicely decorated with azulejos, range from 14,000$00 (with breakfast).

Across the other side of the Avenida da Liberdade is another classy little 1950s hotel, the 112-room *Hotel Lisboa Plaza* (Map 6; ☎ 346 39 22; fax 347 16 30; plaza. hotels@mail.telepac.pt) in a quiet location at Travessa do Salitre 7. Recommended by one

Pick of the Best

Lisbon's three most distinctive hotels can be found in the Alcântara and Lapa districts, west of the centre. At Rua das Janelas Verdes 47, near the Museu Nacional de Arte Antiga, an aristocratic 18th century mansion which once belonged to the famous Portuguese novelist Eça de Queirós has now become a small 17-room hotel, *Janelas Verdes* (Map 5; ☎ 396 81 43; fax 396 81 44). Richly furnished singles/doubles are 23,900$00/26,000, including breakfast served in the room.

Almost opposite, at No 32, you climb an ivy-trellised stone stairway to the enchanting little garden of *York House* (Map 5; ☎ 396 24 35; fax 397 27 98), a former 17th century convent. The 36 rooms, furnished with antiques from Portugal and England, are 24,200$00/28,300. You need to book well ahead at both these places.

The former residence of a noble Portuguese family in the 19th century is now the very exclusive *Hotel da Lapa* (Map 5; ☎ 395 00 05; fax 395 06 65) in Lisbon's most elegant suburb, at Rua do Pau de Bandeira 4. There's an abundance of marble, stucco and azulejos in the 94 rooms; a beautifully landscaped garden; a health club with indoor swimming pool (plus an outdoor pool); and even a presidential suite if you've won the lottery. Rates for doubles range from 28,000$00 at weekends to 33,000$00 on weekdays. Breakfast is 2200$00 extra. ■

reader for its friendly staff, its well-equipped and recently refurbished doubles are around 19,000$00, including a generous buffet breakfast.

Just off Avenida da Liberdade at Rua Mouzinho da Silveira 3, the well-run *Hotel Jorge V* (Map 6; ☎ 356 25 25) has rooms with shower, TV and telephone for 8000$00/ 10,000, with breakfast. It's midway between Avenida and Rotunda metro stations.

Larger and less personal, but offering plenty of comforts are *Hotel Sofitel* (Map 6; ☎ 342 92 02; fax 342 92 22), at Avenida da Liberdade 123, where doubles (not including breakfast) are 35,000$00; and the ugly *Hotel Tivoli Jardim* (Map 6; ☎ 353 99 71; fax 355 65 66) at Rua Júlio César Machado 7, where doubles are 28,000$00, including breakfast; guests can use the open-air swimming pool and tennis court in the nearby Tivoli Lisboa.

Praça Marques de Pombal & Saldanha (Map 3)

Right on the praça, at No 8, is the 123-room *Hotel Fénix* (☎ 386 21 21; fax 386 01 31; h.fenix@ip.pt), a traditional 1st class hotel with a cosy old-fashioned feel. Rooms are 13,900$00/16,000. *Hotel Eduardo VII* (☎ 353 01 41; fax 353 38 79), at Avenida Fontes Pereira Melo 5, just a short walk from the park of the same name, has similar rates and atmosphere. In a quieter location, at

Avenida Sidónio Pais 12, the *Hotel Miraparque* (☎ 352 42 86; fax 357 89 20) manages to retain a personal touch despite frequently hosting group tours. Plain rooms are a reasonable 11,500$00/13,000 and street parking is usually available. The newish *Hotel Real Parque* (☎ 357 01 01; fax 357 07 50), at Avenida Luís Bivar 67, is a more posh outfit: spacious rooms are 17,000$00/19,000 (less at weekends) and there's a floor exclusively for non-smokers.

Top of the range is the modern high-rise *Sheraton Lisboa Hotel & Towers* (☎ 357 57 57; fax 354 71 64), at Rua Latino Coelho 1, which has 384 rooms, including 63 executive club rooms and 23 'smart' rooms designed for the business traveller. There's a health club including a swimming pool, gym and sauna. Rooms start at 32,000$00/ 35,000.

Elsewhere

At Rua Mãe d'Água 16-20, a few steps from the botanical gardens, is the bland but pleasant *Hotel Botânico* (☎ 342 03 92; fax 342 01 25), where doubles with TV, telephone, aircon and minibar are 13,000$00 with bath and breakfast. *Casa de São Mamede* (Map 7; ☎ 296 31 66) is a small hotel in an elegant townhouse at Rua Escola Politécnica 159. Doubles/triples with bath, TV and telephone start at 11,000$00/13,000, including break-

Top: Café life on Rua Augusta
Bottom Left: Repairing one of the many cobbled paths in Lisbon
Bottom Right: Elevador da Bica

Top: Ceiling detail, Palácio Nacional, Sintra
Bottom Left: Jerónimos Monastery, Belém
Bottom Right: Mafra Basîlca

fast. It's a long climb from Rossio, or you can take bus No 15 from Cais do Sodré and get off a couple of blocks past the Universidade Internacional (Map 6).

At one of Lisbon's most stunning viewpoints – the Miradouro da Senhora do Monte – is the *Albergaria Senhora do Monte* (Map 7; ☎ 886 60 02; fax 887 77 83), Calçada do Monte 39. Comfortable rooms with breakfast are 14,000$00/17,500 (or 25,000$00 a double with terrace); free car parking is available on the quiet street outside. You can take a slow tram No 28 from the Baixa district to get to nearby Largo da Graça.

In the far north of the city (near Alto dos Moinhos metro station) is Lisbon's only Turismo de Habitação – the *Quinta Nova da Conceição* (Map 1; ☎ & fax 778 0091). Set in a large garden, this 18th century house (once the residence of the Count of Benfica) has just three rooms (17,500$00) and a grand piano in the lounge.

If you want to wake up in the presence of the Mosteiro dos Jerónimos in Belém, the *Hotel da Torre* (Map 13; ☎ 363 62 62; fax 364 59 95) is just around the corner, at Rua dos Jerónimos 8. Rooms are 12,000$00/14,000 and include breakfast.

LONG-TERM RENTALS

If you just need a room, your best bet would be to negotiate a long-term price with your preferred hotel or residêncial. For a studio room with kitchenette, there's the *Orion*

Eden Lisboa (see Places to Stay – top end) which is central, secure, and functional. Every studio flat or larger one-bedroom apartment here has a small desk, direct phone line with private number, satellite TV and kitchen facilities. Fax and photocopying services are available at reception. Daily rates if you stay for a month drop from 14,900$00 (for a studio flat) to 12,900$00. Cheaper rates for longer periods can be negotiated.

The best choice of other aparthotels are in Cascais or Estoril (see the Excursions chapter). But for more aesthetic surroundings, and space for kids to run around, consider a private apartment in nearby Sintra. Daily rates for a one or two-bedroom place with kitchen average 8000$00 but for extended periods it could be much cheaper, especially in low season. Contact Sintra's turismo for details.

For more up-market, long-term rentals, check the classified section of the *Público* daily newspaper. Another option would be to contact reputable estate agents such as Claustro (☎ 388 72 80; fax 387 54 10) at Largo Hintze Ribeiro 2, or Cobertura (☎ 385 17 00; fax 385 16 97; Cobertura@ mail.telepac.pt) at Rua Silva Carvalho 347. Both deal in commercial facilities and offices as well as housing.

For basic student flats in or near the city centre, check the notice boards at the Espaço Ágora student complex (see Campuses in the Facts for the Visitor chapter).

Places to Eat

FOOD

Eating and drinking get serious attention in Portugal, where hearty portions and excellent value for money are the norm. The only meal that may fail to fill your stomach is *pequeno almoço* (breakfast), which is traditionally just coffee and a bread roll (often taken in a café). *Almoço* (lunch) is a far bigger affair, lasting at least two hours (usually 1 to 3 pm) and, like the *jantar* (evening dinner), features three courses, including a hot main dish, invariably served with potatoes (and sometimes rice as well). As most main dishes in the cheaper eateries cost less than 1200$00 each, you'll find it easy to gorge yourself on a full three-course meal for under 1800$00.

Although restaurants open at about 7 pm for dinner (with last orders at around 10.30 pm), most locals don't eat until at least 8 or 9 pm. Restaurants are usually closed for service between 4 and 7 pm, even if they say they're open all day. But you'll always be able to find something to eat somewhere. In addition to the *restaurantes*, hordes of places serve snacks throughout the day: a café, café-bar or snack-bar sells sandwiches and cakes as well as coffee, tea and alcoholic drinks; some may even serve simple meals at lunch time, often at the bar counter as well as at tables. Several packed-out lunch eateries in Lisbon are almost entirely stand-up. (Non-smokers should avoid these rush hours:

Portuguese restaurants rarely have non-smoking sections.)

Another popular place, especially at lunch times, is a *casa de pasto*, a casual eatery with cheap, simple meals. Slightly more up-market and popular with locals for both lunch and dinner is a *tasca*, a simple tavern, often with rustic décor. A *cervejaria*, literally 'beer house', serves food as well as drinks, while a *marisqueira* specialises in seafood (and is therefore often expensive). The *churrasqueira* (or *churrascaria*), literally a barbecue or grill, is actually a popular family-style restaurant serving grilled foods, especially chicken.

Traditional Portuguese cuisine is far from fancy (it's basically the honest fare of farmers and fisherfolk) but it's always filling. If you can't face the huge servings (rice and chips with at least two pieces of meat or fish is considered quite normal for an ordinary portion), you can ask if a *meia dose* (half-portion) is available. This is standard practice in many restaurants, though the cost usually works out to be about two-thirds of a *dose*, not one-half. A better bargain is the *prato do dia* (dish of the day), often an excellent deal at about 800$00.

Many restaurants also advertise an *ementa turística* (tourist menu), a set meal of the day with a choice of dishes and a glass of beer or half-bottle of wine. Sometimes these can be genuine bargains (popular with locals, too); often, however, they offer miserable portions.

Beware, too, of those tempting little titbits of olives and cheese spread or plain bread and butter which are put on the table at the start of your meal; if you start nibbling them, you'll be charged (they're usually listed as a *couvert* or cover charge on the bill, or as *pão e manteiga*, bread and butter). If you don't want them, play it safe and send them back at the outset.

To order the bill, ask for *a conta, se faz favor*. Cafés don't usually charge for service

An Order of Bull, Please
Be careful not to get *uma torrada* and *uma tourada* mixed up: the first means a piece of toast; the second, a bullfight! ∎

(a tip of small change is acceptable). In other establishments it's invariably included in the bill; if not, it's customary to leave about 10% (a 17% IVA tax may also be added in up-market restaurants).

Snacks

Snacks include *sandes* (sandwiches), typically with *queijo* (cheese) or *fiambre* (ham); *prego no pão* (a slab of meat sandwiched in a roll, often with a fried egg as well); *pastéis de bacalhau* (cod fishcakes); and *tosta mista* (toasted cheese-and-ham sandwich). Prices start at about 250$00. Soups are also cheap (about 200$00) and delicious; see the Portuguese Food Glossary boxed aside. Keep an eye out for cafés advertising *combinados*: these tasty little bargains, costing about 700$00, are miniature portions of a regular meat or fish dish, invariably served with chips (and sometimes salad).

Main Meals

Before delving into the menu (*a ementa* or *a lista*) it's always worth asking if there's a *prato do dia* (dish of the day) or *especialidade da casa* (speciality of the house). Greedy tourist-geared eateries may simply suggest the expensive *arroz de marisco* – a rich seafood and rice stew, usually for a minimum of two – but elsewhere you could well end up with some unusual dish that's far more exciting than some of the standard menu items.

Among *entradas* (starters), the best value are the excellent home-made soups. Especially popular is *caldo verde*, a jade-green potato and cabbage soup. In more up-market restaurants, specialty items such as cheese from the Serra de Estrela region may be included on the entrada menu, as well as the

occasional *queijo fresco* (fresh goat's cheese).

For main meals, *peixe* (fish) and seafood are very popular and often good value. There's an amazing variety available, from favourites such as *linguada* and *lulas grelhado* (grilled sole and squid) and *pescada* (hake) to *bife de atúm* (tuna steak), and *espadarte* (swordfish) – not to be confused with *peixe espada* (scabbard fish).

The cheapest and most ubiquitous fish are *sardinhas assadas* (charcoal-grilled sardines), a delicious feast when eaten with salad and chilled white port. And you won't get far before discovering Portugal's favourite fish dish: *bacalhau* or salted cod, which has been a Portuguese culinary obsession for 400 years (see the Bacalhau, The Faithful Friend boxed aside).

For more exotic fish specialities, there's the popular but expensive arroz de marisco (seafood paella); *caldeirada* (fish stew) or *açorda de marisco* if it's bread-based;

'Bacalhau, The Faithful Friend'
The Portuguese have been obsessed with bacalhau – salted cod – since the early 16th century. It was at this time that Portuguese fishing boats started to fish for cod around Newfoundland (claimed by the Corte Real brothers in 1500). The sailors salted and sun-dried their catch to make it last the long journey home, thereby discovering the perfect convenience food both for their compatriot sea-faring explorers (who were sailing as far as India at the time) and for their fish-loving but fridgeless folk back home. Indeed, so popular did bacalhau become throughout Portugal that it soon became known as *fiel amigo*, the faithful friend.

Most of today's cod is imported from Norway and is fairly expensive, but as it more than doubles in volume after soaking, keeps well and is extremely nourishing, it's still widely popular. If you join the fan club, you're in for a treat – there's said to be a different bacalhau recipe for every day of the year.

It takes a few centuries to get addicted: try the *bacalhau à Gomes de Sá*, a tastier version than most of the 364 other recipes (this one features flaked cod baked with potatoes, onions, hard-boiled eggs and black olives). ∎

cataplana, a combination of shellfish and ham cooked in a sealed wok-style pan (a dish originating from the Algarve region); and all the varieties of shellfish, from *amêijoas* (clams) and *camarões* (shrimps) to *lagostins* (crayfish) and *chocos* (cuttlefish).

Carne (meat) and *aves* (poultry) are often hit-and-miss in Portuguese cuisine: strike it

Portuguese Food Glossary

Entradas (Starters)

cocktail de gambas	prawn cocktail	*omeleta de marisco/*	shellfish/smoked ham/
salada de atum	tuna salad	*presunto/cogumelos*	mushroom omelette

Sopa (Soup)

caldo verde	potato and shredded-cabbage broth	*sopa à alentejana*	bread soup with garlic and poached egg
gazpacho	refreshing cold	*sopa de legumes*	vegetable soup
canja de galinha	chicken broth and rice	*sopa de feijão verde*	green-bean soup

Peixe e Mariscos (Fish & Shellfish)

amêijoas	clams	*lampreia*	lamprey (like eel)
atum	tuna	*linguada*	sole
bacalhau	salted cod	*lulas*	squid
camarões	shrimp	*pargo*	sea bream
carapau	mackerel	*peixe espada*	scabbard fish
chocos	cuttlefish	*pescada*	hake
caldeirada	fish stew with onions, potatoes and tomatoes	*polvo*	octopus
		robalo	sea bass
enguia	eel	*salmão*	salmon
espadarte	swordfish	*sardinhas*	sardines
gambas	prawns	*savel*	shad
lagostins	crayfish	*truta*	trout

Carne e Aves (Meat & Poultry)

borrego	lamb	*frango*	young chicken
bife	steak	*galinha*	chicken
cabrito	kid	*leitão*	suckling pig
carne de vaca (assada)	beef (roast)	*lombo*	fillet of pork
carneiro	mutton	*pato*	duck
chouriço	spicy sausage	*perú*	turkey
coelho	rabbit	*presunto*	smoked ham
costeleta	chop	*salsicha*	sausage
entrecosto	rump steak	*tripas*	tripe
fiambre	ham	*vaca*	beef
fígado	liver	*vitela*	veal

Legumes (Vegetables)

alface	lettuce	*espargos*	asparagus
alho	garlic	*espinafres*	spinach
arroz	rice	*favas*	broad beans
batatas	potatoes	*feijão*	beans
cebolas	onions	*lentilhas*	lentils
cenouras	carrots	*pepino*	cucumber
cogumelos	mushrooms	*pimentos*	peppers
couve	cabbage	*salada*	salad
couve-flor	cauliflower	*salada mista*	mixed salad
ervilhas	green peas		

lucky and you'll find delicious specialities such as *leitão assado* (roast suckling pig), *borrego* (lamb), and *presunto* (smoked ham). One of Portugal's rare culinary coups is *carne de porco à alentejana*, an inspired combination of pork and clams.

Even the cheapest menus invariably feature *vitela* (veal) and *bife* (beef steak),

Ovos (Eggs)

cozido	hard boiled	*mexido*	scrambled
escalfado	poached	*omeleta*	omelette
estrelado	fried	*quente*	boiled

Frutas (Fruit)

alperces	apricots	*limões*	lemons
ameixas	plums	*maças*	apples
amêndoas	almonds	*melões*	melons
ananás	pineapple	*morangos*	strawberries
bananas	bananas	*pêras*	pears
figos	figs	*pêssegos*	peaches
framboesas	raspberries	*uvas*	grapes
laranjas	oranges		

Sobremesas (Desserts)

arroz doce	sweet rice pudding	*leite creme*	custard
doce	sweet pudding	*mousse de chocolate*	chocolate mousse
gelado	ice cream	*pudim*	crème caramel

Condiments, Sauces & Appetisers

azeite	olive oil	*piri piri*	chilli sauce
azeitonas	olives	*sal*	salt
pimenta	pepper		

Cooking Methods

assado	roasted	*grelhado*	grilled
cozido	boiled	*na brasa*	braised/charcoal grilled
ensopada de ...	stew of...	*no espeto*	on the spit
estufado	stewed	*no forno*	in the oven (baked)
frito	fried		

Eating Places

casa da chá	teahouse	*marisqueira*	seafood restaurant
casa de pasto	a casual eatery with cheap, simple meals	*pastelaria*	pastry and cake shop
cervejaria	literally a beer house	*salão de chá*	teahouse
churrasqueira	literally a barbecue or grill		

Snacks & Supplements

arroz	rice	*queijo*	cheese
batatas fritas	chips/French fries	*salada*	salad
manteiga	butter	*sandes*	sandwich
pão	bread		

Miscellaneous

almoço	lunch	*jantar*	evening dinner
balcão	bar/counter	*meia dose*	half-portion of a dish
conta	bill (check)	*mesa*	table
couvert	cover charge	*pequeno almoço*	breakfast
ementa	menu	*prato do dia*	dish of the day

while *coelho* (rabbit) and *cabrito* (kid) are unexpected culinary delights. Most popular of all poultry dishes is *frango* (chicken), widely available grilled on outdoor spits (*frango assado*), and perfect for a takeaway meal.

Strike it unlucky, however, and you'll end up with *tripas* (tripe), a specialty of Porto; the stomach-sticking *migas alentejanas*, a bread and fatty pork stodge; the unbelievably meaty *cozido à Portuguesa* stew; or worst of all, a bloody bread-based slop called *papas de sarrabulho*.

Vegetarian Food

Vegetarians can have a miserable time in carnivorous Portugal, where meat and offal are consumed with relish. Servings of vegetables just don't figure in traditional cuisine

---

Caldo Verde

This is the most typical of Portugal's soups and is made with kale or cabbage. The stalk and tough parts of the kale are removed and the rest is shredded finely so that it resembles grass. The soup is sometimes served with a slice of maize bread and a side dish of small black olives.

Serves 4

500g (1lb) floury potatoes, peeled and cut into quarters
4 cups (1L) water
salt
3 tablespoons olive oil
1 onion, finely chopped
250g (8 oz) kale or cabbage leaves, very finely shredded
1 small clove of garlic (optional)
freshly ground black pepper
4 thin slices of chouriço (optional)

Cook the potatoes in salted water until they are soft enough for mashing. Remove, mash and return to the water, along with the oil, onion and shredded cabbage, and boil for three to four minutes (the cabbage should not be over-cooked or mushy). Season and serve hot. Place a slice of chouriço (a Portuguese spicy pork sausage) in each soup bowl if desired. ■

---

here. And although many restaurants in Lisbon and other tourist areas now include a token few vegetarian dishes on their menus, exclusively vegetarian restaurants are few and far between: in Lisbon, we've tracked down just half-a-dozen.

The most easily available but utterly boring choices of unadulterated vegetarian fare are *omeleta*, and *batatas fritas* (chips), *salada mista* (mixed salad), and *sandes do queijo* (cheese sandwiches). But there are some delicious vegetable soups on nearly every menu – from sopa de legumes, the good old vegetable purée stand-by, to the more uniquely Portuguese *sopa à alentejana*, a bread, garlic and poached egg soup (better than it sounds). Even here, however, something that should be reliably vegetarian (the popular caldo verde soup, for instance) can often be tainted with slices of chouriço or bits of fatty pork, and there's no knowing whether the stock is made with meat.

Among more filling dishes, Portuguese specialities that avoid meat are some of the simple peasant *migas* (bread soup) dishes, notably *migas do Ribatejo* and *migas à moda da Beira Litoral*. They look disgusting (their main ingredient is soaked maize bread, with lots of olive oil and garlic to taste) and to many people, they are. Keep an eye out instead for *arroz de tomate* (tomato rice) or *favas com azeite* (broad beans with olive oil).

Or head for the markets and do your own vegetarian shopping: in addition to excellent fruit and vegetable stalls (along with the fish and meat), you'll nearly always find freshly baked bread and cheeses – the soft, hand-made ewe's or goat's milk cheeses are well worth trying, and perfect for a picnic. Markets are best on Saturdays, worst on Mondays and closed on Sundays.

Desserts & Pastries

Sobremesas (desserts) are a surprising disappointment in restaurants, though you're in for a treat if a home-cooked *doce* (sweet pudding) such as a *leite creme* (custard) or *mousse de chocolate* is available. More often than not, however, you'll be offered the same old *pudim* (crème caramel), *arroz doce* (sweet rice) or *gelado* (ice cream) – often the expensive Ola or Motta commercial varieties. But fresh fruit is usually available, as well as cheese (the best and most expensive is a Brie-like cheese, *queijo da serra*, made in the Serra da Estrela region from pure ewe's milk).

If you're hankering for some really effective tooth-decaying desserts, head for the nearest pastelaria or *casa de chá* where you can find the sweetest concoctions imaginable, invariably made from egg yolks and sugar. Nuns of the 18th century created many of the recipes, bestowing tongue-in-cheek names on the results, such as *papos de anjo* (angel's breasts) or *barriga de freira* (nun's belly). Local specialities in this department include the cheesecakes *(queijadas)* and almond pastries *(travesseiros)* from Sintra.

DRINKS
Nonalcoholic Drinks
Surprisingly, *sumo de fruta* (fresh fruit juice) is rare, although the local Tri Naranjus bottled varieties are a reasonable substitute. But Portuguese *gua mineral* (mineral water) is excellent and widely available, either *com gás* (carbonated) or *sem gás* (still).

Coffee drinkers are in for a high time: it's freshly brewed, even in the humblest café, and comes in all varieties with its own convoluted nomenclature.

For a small black espresso (the most popular form) simply ask for *um café* (or *uma bica* to be more precise: many waiters don't believe foreigners want the real thing – strong, black and punchy). You may soon graduate to a double dose, *um café duplo*, or retreat to something weaker, *um carioca*. If you want milk, ask for *um garoto* (small size) or *um café com leite*. Popular at breakfast time is the caffè latte-style *um galão*, a large milky coffee served in a glass (usually with a good deal more milk than coffee). For equal portions (in a cup) ask for *um meia de leite*. Depending on where you drink it, *uma bica* usually costs about 70$00: a typical Lisbon pastelaria might charge 80$00 if you drink your coffee standing up by the *balcão* (counter), 120$00 seated at the *mesa* (table)

or as much as 200$00 outside at the *esplanada* (street tables).

Chá (tea) is usually served rather weak, in the style of Catherine of Bragança, who is best remembered not for being the wife of Charles II but for starting England on its long love affair with tea (and toast). You can ask for it *com leite* (with milk) or *com limão* (lemon), but if you ask for *um chá de limão*, you'll get a glass of hot water with a lemon rind (which is actually quite refreshing).

Also available in cafés and teahouses is *um chocolate quente* (hot chocolate), or simply *um copo de leite* (a glass of milk).

Alcoholic Drinks
Portuguese people like their tipple: you can pick up anything from a glass of beer or wine to a shot of *aguardente* (firewater) at cafés, restaurants and bars throughout the day (and most of the night). And bartenders aren't stingy with their tots, either: most of them don't even bother with spirit measures. A single brandy here often contains the equivalent of a double in the UK or USA.

In most places you pay when you're ready to leave (as in a restaurant) but in some foreign-owned bars there's a pay-as-you-order system *(pronto pagamento)*.

Wines Portuguese wine offers great value in all its varieties – red, white, or rosé; mature or young (and semi-sparkling). You can find decent *vinho da casa* (house wine) everywhere, for as little as 250$00 for a 350mL bottle or jug. And for less than 800$00 you can buy a bottle to please the most discerning taste buds. In shops and supermarkets wine is available by the bottle, box or 5L container (and you can leave your empty bottles at the ubiquitous bottle banks, or at supermarket checkouts).

Restaurant wine lists differentiate not only between *tinto* (red) and *branco* (white), but between *maduros* (mature wines) and *vinhos verdes* (semi-sparkling young wines). As there are over a dozen major regional wines (usually produced by cooperatives), with new ones coming onto the market all the time, you're spoilt for choice.

A Glossary of Wines & Their Labels

adega	winery or cellar
ano	year
branco	white
bruto	extra dry
colheita	a single-harvest vintage tawny port, aged for at least seven years
doce	sweet
engarrofado por ...	bottled by ...
espumante	sparkling
garrafeira	wines of an outstanding vintage, at least three years old for reds and one year for whites
generoso	fortified wine
LBV	late-bottled vintage; a vintage port aged for four to six years in oak casks before bottling
licoroso	sweet fortified wine
meio seco	medium dry
quinta	a country property or wine estate
região demarcada	officially demarcated wine region
reserva	wine from a year of outstanding quality
ruby port	the cheapest and sweetest port wine
seco	dry
tawny port	a sweet or semi-sweet port, the best of which has been aged for at least 10 years; less likely than a vintage port to give you a hangover
tinto	red
velho	old
vinho branco/tinto	white/red wine
vinho da casa	house wine
vinho do Porto	port wine
vinho maduro	wine matured for more than a year
vinho regionão	a new classification for superior country wines, similar to the French vins de pays
vinho verde	young (literally 'green wine') wine, slightly sparkling and available in red, white and rosé varieties
vintage character porto	a cheap version of a vintage port, blended and aged for about four years
vintage port	the unblended product of a single harvest of outstanding or rare quality, bottled after two years and then aged in the bottle for up to two decades, sometimes more
white port	usually dry, crisp and fresh; popular as an apéritif

The most famous of the maduro wines are probably the red *Dão* table wines produced from just north of the Serra da Estrela. Sweet and velvety, they resemble a Burgundy. Other maduros worth trying are the increasingly popular wines from the Alentejo (the reds from Reguengos are excellent); the reds and whites of Buçaco, near Coimbra; the dry, straw-coloured whites of Bucelas in Estremadura; the table wines of Ribatejo, especially the reds of Torres Vedras and whites from Chamusca; and the expensive but very traditional-style red Colares wines (famous since the 13th century) from near Sintra – where the vines, grown on sand dunes, have never been touched by phylloxera (a fungus that has ravaged many a European wine region over the years).

The vinho verde (literally 'green wine') of the northern Minho and lower Douro valley area is also very popular: young (hence its name) and slightly sparkling, it has a low alcohol content and comes in red, white and rosé varieties, though the white is undoubtedly the best (try it with shellfish). The best known vinho verde label is *Casal Garcia*, but well worth the extra escudos are the *Alvarinho* whites, especially those from Quinta da Brejoeira; the reds from Ponte da Barca; and whites from Ponte de Lima.

Portugal's most internationally famous rosé wine is, of course, the too-sweet, semi-sparkling Mateus rosé. The Portuguese themselves prefer their bubbles either in vinho verde form or as *espumantes naturais* (sparkling wines). The best of these are from the Bairrada region near Coimbra and the Raposeira wines from Lamego. Sweet dessert wines are rare – the *moscatel* from Setúbal and Favaíos and the Carcavelos wine from Estremadura offer the fruitiest flavours.

Port & Madeira Vinho do Porto (port), a fortified wine made exclusively from grapes grown in the northern Douro valley, is Portugal's most famous export. Fortified by the addition of grape brandy it is matured in casks or large oak vats, traditionally at Vila Nova de Gaia, across the Douro river from Porto – from which it took its name. (See the Solar do Vinho do Porto boxed aside in the Entertainment chapter for information on Lisbon's port wine institute). Port can be red or white, dry, medium or sweet. The main difference in price and quality is between blended ports taken from a number of different harvests, and vintage port from a single high-quality harvest. All genuine ports carry the Port Wine Institute's seal. You don't need to shell out for a whole bottle just to try some port (though a cheap white or ruby only costs about 700$00 a bottle): any café, bar or restaurant can serve you a glass of port for about 150$00. For the better quality vintage brews, be prepared to pay at least 2500$00 a bottle.

Cheapest and sweetest are the ruby and red ports, made from a blend of lesser wines, bottled early and drunk young (after about three years). Also blended are semi-sweet or sweet tawny ports, named after the mahogany colour they gain after years aged in wooden oak casks, and very popular as an apéritif (especially with the French, who drink several million cases of the stuff every year). Check out the label ('10 Years Old', '20 Years Old' etc) for an indication of the best-quality tawnies. Vintage character port is a cheap version of a vintage (but with similar characteristics), blended and aged for about four years.

The single harvest ports range from the colheita port, a tawny made from high-quality wines and aged for at least seven years before bottling, to late-bottled vintage (LBV) ports, which are produced from an excellent harvest and aged for four to six years before bottling. The most sublime (and most expensive) port of all – vintage port – is produced in a year of outstanding quality, bottled within two years and aged for up to two decades, sometimes more. This is your ultimate after-dinner drink, always served from a decanter (not because it's classy but because there's always sediment in the bottle). Little known outside Portugal but well worth trying are white ports, ranging from dry to rich and sweet. The dry variety is served chilled with a twist of lemon.

Vinho da Madeira (Madeira) is one of the oldest fortified wines of all: vines were first introduced to this Atlantic Ocean island province of Portugal soon after it was claimed by Portuguese explorers in 1419. The English (who called the sweet version of the wine 'malmsey') became particularly partial to it (the Duke of Clarence drowned in a butt of the stuff). In addition to the malmsey dessert wine, there's a dry apéritif version called *sercial* and a semi-sweet *verdelho*.

Spirits Portuguese gin, whisky and brandy are all much cheaper than elsewhere in Europe, although the quality isn't as good. If you fancy something with a more unique taste and punch, try some of the aguardente firewaters: *medronho* (made from arbutus berries), *figo* (figs), *ginginha* (cherries) and *licor beirão* (aromatic plants) are all delicious – and safe in small doses. For some rough stuff that nearly destroys your throat, ask for a *bagaço* (made from grape husks).

Beer Stronger and cheaper than in the UK or the USA, Portugal's *cerveja* (beer) comes in three main brands of lager: Sagres, Cristal and Super Bock. There's little difference between them. Empty bottles can be exchanged at supermarket checkouts for a refund.

You can order beer in bars by the bottle or on draught – *um imperial* or *um fino* for a quarter-litre, *uma caneca* for a half-litre, *um girafe* for a litre. A 300mL glass of draught costs about 200$00 (equivalent to about 150$00 for a half-pint). Some bars frequented by tourists often have popular foreign brews such as bitter or stout, pricey at 400$00 for 400mL.

PLACES TO EAT

Lisbon is not a gastronomic paradise, but you can fill up and enjoy without spending a lot of money.

Restaurants & Cafés

Good (and good-value) restaurants and cafés are concentrated in the Baixa and Bairro Alto districts. With a few exceptions noted here, places off Rossio and Praça dos Restauradores, while sometimes very good, tend to be poorer value for money. If you want to avoid the crowded rush-hours you'll have to grab a table before noon (for lunch) or 8 pm for dinner.

Rossio & Praça dos Restauradores Not

for vegetarians is a good little casa de pasto called *Casa Transmontana* (Map 8; ☎ 342 03 00) at Calçada do Duque 39. It serves one or more strong-tasting northern Portuguese specialities, eg chicken or rabbit cooked in its own blood, at a modest 700$00 to 1100$00 per plate. Also recommended is the sweet pudim de castanhas (chestnut pudding). It's open daily from noon to 3 pm and 7.30 to 11.30 pm (but on Sundays in the evening only); on weekends, book ahead or arrive early.

For a coffee or a meal, the handsome Art Deco *Café Nicola*, (Map 9), at Rua 1 de Dezembro 16-26 (through to Rossio 24) is the grande dame of Lisbon's turn-of-the-century cafés, its maroon walls lined with paintings. It's recently been closed because of metro expansion: you might have to settle for pricey coffee and a fraction of the atmosphere at *Nicola Gourmet*, Rua 1 de

Dezembro 10. It's closed on Sundays. One of the few Art Deco cafés unaffected by the metro works is the *Casa Chineza* (Map 9) stand-up only café at Rua Áurea 274.

A good spot close to the turismo is the unpretentious *Restaurante O Brunhal* (Map 8; ☎ 347 86 34) at Rua da Glória 27. It has well-prepared standard pratos do dia for 700$00 to 900$00 and service beyond the call of duty.

Opposite the turismo at Praça dos Restauradores 79 is *Pinóquio* (Map 9; ☎ 346 51 06), with pricey but tasty seafood specials. A block back, along Rua das Portas de Santo Antão, a string of restaurants offers good – but seriously overpriced – seafood at sunny outdoor tables for tourists who cannot find their way out of the centre. A genuinely superb fish restaurant here is *Gambrinus* (☎ 342 14 66) at No 23 (see the Celebrity Haunts boxed aside in this chapter). You can enjoy the rich ambience without breaking the bank by eating snacks at the counter.

Another treat – but much more fun – is *Casa do Alentejo* (Map 9; ☎ 346 92 31) at No 58 which boasts an extraordinary 19th century mélange of Franco-Arabic décor with a huge ballroom and two azulejo-adorned dining rooms. Surprisingly, the menu prices are comparatively modest. It's closed on Mondays and summer-time Saturdays.

Cervejaria Ribadouro (Map 6; ☎ 354 94 11) at Rua do Salitre 2, is a traditional beerhouse whose looks have been modernised, but the menu is still reliably good, with prices around 1300$00. There are some scales outside if you need to check whether you've over-eaten.

Baixa The Baixa has plenty of burgers and

beer if that suits you, but also some of the best modestly priced food in Lisbon. Our favourite is *Restaurante João do Grão* (Map 9; ☎ 342 47 57) at Rua dos Coreeiros 228, open daily from noon to 4 pm and 7 to 11 pm (closing earlier in winter). Don't confuse the decades-old 'Inglish Menu Trnsletion' (sic) with the real thing, which has a long list of salads, soups and fish and meat standards, helpfully arranged in order of price. You can eat well here for under 2000$00. Two other good-value places on the same street are *Restaurante Ena Pãi* (Map 9; ☎ 342 17 59) at No 180 and the casual casa de pasto *Lagosta Vermelha* (Map 9; ☎ 342 48 32) at No 155 (closed Sunday). A classier outfit is *Restaurante Múni* (Map 11; ☎ 342 89 82) at No 115 where dishes are around 1800$00 each.

Down at Praça do Comércio 3, *Martinho da Arcada* (Map 11; ☎ 887 92 59) makes much of the fact that it has been in business since 1782. It was once a haunt of the literary set, including Fernando Pessoa, though renovation has altered its clientele from literati to tourists. The café, good value for a stand-up or sit-down lunch (daily specials are about 800$00), is open from 7 am to 9 pm; the much pricier restaurant closes at 10 pm, and both are closed on Sunday.

Bairro Alto & Chiado Mention Bairro Alto and most tourists think '*fado*', although most casas de fado are better known for their music than their menus. See the Entertainment chapter for several tourist-friendly fado houses with adequate food, most of them in the Bairro Alto.

The informal, family-run *Tasca do Manel* (Map 8; ☎ 346 38 13), at Rua da Barroca 24, serves plain, tasty Portuguese standards that are good value at 1000$00 to 1800$00 per dish. Similarly priced dishes (emphasising Alentejan specialities) can be found in the cosy, rural-decor *O Cantinho do Bem Estar* (Map 8; ☎ 346 42 65) at Rua do Norte 46. It's tiny and very popular so you need to get here early. *Bota Alta* (Map 8; ☎ 342 79 59), at Travessa da Queimada 35, has fewer décor frills but similar prices and ambience. It's closed on Sunday. On the southern fringe of the bairro, *Tendinha da Atalaia* (Map 10; ☎ 346 18 44) at Rua da Atalaia 4, is an easily-overlooked little place, with attractive azulejos inside and a friendly management. Dishes are around 1000$00.

The bright and brisk *Vá e Volte* (☎ & fax 342 78 88), at Rua Diário de Noticias 100, is another local favourite, with lunchtime specials around 1000$00. It's closed on Monday. *O Cantinho da Rosa* (Map 8; ☎ 342 03 76), at Rua da Rosa 222, has mini pratos for 700$00 at lunchtimes and a friendly family atmosphere. *Até Lá Lá* (☎ 342 28 22), at Rua da Atalaia 176, serves cheap meals at night only.

Fancy a change from sardines and bacalhau? Try *Ali-a-Papa* (Map 8; ☎ 347 21 16), at Rua da Atalaia 95, which serves Moroccan specialities such as couscous and tagines from 1400$00. Or head for the unabashed American *Henry J Bean's* (Map 8; ☎ 343 07 77), at Rua da Misericórdia 74, which serves up everything from hot dogs to T-bone steaks with accompanying sports videos. At No 35 on the same road, the riff-raff can enjoy the famously superb food of *Tavares Rico* (Map 8; ☎ 342 11 12) at the cheaper 1st floor, self-service restaurant (the chandeliers and pricier menu are downstairs; see the Celebrity Haunts boxed aside).

Cavernous *Cervejaria da Trindade* (Map 8; ☎ 342 35 06), at Rua Nova da Trindade 20-C, is a former convent with arched ceilings, gorgeous 19th century tilework and a robust, busy atmosphere. They've been serving food here for over 150 years. It's a bit pricey (grilled beef and seafood specialities start at 1200$00) but it makes a great lunch stop. It's open daily, except holidays, from noon to 1 am.

A great outdoor spot for a quiet, shady meal is *Leitaria Académica* (Map 9; ☎ 346 90 92) in Largo do Carmo. The indoor version of the restaurant at No 13 Largo do Carmo is so small it's like eating in a cell but the prices are cheaper (around 700$00 for daily specials) than outside.

Similarly short on atmosphere but with equally well-priced daily specials is the bright, plain *Cafetaria Brasil* (Map 8) at Rua de São Pedro de Alcântara 51. Check out the unusual décor at *Restaurante O Tacão Pequeno* (Map 8; ☎ 347 28 48), around the corner at Travessa da Carra 3-A.

In the Santa Catarina neighbourhood, on the western edge of Bairro Alto, the Rua do Poço dos Negros provides some surprises. *Cantinho do Paz* (Map 6; ☎ 390 8638),

---

Celebrity Haunts

If you want to rub shoulders with the rich and famous (or simply those aspiring to be famous) these are the places to head for. Expect to pay at least 3500$00 a dish.

Belcanto (Map 10; ☎ 342 0607), Largo de São Carlos 10; favourite haunt of bankers and politicians; famous for its bacalhau dishes; closed Saturday lunch time and Sunday

Gambrinus (Map 9; ☎ 342 14 66), Rua das Portas de Santo Antão 23 ; popular with the élite for over 70 years; refined ambience; superb fish and roast beef; open noon to 2 am daily

Pap' Açorda (Map 8; ☎ 346 48 11), Rua da Atalaia 57; startling minimalist décor and excellent, expensive açorda (bread and shellfish mush served in a clay pot); advance bookings essential; closed Saturday evening and Sunday

Restaurante Novo Bonsai (Map 8; ☎ 346 25 15), Rua da Rosa 244; elegant and traditional décor, with tatami mats and rice paper screens; special lunch menu of Japanese specialities; closed Monday and Saturday lunch times and all day Sunday

Tagide (Map 11; ☎ 346 05 70), Largo da Academia Nacional de Belas Artes 18; wonderful river views outside and 17th century azulejos inside; Portuguese and French menu; closed Saturday evening and all day Sunday

Tavares Rico (Map 8; ☎ 342 11 12), Rua da Misericórdia 35; strong on tradition (it was founded in 1784) and palatial-style chandeliers; closed for lunch on Saturday and Sunday

---

located at No 64, offers Indian and African food (evenings only) with live music at weekends. Plenty of more traditional places can be found on Rua da Bica Duarte Belo (the street with the funicular), notably *Restaurante Alto Minho* (Map 10; ☎ 346 81 83) at No 61, which is a great favourite with both locals and visitors for its cheap and wholesome fare. It's closed on Saturday. If you can't get a table here, go for the fun atmosphere, day and night, of *A Bicaense* (Map 10; ☎ 346 58 00), at No 38.

High on style and ambience is *La Brasserie de L'Entrecôte* (Map 10; ☎ 342 83 43; fax 347 36 16) on the southern edge of the neighbourhood at Rua do Alecrim 117. This high-ceilinged, modernist venue offers a simple French menu – entrecôte, salad and chips (2450$00) – cooked to perfection, with some famously superb herb and nut sauces.

Praça Principe Real One of the artiest places in this northern Bairro Alto area is the chic bar and restaurant, *Real Fabrica* (Map 5; ☎ 387 20 90) at Rua Escola Politécnica 275: this converted 19th century silk factory looks expensive, but you can eat lunchtime specials here for under 1000$00, and even main evening meals are under 2000$00. There's a very pleasant terrace, too.

Just south of this road, around the romantic Praça das Flores, there's the up-market *Conventual* (Map 6; ☎ 60 91 96), at No 45, where you'll pay at least 4000$00 per dish for superb and often unusual Portuguese food; and the more congenial *Casa de Pasto Flores* (Map 6), at No 40, which has long been highly regarded; prices used to be reasonable, though it was undergoing refurbishment at the time of my visit.

One of several typically unpretentious little lunchtime eateries around here is *Tascardoso* (Map 6; ☎ 342 75 78) at Rua do Século 244; it has just half-a-dozen tables, and dishes are under 900$00.

Cais do Sodré (Map 10) A short walk uphill along Rua do Alecrim, at No 47, there's the zany new *Pano Mania* (☎ 342 24 74) self-service restaurant, offering some great salads, soups, hamburgers and daily specials for 650$00. *Restaurante Cervejaria Solar do Kadete* (☎ 342 72 55), at Cais do Sodré 2, is more traditional, with huge servings of Portuguese specialities for around 1200$00; its outdoor tables are a bonus. *Restaurante Porto de Abrigo* (☎ 346 08 73), Rua dos Remolares 18, has good fish and seafood dishes for 800$00 to 1700$00. One of several basic cheapies in the same area is

Pastelaria & Snack Bar Brasilia (☎ 346 69 02) at Praça do Duque da Terceira 10, with daily specials for about 800$00.

These and most other places in this neighbourhood are closed on Sundays and holidays, though you can always find a snack at the Espaço Ágora's *Ágora Café*, on the riverfront Avenida da Ribeira das Naus (near Cais do Sodré car ferry pier): it's open 24 hours a day, like many of the other student-oriented services in this complex, and there are discount prices for students.

Praça Marquês de Pombal & Saldanha A

pastelaria and café crammed with Portuguese at lunch time is *Balcão do Marquês* (Map 3; ☎ 354 50 86) at Avenida Duque de Loulé 119, two blocks from Rotunda metro station. Eating is mainly stand-up (balcão means counter) and there are stacks of sandwiches or a large daily menu of meaty dishes for under 800$00, plus soups, salads and sweets. Take an ordering ticket when you enter; service is crisp and cheerful. It's open weekdays from 7 am to 9 pm and Saturday from 7 am to 3 pm.

Just east of Avenida da Liberdade, Rua de Santa Marta is good hunting ground for unpretentious and reasonably priced restaurants, crammed at lunchtimes. Go early to get a seat at *Restaurante Estrela de Santa Marta* (Map 6; ☎ 354 84 00), at No 14-A, where daily specials are under 900$00; or *O Coradinho* (Map 6; ☎ 355 59 50), at No 4, where generous half-portions are even cheaper.

If you're nostalgic for pizzas and burgers, try the cheerful *Big Apple Restaurante* (Map 6), at the rear of a shopping arcade at Rua Barata Salgueiro 28, a block off Avenida da Liberdade. It's open from noon to 3.30 pm on weekdays, and Friday and Saturday nights from 7 to 11 pm; fuel up here for the Ad Lib disco upstairs (see the Entertainment chapter).

One of the best Chinese restaurants in Lisbon is *Li Yuan* (Map 3; ☎ 357 77 40) at Rua Viriato 23, not far from Picoas metro station. You can eat your favourite Chinese dishes here for under 1800$00.

Chic & Open-Air

At the last count, the trendy new Doca de Santo Amaro (Map 4) in the Alcântara area of western Lisbon had a dozen restaurants-cum bars. Overlooking the yachts in the marina, and with a view of the massive Ponte de 25 Abril above, it's a great place for open-air dining and late-night boozing. The following places (from east to west along the dockside) are just some of the places which are open both day and night.

Doca de Santo Esplanada (☎ 396 35 22); large outdoor dining area and extensive menu of dishes (including some great salads) for under 1000$00; open till very late

Havana (☎ 397 98 93); colourful décor and a simple menu of hamburgers, salads or tapas; live music Tuesday to Friday

Tertúlia do Tejo (☎ 395 55 52; fax 395 55 96); one of the poshest and most expensive in the strip, with traditional Portuguese fare from 2500$00 to 5000$00 per dish

Cosmos (☎ 397 27 47); specialises in pizzas, salads and pastas for under 1500$00

Cafe Zonadoca (☎ 397 20 10); zany décor and classy music, plus a stylish menu of salads, crêpes and ices

Cafe da Ponte (☎ 395 76 69); known for its charismatic bar staff and billed as 'Lisbon's craziest cafe'; small and simple, with a menu equally modest; closed on Tuesday

For more on the evening-only bars in this strip, see the Entertainment chapter, and for transport to the area see the Doca de Santo Amaro boxed aside in the same chapter. ■

Alcântara & Lapa The pricey *Alcântara Cafe* (Map 4; ☎ 363 71 76) at Rua Maria Luisa Holstein 15, is a design eye-opener combining neoclassical and Art Deco features. It's open evenings only, from 8 pm to 3 am.

In one of Lisbon's most elegant suburbs, *Sua Excelência* (Map 5; ☎ 360 3614) at Rua do Conde 42 is small and deluxe, with an international menu and dishes at least 4000$00 each. It's open every day except Wednesday.

Stylish but far more modest, *Picanha* (Map 5; ☎ 397 54 01), at Rua das Janelas Verdas 96, serves a set 2100$00 menu of *picanha* (a Brazilian tenderloin beef dish) with potatoes, salad, rice, beans and various sauces. There's a good choice of desserts, too.

Alfama Top of the range, on both the geographic and culinary scale, is *Casa do Leão* (Map 12; ☎ 887 59 62), right inside the Castelo São Jorge, with a terrace offering panoramic views. Expect to part with at least 3000$00 for a main dish.

Just outside the castle entrance, *Castelo Mourisco* (Map 12; ☎ 886 78 52) at Rua Santa Cruz do Castelo 3, is considerably cheaper, offering a good menu of dishes under 1500$00. In the former Mouraria area, at Rua das Farinhas 1, *Algures na Mouraria* (Map 9; ☎ 887 24 70) is a fashionable little place offering a choice of Portuguese or African dishes at reasonable prices. It's closed on Sundays. Across the road, at No 30, the scruffier *Restaurante São Cristóvão* (Map 9) advertises vegetarian dishes as well as standard Portuguese fare.

Moving downhill, to Rua da Madalena 94, *Churrasqueira Adega do Manel* (Map 11; ☎ 886 91 64) offers meat-lovers a wide choice of dishes for under 1400$00. Down at Baixa level, the popular *Hua Ta Li* (Map 7; ☎ 887 91 70). at Rua dos Bacalhoeiros 109, has an east-meets-west menu and other more traditional Chinese dishes for around 1000$00 each.

The Alfama's waterfront restaurants can be expensive and touristy: head up one of the alleys for simpler places like *Snack-Bar Arco Iris* (Map 12; ☎ 886 45 36). at Rua São João da Praça 17, which has more space than most

---

Azulejos for Lunch?
One of the finest settings for a light lunch is the restaurant of the *Museu Nacional do Azulejo*, in the old convent of Nossa Senhora da Madre de Deus Church; take bus No 104 from Praça do Comércio or No 105 from Praça da Figueira. Choose from a small menu of salads, crêpes or meat and fish dishes for 1000$00 to 1300$00, and eat in the bright, traditional kitchen (tiled with azulejos, of course) or the plant-filled garden. ■

---

for its half-a-dozen outdoor tables. In the heart of the Alfama, the tiny *O Bêco Restaurante Típico* (Map 12; ☎ 887 49 14). at Rua de São Miguel 87, is reasonably priced and unpretentious – despite attracting tourists for its nightly, amateur fado performances.

Very much a locals' spot is *Estrela de Alfama* (Map 12; ☎ 888 13 89) on the same street at No 2: it's mostly meat dishes on the menu (for under 800$00) and no frills inside. There are several tourist-geared places around Largo do Chafariz de Dentro but *Restaurante Cais D'Alfama* (Map 12; ☎ 887 32 74), at no 24 attracts the locals, too, with its extensive menu (including fresh sardines grilled outdoors) and prices under 1000$00.

Restaurante Tolan (Map 12; ☎ 887 22 34), at Rua dos Remédios 134, is another locals' favourite; dishes (accompanied by constant TV) are under 900$00 (the bacalhau is especially good). Lastly, high above it all, the outdoor tables at *Bar Cerca Moura* (Map 12; ☎ 887 48 59), Largo das Portas do Sol 4, are worth the extra escudos just for the fantastic view over the Alfama neighbourhood.

Belém (Map 13) One of the best places for an open-air (or indoor) snack and coffee is the terrace café in the *Centro Cultural* on the western side of Praça do Império. There are lots of other cafes and pastelarias on Rua de Belém, just east of the monastery, although they inevitably get packed out with tourists most of the time. One not to miss is the *Pasteis de Belém* (see the following Pastelarias & Confeitarias section). And one to avoid is the over-priced *Café Astrolabio* opposite the Museu da Marinha.

Among the less expensive restaurants on Rua de Belém are *Os Jerónimos* (☎ 363 84 23) at No 74 which serves up tasty lunches for around 700$00 a dish; *Nau de Belém* (☎ 363 81 33), opposite at No 29, which has slightly more expensive dishes but a pleasant outdoor area; and *Adamastor* (☎ 363 61 16) at No 83, which has a cosy first-floor dining area as well as its more casual street-level restaurant, with an extensive menu of dishes at both for under 1000$00.

Vegetarian Food

Thankfully, in this country that so loves its meat, the capital has a few good, modestly priced vegetarian eateries.

Our choice for best value is *Restaurante Os Tibetanos* (Map 6; ☎ 314 20 38), part of a school of Tibetan Buddhism in an old house topped with prayer flags at Rua do Salitre 117, on the northern side of the botanical garden (metro: Avenida). It offers a changing 750$00 rice and vegetable dish plus soups, salads and pastries in a fresh, peaceful atmosphere. It's open for meals from noon to 2.30 pm and 7.30 to 10 pm on weekdays, and to 10.30 pm on Saturday. It serves teas, coffee and munchies from 4.30 to 7 pm.

Also recommended is the *Restaurante Espiral* (Map 3; ☎ 357 35 85), at Praça Ilha da Faial 14-A in the Estefânia district (metro: Saldanha). Open daily from 10 am to 10 pm, it sells macrobiotic rice and vegetable dishes, Chinese-style vegetables and light meals for less than 600$00 per course, plus lots of sweet snacks and desserts – and sometimes live music. Next door at No 14-B is a food shop and snack bar with soups, salads and sandwiches for under 300$00; it's open from 10 am to 8.30 pm.

The *Centro de Alimentação e Saúde Natural* (Map 6; ☎ 315 08 98) is a small restaurant with a weedy, meditative courtyard at Rua Mouzinho da Silveira 25 in Rato (between Avenida and Rotunda metro stations). On weekdays from noon to 9 pm and Saturday from noon to 2 pm it has a small selection of vegetarian and macrobiotic plates for under 1000$00, plus soups and desserts. Next door is a health-food shop, and courses in massage and Zen meditation are offered upstairs.

At Rua 1 de Dezembro 65, by Rossio train station, is a health-food shop called *Celeiro*, open weekdays from 8.30 am to 8 pm and Saturdays to 7 pm. The self-service macrobiotic restaurant downstairs (Map 9; ☎ 342 24 63) is open Monday to Friday from 9 am to 7 pm, serving everything from herbal teas to Chinese crêpes. On the next block is an excellent supermarket, also called Celeiro.

Restaurante Yin-Yang (Map 11), a vegetarian place upstairs at Rua dos Coreeiros 14 in the Baixa, is open Monday to Friday from noon to 3 pm and 6.30 to 8.30 pm, serving macrobiotic meals from 750$00. Similar fare and prices can be found at *A Colmeia* (Map 10; ☎ 347 05 00), tucked away on the 2nd floor of Rua da Emenda 10. It's open Monday to Friday from noon to 7 pm and Saturday from 12.30 to 2.30 pm.

Pastelarias & Confeitarias

Lisbon has enough pastry shops and coffee shops to keep you buzzing all day, and the Portuguese love 'em. Many restaurants also have a separate area devoted to this excellent Portuguese pastime. You'll often pay less to have your snack at the balcão, and quite a lot more to have it at a table out on the esplanada.

Our favourite spot around the Rossio is a big pastelaria called *Casa Suiça* (Map 9; ☎ 342 80 92) at Rossio 96-101 (through to Praça da Figueira 3-A). It has good coffee and a dizzying array of pastries and sweets available daily from 7 am to 10 pm. At the time of research it had fallen temporary victim to metro works. Short on ambience but strong on its choice of diet-defying cakes (and with great window seats for watching shoppers down below) is *Chiadomel* (Map 9; ☎ 347 44 01) right by the Elevador de Santa Justa, above Rua de Santa Justa 105.

With strong literary associations and art all over the walls, *Café A Brasileira* (Map 10; ☎ 346 95 47), open daily from 8 am to 2 am at Rua Garrett 120 (now directly above a new metro station) in the Chiado, is a very elegant setting for a snack. The bronze statue (by Lagoa Henriques) sitting outside is of the famous Portuguese poet and writer Fernando Pessoa, a frequent habitué of the café in his day.

Beloved of students and senior citizens from the neighbourhood, for its pastries and big coffees, is cheerful *Confeitaria Císter* (Map 6), at Rua da Escola Politécnica 107.

At Rua Bernardino Costa 34-36 in Cais do Sodré is a fine little bakery and pastelaria called *Caneças* (Map 10), with hot fresh bread, croissants, cakes and light snacks. It's open weekdays from 6 am to 7.30 pm and Saturday from 8 am to 2 pm.

Finally, when you go to Belém, don't miss the *Pastéis de Belém*, Rua de Belém 88, where the traditional custard tarts called pastéis de Belém are made on the premises and consumed in vast quantities.

Entertainment

Probably the most famous form of entertainment in Lisbon (though not necessarily among *lisboêtas* themselves) is listening to *fado*, the haunting, melancholy Portuguese equivalent of the blues (see Arts in the Facts about Lisbon chapter for more on fado). Tourists get stylised versions in the *casas de fado* of the Bairro Alto district, while shelling out minimum charges of 2000$00 to 3000$00. If you're lucky, a local fan may direct you to the real thing, in obscure cafés that stay open most of the night.

More conventional bars, pubs and discos abound in Lisbon, especially in the traditional nightlife neighbourhoods of Bairro Alto, Alcântara and Avenida 24 de Julho and up-and-coming riverside areas such as Doca de Santo Amaro. But bear in mind that clubs come and go like the wind; those listed here are only a drop in the bucket. Your best bet may be to do what everybody else does: trawl the neighbourhoods to find what appeals to you. Note that evening revels start late – around 11 pm at the earliest – and stagger to a stop any time up until dawn. And don't be surprised if some clubs (eg the very popular Frágil) refuse you entry: they can be infuriatingly and unpredictably choosy about their clientele.

Traditional Portuguese entertainment – such as folk songs and folk dancing, parades and processions – can best be enjoyed during traditional *festas* (festivals) and *feiras* (fairs). Many are centred on local saints' days and associated religious processions, or are part of a *romaria* (pilgrimage). Lisbon's best such event is the Festa de Santo António on 12-13 June, part of the month-long Festas dos Santos Populares (for more on this, see Public Holidays & Special Events and the Festas dos Santos Populares boxed aside, both in the Facts for the Visitor chapter).

During the summer there's a number of cultural programmes in and around Lisbon: one of the country's best known international music festivals is held in Sintra in July-August. Others of interest include a jazz festival in Estoril and Cascais, also in July, and the Lisboa Mexe-me Festival in August (see the Excursions chapter and Music Festivals under Public Holidays & Special Events in the Facts for the Visitor chapter for details).

In addition to Lisbon's main performance halls – at the Fundação Calouste Gulbenkian and the Centro Cultural de Belém – there are over half-a-dozen other major theatres, listed in the following Theatres & Concert Halls section. Several of these (notably Culturgest) host changing art exhibitions as well as occasional music and other performances. Once EXPO '98 ends, the Multipurpose (during EXPO '98 called the Utopia) Pavilion will become another major venue for large scale shows. Free concerts are often held on weekends – and almost daily during the Festas dos Santos Populares in June – at several city churches and former churches, including the Basílica da Estrela (Map 5), Igreja de São Roque (Map 8), Convento do Carmo (Map 9), Basílica da Nossa Senhora dos Mártires (Map 10) and the Sé (Map 12). During July and August, the Centro Cultural de Belém (Map 13) has a programme of free performances on Thursday, Friday and Saturday from 10 pm to midnight at the Jardim das Oliveiras inside the Centro. Also during this time, amateur student performers strut their stuff on a tiny riverside stage at the Espaço Ágora (Map 10), near Cais do Sodré ferry terminal.

For current listings, pick up the free monthly publications available at the turismo (see Tourist Offices in the Facts for the Visitor chapter) or see the listings in the daily *Público* newspaper. The Gulbenkian and the Centro Cultural de Belém publish their own schedules as well. The city operates a 24-hour 'what's on' hotline (☎ 790 10 62), providing information (in Portuguese) about theatre, dance, classical music, rock concerts, cinema, galleries, exhibitions and so on. You'll find that performances often start late, around 9.30 pm.

As for getting tickets, the ABEP ticket agency (Map 9), on Praça dos Restauradores opposite the turismo, is fine for bullfights, cinemas, football and stadium concerts, but you're better off buying concert and theatre tickets at the relevant venues.

CINEMAS

European and American films (most of them thankfully subtitled, not dubbed) seem to edge out local competition in Lisbon's cinemas. Tickets are fairly cheap, typically 500$00 to 700$00; prices are often further reduced one day a week in an effort to lure audiences away from their home videos.

There are something like 60 cinemas in Lisbon. Among at least seven multiscreen theatres, the biggest are the 10-screen *Amoreiras* (☎ 383 12 75), at the Amoreiras shopping centre (Map 2) on Avenida Engenheiro Duarte Pacheco, and the similar multi-screen theatre at the new Colombo shopping centre on Avenida Colégio Militar. For listings (and star ratings), see the comprehensive section in the daily *Público* paper.

DISCOS

Lisbon has scores of discos, though they boom and bust at lightning speed. Some have occasional live bands. Rua Nova do Carvalho (near Cais do Sodré) is the traditional den of discos, many rather seedy, though *Jamaica* (Map 10; ☎ 342 18 59) at No 5 often has some good reggae sounds. Other possibilities are:

Bairro Alto

Frágil (Map 8; ☎ 346 95 78), Rua da Atalaia 126-128; open 10 pm to 4 am (closed Sundays); well established but still trendy

Três Pastorinhos (Map 8; ☎ 346 43 01), Rua da Barroca 111-113; open 11 pm to 4 am

Incógnito (Map 6; ☎ 60 87 55), an unmarked door at Rua dos Poiais de São Bento 37; open 11 pm to at least 4 am (3 to 7 am Tuesdays; closed Sundays)

Avenida 24 de Julho

Absoluto (Map 6; ☎ 395 50 09), Rua Dom Luís I 5 (24 de Julho); open to 4 am, Thursday to Saturday only; restaurant and bar, too

Kapital (Map 5; ☎ 395 59 63), Avenida 24 de Julho 68; open 11.30 pm to 4 am (closed Mondays and Wednesdays); hypertrendy; disco, bar and roof terrace

Kremlin (Map 5; ☎ 60 87 68), Escadinhas da Praia 5; open 1 am to 7 am (to 8 am Fridays and Saturdays; closed Sundays and Mondays); acid and techno; young and very trendy

Metalúrgica (Map 5; ☎ 397 14 88), Avenida 24 de Julho 110; open 10 pm to 4 am; blues, rock and pop; all ages; good vibes

Alcântara

Alcântara Mar (Map 4; ☎ 363 64 32), Rua da Cozinha Económica 11; open 11.30 pm to 6 am (closed Mondays and Tuesdays); rock on Wednesdays and Thursdays, funk on weekends; also a café (☎ 363 71 76); outside is the 'Souk de Alcântara', a row of trailers dishing up munchies all night

Benzina (Map 4; ☎ 363 39 59), Travessa de Teixeira Júnior 6; open midnight to 6 am; soul, funk, acid jazz, rock and pop in good ship *Titanic* décor

Blues Cafe (Map 5; ☎ 395 70 85), Rua da Cintura do Porto de Lisboa, Armazém H; open daily except Sundays; a hot new spot with a Cajun menu and Louisiana-style atmosphere

Cais S (☎ 395 81 10), Doca de Santo Amaro (Map 4), Armazém 1; bar-cum-disco open daily until 4 am except Sundays (disco starts at 9pm); surf shop by the bar; seats by the river; bizarre décor of huge metal insects hanging from the ceiling and a giant screen relaying radical sports shows

Dock's Club (Map 5; ☎ 395 08 56), Rua da Cintura do Porto de Lisboa 226, Armazém H; open 10 pm to around 4 am (closed Sundays); among the new strip of bars overlooking the Doca de Alcântara; plenty of open-air space

Gartejo (Map 4; ☎ 395 59 77), Rua João de Oliveira Miguens 38; open 10 pm to at least 4 am (closed Sundays); young and very trendy, some live bands

Discoteca Kings and Queens (Map 5; ☎ 397 76 99), Rua da Cintura do Porto de Lisboa (near Dock's Club); open 10.30 pm to 5 am (closed Sundays); lively and loud

Ultramar (Map 5; ☎ 396 18 86), Rocha do Conde de Óbidos; open 10 pm to around 4 am (closed Mondays and Tuesdays); easy-going atmosphere; restaurant and great esplanade, too

Rato

Ad Lib (Map 6; ☎ 356 17 17), Rua Barata Salgueiro 28, 7th floor; open 11 pm to whenever (closed Sundays and Mondays); yuppies and business types

THEATRES & CONCERT HALLS

Lisbon's main theatres, concert and dance halls are at the Fundação Calouste Gulbenkian (Map 3; ☎ 795 02 36) and Centro Cultural de Belém (Map 13; ☎ 301 96 06). The following venues also host musical and theatrical events:

Agência 117 Theatre (Map 8; ☎ 346 12 70), Rua do Norte 117, Bairro Alto; one of the more unusual venues, doubling as a clothes shop and hairdresser's salon as well as an ad-hoc venue for off-beat performances

Culturgest (Map 3; ☎ 790 51 55), Edificio Caixa Geral de Depósitos, Rua Arco do Cego (metro: Campo Pequeno); art gallery and exhibition venue as well as theatre (galleries open weekdays, except Tuesdays, from 10 am to 5.30 pm and weekends from 3 to 7 pm); theatre often hosts unusual performances

Institut Franco-Portugais (Map 3; ☎ 311 14 77), Avenida Luís Bívar 91, Saldanha; occasional performances by visiting French artists and companies

Teatro Aberto (Map 2; ☎ 797 09 69), Praça de Espanha, Rato

Teatro Maria Matos (Map 1; ☎ 849 70 07), Avenida Frei Miguel Contreras 52 (metro: Roma); Teatro Infantil de Lisboa (Lisbon Children's Theatre) events during term time

Teatro Maria Vitória (Map 6; ☎ 346 17 40), Parque Mayer (Avenida da Liberdade)

Teatro Municipal de São Luís (Map 10; ☎ 342 71 72), Rua António Maria Cardoso 54, Chiado; venerable venue with major shows at its studio theatre, Teatro Estúdio Mário Viegas (☎ 347 12 79)

Teatro Municipal de Trinidade (Map 8; ☎ 342 32 00), Rua Nova da Trinidade 9, Bairro Alto; dance, jazz and popular musical shows

Teatro Nacional de Dona Maria II (Map 9; ☎ 342 22 10), Praça Dom Pedro IV, Rossio; historic city centre theatre

Teatro Nacional de São Carlos (Map 10; ☎ 346 59 14), Rua Serpa Pinto 9, Chiado; opera and other serious stuff at Lisbon's handsome 18th century opera house

Teatro Villaret (Map 3; ☎ 353 85 86), Avenida Fontes Pereira de Melo 30A (metro: Picoas)

MUSIC
Rock & Pop

Fancy some good old baby-boomer boogie? Here are a few suggestions.

Álcool Puro (Map 5; ☎ 396 74 67), Avenida Dom Carlos I 59 (24 de Julho); open 11 pm to 4 am (closed Sundays); live rock and dancing

Anos 60 (Map 7; ☎ 887 34 44), Largo do Terreirinho 21 (Mouraria); open 9.30 pm to 3 am (closed Sundays), live 60s music on Fridays and Saturdays

Até Qu'Enfim (Map 5; ☎ 396 59 39), Rua das Janelas Verdes 2, Lapa; open 10 pm to 2 am daily

Rock City (Map 6; ☎ 342 86 40), Rua Cintura do Porto de Lisboa, Armazém 225 (five minutes walk along the riverfront west of Cais do Sodré station); live rock music from midnight to 4 am (closed Mondays); restaurant and four bars (two in a tropical garden)

Jazz

The Fundação Calouste Gulbenkian and Hot Clube de Portugal organise an excellent international jazz festival at the fundação's open-air amphitheatre (see the Gulbenkian boxed asides in the Things to See & Do

---

Chapitô

If you pop into the *Chapitô* bar (Map 12; ☎ 887 82 25), below Castelo São Jorge at Costa do Castelo 7, you'll discover that it's more than an open-air pub with a great view. It's actually part of a school of circus arts and show business, run by the Collectividade Cultural e Recreativa de Santa Catarina (Santa Catarina Cultural & Recreation Collective), founded in the mid-1980s.

Next door at No 1 are the collective's office, library, theatre, gallery, recording studios, classrooms and a day-care centre. On the patio you may see street-theatre or juggling workshops; in the bar you may hear live music, poetry readings or other late-evening entertainment. The collective runs evening courses in dance, music, singing, juggling, circus techniques and TV acting, and presents performances, films and exhibitions – all listed in its own monthly programme (in Portuguese), and also usually in the newspapers, in the *Agenda Cultural* and at the turismo.

There is also a small restaurant, *Gargalhada Geral*, serving salads, soups and sandwiches from 7.30 pm to 2 am. The bar is open from 9.30 pm to 2 am. Both are closed on Sundays and practically everything comes to a stop during August. ∎

chapter) each year in early August. The box office (☎ 793 51 31, ext 3402; fax 795 52 06) is open Tuesday through Saturday from 1 to 7 pm, and before each show. Tickets are 1500$00 and there are discounts available for young people, over-65s, musicians and actors.

Hot Clube de Portugal (Map 6; ☎ 346 73 69; www.isa.utl.pt/HCP/HCPhome.html), Praça da Alegria 39 (metro: Avenida); open 10 pm to 2 am (closed Sundays and Mondays), the centre of the jazz scene; live music at least three or four nights a week, with sessions at 11 pm and 1.30 am

Café Luso (Map 8; ☎ 342 22 81), Travessa da Queimada 10, Bairro Alto; open 8 pm to 3.30 am (closed Mondays); casa de fado with jazz on weekends

Tertúlia (Map 8; ☎ 346 27 04), Rua do Diário de Notícias 60, Bairro Alto; open 10.30 pm to 2 am (closed Sundays); some live jazz plus a piano for anyone to tinkle

Speakeasy (Map 5; ☎ 386 42 57), Cais da Rocha do Conde de Óbidos, Doca do Alcântara; open noon to 4 am daily; jam sessions on Tuesdays

Fado

Listening to Portugal's 'blues' in its authentic form is a wonderfully melancholy way to drink your way through the night (for more about *fado*, see the Arts section in the Facts about Lisbon chapter), and the Alfama district is said to be its true home.

But every tourist wants to say they've heard it, and the sad truth is that many of Lisbon's casas de fado now offer pale imitations – 'tour-bus meets Greek taverna', as one travel writer put it – and often at prices to make you moan along with the fadista. Nearly all are restaurants, and insist that you spend a minimum (*consumo mínimo*) of 2000$00 to 3500$00 on their food and drinks in order to stay and hear the music; you're likely to spend twice that amount if you have dinner.

Following are many of Lisbon's better known fado houses, with an indication of minimum charges.

Adega do Machado (Map 8; ☎ 342 87 13), Rua do Norte 91, Bairro Alto; music from 9.30 pm to 3 am (closed Mondays); minimum 2500$00

Adega do Ribatejo (Map 8; ☎ 346 83 43), Rua Diário de Notícias 23, Bairro Alto; music 8.30 pm to midnight (closed Sundays); minimum 1800$00, reasonable food prices, better value than most

Adega Mesquita (Map 8; ☎ 346 20 77), Rua Diário de Notícias 107, Bairro Alto; 8 pm to 3.30 am; minimum 2000$00

Café Luso (Map 8; ☎ 342 22 81), Travessa da Queimada 10; open 8 pm to 3.30 am (closed Mondays), minimum 2000$00; jazz on weekends

Lisboa à Noite (Map 8; ☎ 346 26 03), Rua das Gáveas 69, Bairro Alto; open 8 pm to 3 am (closed Sundays); minimum 2750$00

Nono (Map 8; ☎ 346 86 25), Rua do Norte 47, Bairro Alto; open 8 pm to 3.30 am (closed Sundays); minimum 1500$00

O Bêco Restaurante Típico (Map 12; ☎ 887 49 14), Rua de São Miguel 87, Alfama; amateur fadistas sing at this small restaurant nightly from 8.30 pm to midnight; reasonable menu prices, plus 500$00 extra per person for the music

Fado Uproar

There are two styles of fado music: one comes from Lisbon and the other from the university town of Coimbra (about 200km north of Lisbon). The Lisbon style is still considered by aficionados to be the most genuine, but there's something about Coimbra's roving bands of romantic, fado-singing students during their May celebration week that pulls at the heart-strings far more effectively than the Lisbon performers in their nightclubs. Indeed, in many ways, the Coimbra singers surpass their Lisbon colleagues in tradition. When singer Manuela Bravo announced in April 1996 that she was going to record a CD of Coimbra fados, there was an outcry by the fado department of Coimbra University. Why? Because Coimbra fado – which praises the beauty of women – is traditionally sung by men only. Her opponents, described Bravo's supporters as 'Salazaristic, old-fashioned and musty', warn that the gutsy *fadista* will 'debauch' tradition. To their horror, she even won the support of one of Portugal's best fado guitarists, António Pinho Brojo. Even the Mayor of Coimbra got involved (on the side of Bravo), and the album, entitled *Intenções*, went ahead. Few things arouse such emotion in Portugal as fado, and nowhere more so than in Lisbon and Coimbra. ■

Os Ferreiras (Map 6;☎ 885 08 51), Rua de São Lázaro 150, near Largo Martim Moniz (metro: Socorro); open midnight to 2 am; minimum 1500$00

O Forcado (Map 8; ☎ 346 85 79), Rua da Rosa 219, Bairro Alto; open 8 pm to 2 am (closed Wednesdays); minimum 2500$00

Parreirinha de Alfama (Map 12; ☎ 886 82 09), Beco do Espírito Santo 1, Alfama; open 8 pm to 3 am; minimum 2000$00

Senhor Vinho (Map 5; ☎ 397 26 81), Rua do Meio à Lapa 18, Lapa; open 8.30 pm to 3 am (closed Sundays); minimum 3000$00

Taverna do Embuçado (Map 12; ☎ 886 50 88), Beco dos Cortumes 10, Alfama; open 9 pm to 2.30 am (closed Sundays); no minimum

Tímpanas (Map 4; ☎ 397 24 31), Rua Gilberto Rola 24, Alcântara; open 8 pm to 2 am (closed Wednesdays); minimum 2000$00

Voz do Operário (Map 7; ☎ 886 21 55), Rua Voz do Operário 13, Alfama; amateur fado performances at this workers' club on occasional Saturdays (except August) from around 11 pm; 1000$00 admission

African Music

The African music scene (with its roots predominantly in Cape Verde, but also Mozambique, Guinea Bissau and Angola) bops in bars all over town.

Discoteca A Lontra (Map 5; ☎ 369 10 83), Rua de São Bento 155, Bairro Alto; music starts after midnight (closed Mondays); one of the best known venues in town

Banana Power (Map 4; ☎ 363 18 15), Rua de Cascais 51-53, 2nd Floor, Alcântara

Café Be Pop (Map 8; ☎ 342 1626), Rua Luz Soriano 18; live Latin-African (eg from Guinea Bissau) and jazz sounds, especially Saturday nights; closed Sunday and Monday

Ritz Clube (Map 8; ☎ 346 59 98), Rua da Glória 57, just off Avenida da Liberdade; open 10 pm to 4 am (closed Sundays); mainly Cape Verdean; late meals

South American Music

For live Brazilian rhythms, ring the bell at Largo de São Martinho 6, Alfama for the *Pé Sujo* bar (Map 12; ☎886 56 29); it's closed on Mondays. Or try the following:

Havana (Map 4;☎ 397 98 93), Doca de Santo Amaro, Armazém 5; open daily from noon to 4 am; a Cuban bar and restaurant with live Brazilian music on Fridays

---

❦❦❦❦❦❦❦❦❦❦❦❦❦❦❦❦❦❦❦❦❦

Solar do Vinho do Porto

The Instituto do Vinho do Porto (Port Wine Institute) is an autonomous agency, based in Porto, with the job of maintaining the reputation of the port wine appellation by controlling its quality and output and promoting it generically. Among other things, it operates the *Solar do Vinho do Porto* (☎ 342 33 07) in an old palace at Rua de São Pedro de Alcântara 45, right at the top of the Elevador da Glória in the Bairro Alto. Here you can sample various port wines, from about 150$00 a glass, in a subdued, living-room-like setting, and peruse (or buy) books and other information on port wine. It's open weekdays from 10 am to 11.45 pm and Saturdays from 11 am to 10.45 pm. ■

❦❦❦❦❦❦❦❦❦❦❦❦❦❦❦❦❦❦❦❦❦

Salsa Latina (Map 4; ☎ 395 05 50), Gare Marítima de Alcântara; restaurant-cum dance hall open weekdays from noon to 4 am, Saturday from 8 pm to 4 am (closed Sundays); live music nightly, with a salsa dance teacher at hand on Fridays

Irish Music

Homesick Dubliners should head down to *Ó Gilíns Irish Pub* (Map 10; ☎ 342 18 99), at Rua dos Remolares 8-10, Cais do Sodré, where Conor Gillen will fill your glass with draught Guinness daily from 11 am to 2 am; there's live traditional Irish music on most Saturday nights and live jazz with brunch on Sundays.

BARS

This section is for people in search of watering holes. Many places also have music (sometimes live) and dancing, so if that's what you're after, see the sections on discos and live music too. Avenida 24 de Julho has the heaviest concentration of discos and bars while Doca de Santo Amaro is the hottest new area for late night restaurants and bars.

Alfama (Map 12)

Chapitô (☎ 887 82 25), 7 Costa do Castelo, corner of Costa do Castelo and Calçada do Marquês de Tancos; open 10 pm to 2 am (closed Mondays); bar/restaurant with city views

O Esboço (☎ 887 78 93), Rua do Vigário 10; open 11 pm to 2 am (closed Sundays); cheap meals

Ópera (☎ 886 23 18), Travessa das Mónicas 65; open 10 pm to 2 am (Friday and Saturday nights to 3.30 am); cheap meals; occasional art exhibits

Bairro Alto & Chiado

A Capela (Map 8), in a former chapel at Rua da Atalaia 45; open 10 pm to 2 am (Fridays and Saturdays to 4 am); sometimes live jazz

Arroz Doce (Map 8; ☎ 346 26 01), Rua da Atalaia 117; open 6 pm to 2 am (closed Sundays); cheerful and unpretentious

Café Suave (Map 10; ☎ 347 11 44), Rua do Diário do Noticias 6; open 9 pm to 2 am

Cena de Copos (Map 8), Rua da Barroca 103; open 9 pm to 2 am

Fremitus (Map 8;☎ 343 36 32), Rua da Atalaia 78; open nightly 8.30 pm to 3.30 am

Ma Jong (Map 10; ☎ 342 10 39), Rua da Atalaia 3; open 11 pm to 2.30 am; lots of artists

Nova (Map 8; ☎ 346 28 34), Rua da Rosa 261; open 10 pm to 2 am (Fridays and Saturdays to 2.30 am); trendy

Pavilhão Chinês (Map 6; ☎ 342 47 29), Rua Dom Pedro V 89; open 6 pm to 2 am (from 9 pm Sundays); idiosyncratic, turn-of-the-century décor; pool tables

Portas Largas (Map 8; ☎ 846 63 79), Rua da Atalaia 105; converted old tavern open nightly 8 pm to 4 am; casual atmosphere

Primas (Map 8; ☎ 342 59 25), Rua da Atalaia 154; open 9.30 pm to 2 or 3 am; noisy local pub with pinball machines

Snob Bar (Map 6; ☎ 346 37 23), Rua do Século 178; open 4.30 pm to 3 am; favourite watering hole (serving meals, too) for journalists and the advertising crowd

Soul Factory Bar (Map 10), Rua das Salgadeiras 28; open 9.30 pm to 3.30 am; music from reggae to soul, hip hop to funk and rap; closed Tuesdays

Sudoeste (Map 8; ☎ 342 16 72), Rua da Barroca 129; cocktail bar plus disco

Work in Progress (Map 10; ☎ 886 65 32), Rua da Bica Duarte Belo 47; open 10 pm to 4 am; bizarre combination of clothes shop and bar, with live music Wednesdays

Cais do Sodré (Map 10)

Bar do Rio (☎ 346 72 79), in Armazém 7 (on the riverfront just west of the Cais do Sodré bus station); open 11 pm to 6 am daily; minimum consumption 5000$00

British Bar (☎ 342 23 67) at Rua Bernardo Costa 52; open daily, until 2 am at weekends; crammed with pub paraphernalia

Hennessy's Irish Pub (☎ 343 10 64), at Rua Cais do Sodré 38; open 12 noon to 1 am (4 am at weekends); serving Guinness, of course, and Irish food, though in rather dark and drab surroundings

Avenida 24 de Julho (Map 5)

Café Central (☎ 395 61 11), Avenida 24 de Julho 112; open 10 pm to 4 am; rock and blues

Cervejinhas (☎ 60 80 50), Avenida 24 de Julho 78-B

Décibel (☎ 396 17 29), Avenida 24 de Julho 90-B/C; open 11 pm to 3.30 am; psychedelic rock for all ages

Gringo's Café (☎ 396 09 11), Avenida 24 de Julho 116; open until 2 am (closed Sundays); Tex-Mex café-bar with food available until 1 am; margarita-land

Paulinha (☎ 396 47 83), Avenida 24 de Julho 82-A; open 10.30 pm to 4 am (closed Sundays and Mondays); all ages

Doca de Santo Amaro (Map 4)

Celtas & Iberos (☎ 397 60 37), Armazém 7; open daily except Monday, from 12.30 to 2 am; pleasant wood and brick surroundings and lots of Guinness on tap

Santo Amaro Cafe (☎ 397 99 04), Armazém 9; open daily except Tuesdays; modernist chrome and rattan decor; meals available

Lapa (Map 5)

Stones (☎ 396 45 45), Rua do Olival 1; open to 4 am (closed Mondays); 60s and 70s rock

Gay & Lesbian Bars

Many gay and lesbian bars are clustered in the hilly streets of Rato and northern Bairro Alto.

Doca de Santo Amaro

The revamped and revitalised riverside area of Doca de Santo Amaro – just east of the Ponte 25 de Abril – is the city's newest spot for chic outdoor lunch time dining and late-night revelries. Around a dozen bars and restaurants have been converted from the cavernous riverside warehouses and stores (called *armazém*) and more are opening up all the time. A few hundred metres to the east, within walking distance from Doca de Santo Amaro, is Doca de Alcântara, which has its own strip of new bars.

The easiest way to get here is to take a train from Cais do Sodré station to Alcântara-Mar; follow signs for the riverside *(marítima)*, turning right to find Doca de Santo Amaro or left for Doca de Alcântara. Alternatively, catch tram No 15 from Praça da Figueira and get out when you see the Doca de Alcântara's Blues Cafe and Dock's Club on your left. ■

Bar 106 (Map 6; ☎ 342 73 73), Rua de São Marçal 106; open 9 pm to 2 am; one of the best and busiest

Brica Bar (or *O Brica*; Map 6; ☎ 342 89 71), Rua Cecilio de Sousa 84; open 9 pm to 4 am

Finalmente (Map 6; ☎ 347 26 52), Rua da Palmeira 38; closed Mondays; weekend drag shows

Memorial (Map 6; ☎ 66 88 91), Rua da Gustavo de Matos Sequeira 42-A; open 10 pm to 3.30 am (closed Mondays); very popular; gay and lesbian

Tatoo (Map 6; ☎ 67 07 26), Rua de São Marçal 15; open 8.30 pm to 2 am (closed Sundays)

Trumps (☎ 67 10 59), Rua da Imprensa Nacional 104-B; open 11 pm to 4 am (closed Mondays); huge dance floor

SPECTATOR SPORT
Football

Lisboêtas are as obsessed as everybody else in Portugal with football (soccer). When there's a big match on, TVs in bars and restaurants show nothing else. Of Portugal's three good national teams, two – Benfica and Sporting – are based in Lisbon. The two have been rivals ever since Sporting beat Benfica, 2-1, on 1 December 1907.

The season runs from September through May, and most league matches are on Sundays; check the newspapers (especially *A Bola*) or ask at the turismo about upcoming contests. Tickets are fairly cheap and are sold at the stadium on match day, or you can buy them, for slightly inflated prices, at the ABEP ticket agency on Praça dos Restauradores, opposite the turismo.

Benfica (properly Sport Lisboa e Benfica) plays at *Estádio da Luz* (Map 1) in the north-west Benfica district (metro: Colégio Militar, or take bus No 41 from Rossio). For ticket information call ☎ 726 60 53, or contact Benfica's enquiries office (☎ 726 61 29/726 03 21; fax 726 47 61).

Sporting (properly Sporting Clube de Portugal) plays at *Estádio José de Alvalade*, just north of the university. The nearest metro station is Campo Grande, or take bus No 1 or 36 from Rossio. For information, call ☎ 758 90 21 (or fax 759 93 91).

Bullfighting

Bullfighting is still popular in Portugal, despite pressure from international animal-rights activists. Lisbon, like nearly every town and city in the country, has its own *praça de touros* (bullring) – an eye-catching Moorish-style building across Avenida da República from Campo Pequeno metro station (or take bus No 1, 21, 36, 44, 45 or 83 from Rossio).

Man, Bull & Horse

A typical *tourada* (bullfight) starts with a huge bull charging into the ring towards a *cavaleiro*, a horseman dressed in elaborate 18th century-style costume and plumed tricorn hat (so far, there's only one female *cavaleira* or mounted bullfighting woman in the world, the 24-year-old Portuguese Marta Manuela). The 500kg bull has his horns capped in metal balls or leather, but he's still an awesome adversary. The cavaleiro sizes him up as his backup team of *peões de brega* (footmen) distract and provoke the bull with capes. Then, with incredible horse-riding skills, he gallops within inches of the bull's horns and plants a number of short, barbed *bandarilha* spears into the bull's neck.

The next phase of the fight, the *pega*, features a team of eight young, volunteer *forcados* dressed in breeches, white stockings and short jackets, who face the bull barehanded, in a single line. The leader swaggers towards the bull from across the ring, provoking it to charge. Bearing the brunt of the attack, he throws himself onto the animal's head and grabs the horns while his mates rush in behind him to try and immobilise the beast, often being tossed in all directions in the process. Their success marks the end of the contest and the bull is led out of the pen among a herd of steers. Though the rules for Portuguese bullfighting prohibit a public kill, the hapless animal is usually dispatched in private afterwards.

Another style of performance (often the final contest in a day-long *tourada*) is similar to the Spanish version, with a *toureiro* challenging the bull – its horns uncapped – with cape and bandarilhas. Unlike in Spain, however, there's no *picador* on horseback to weaken the bull with lances. It's man against beast. And unlike in Spain, the kill is symbolic, a short bandarilha feigning the thrust of a sword. ■

Fights take place from May through October, usually on Thursdays or Sundays. Tickets, on sale outside the bullring, range from 2500$00 to 4000$00, depending on whether you want a *sol* (sunny), *sol e sombra* (sunny and shady) or *sombra* (shady) seat. You can also buy tickets from the ABEP ticket agency on Praça dos Restauradores.

You can see more traditional bullfights in bull-breeding Ribatejo province, especially in Santarém during its June agricultural fair and in Vila Franca de Xira during the town's July and October festivals. See the Cruelty to Animals section in the Facts about the Country chapter for a discussion of the associated cruelty to animals issue.

Shopping

Lisbon is a tempting place to shop if only because street life moves slowly enough to make browsing a pleasure. In addition, modern shopping malls are still few and far between and tacky souvenir outlets surprisingly rare. Most attractive of all, prices here are among the lowest in Europe, especially for shoes and leather items. During the summer sales many clothes shops – even designer outlets – offer discounts of up to 50%.

Some of the best buys are the uniquely Portuguese products such as *azulejos*, ceramics and handicrafts and, of course, port wine. And if you're into haute couture, this is definitely the place to find all the latest bank-breaking fashions by leading Portuguese designers. Delightful just to look at are the Art Deco speciality shops of the kind your grandmother would recognise, dealing exclusively in shirts, hats or gloves.

Cheaper and tackier – but a lot of fun – are the open-air markets in and around Lisbon (see the Markets boxed aside in this chapter) where you can pick up anything from a souvenir T-shirt or embroidered tablecloth to a cow bell or gilded wooden angel.

The main shopping areas are in the Baixa (especially the pedestrianised Rua Augusta for clothes and shoes, and Rua Áurea for jewellery), the Chiado and Bairro Alto (Rua Garret for clothes and linen and neighbouring streets for ceramics and haute couture) and Avenida da Roma (for high class shoe shops). Among shopping malls, the most popular are the new Centro Comercial Colombo and the Complexo das Amoreiras, M3, (and outside Lisbon, CascaiShopping, near Cascais). The free ANA *Your Guide: Lisboa* booklet, and the Tax Free for Tourists' *Shopping in Portugal* guide (both available at the airport) have a comprehensive listing of shops.

Most city centre shops are open from 9 am to 1 pm and from 3 to 7 pm (but often until 10 pm or 11 pm in the shopping malls). On Saturday some shut at 1 pm. If you live outside the EU and spend more than 11,700$00 at a shop that's a member of the Europe Tax-Free Shopping Portugal scheme, your purchase will be eligible for a VAT refund. See Taxes & Refunds under Money in the Facts for the Visitor chapter for details.

SHOPPING CENTRES

The colossal new Centro Comercial Colombo – the biggest shopping centre in the Iberian peninsula, designed by José Quintela da Fonseca – opened in September 1997 at Avenida Colégio Militar (metro: Colégio Militar/Luz station). With 500 shops, 20 banks, 50 restaurants, 10 cinemas and a 'Play Center' including a bowling alley and karting circuit, it has well and truly stolen the limelight from the Complexo das Amoreiras, which was once the biggest shopping centre in Portugal.

Designed by architect Tomás Taveira, the chrome-plated Amoreiras complex is still an impressive building, looming on a hilltop north-west of the city centre, on Avenida Engenheiro Duarte Pacheco. It contains some 300 boutiques, restaurants, snack bars and cinemas. To get here, take almost any bus west from Rotunda metro station on Rua Joaquim António de Aguiar.

Another huge centre is the Centro Comercial Carrefour, north of the city at Avenida das Nações Unidas, Telheiras (Campo Grande metro then bus No 47). Smaller centres include Centro Comercial Espaço Chiado, at Rua da Misericórdia 12-20, and Galerias Monumental at Praça Duque de Saldanha. Outside Lisbon, CascaiShopping, between Sintra and Cascais, has 130 shops (including Toys 'R Us and C&A), 30 restaurants, seven cinemas and a games area for kids. Bus No 417 from Sintra/Cascais goes past regularly.

ANTIQUES

For up-market antiques, trawl Rua de São

Bento (west of Bairro Alto) or Rua Dom Pedro V (north of Bairro Alto) where you'll find everything from Indo-Portuguese furniture to porcelain and crystal. Far more fun (though not necessarily cheaper) are the shops in Campo de Santa Clara, near Igreja de São Vicente. Especially busy on flea market days (Tuesday and Saturday), they offer everything from glass, ceramics and religious statuettes to furniture, silver and jewellery.

Keep an eye out for the occasional antique shop in the Alfama district, too, eg Casa Domingues, on Rua de Santa Marinha 3, and the posher Antiguidades Outro Era at Largo Santo António de Sé 15. In Bairro Alto, the tiny O Velho Sapateiro (Map 8) at Travessa da Queimada 46 has some intriguing items, including old postcards of Portugal and Spain.

Beyond Lisbon, Sintra's São Pedro district has several antique shops and its twice-monthly fair hosts a few stalls of the flea market variety.

AZULEJOS & CERAMICS

Lisbon has many azulejos factories and showrooms. One of the finest (and priciest) is Fábrica Sant'Ana (Map 10), the pink building at Rua do Alecrim 95. The street-level showroom is open weekdays from 9 am to 7 pm and on Saturday from 10 am to 2 pm. The factory is upstairs, along with what look like the offices of azulejo-makers' guilds.

Another good showroom for azulejos (including made-to-order items) and other ceramic ware is Cerâmica Viúva Lamego (Map 7; ☎ 885 24 02) at Largo do Intendente Pina Manique 25 (metro: Intendente). Pottery fanatics will also like the venerable, family-run Olaria do Desterros (Map 6; ☎ 885 03 29), which is a few blocks away in a neighbourhood of warehouses and hospitals. The factory (there's no obvious showroom) is at entry F in an alley, seemingly within the grounds of the Hospital do Desterro, at Rua Nova do Desterro 14.

More of a gallery than a shop, Ratton (Map 6; ☎ 346 09 48), at Rua da Academia Ciências 2, displays and sells some of the

JULIA WILKINSON

Examples of pottery in São Pedro, Sintra

best hand-made contemporary azulejo creations in Portugal, by such leading names as Jorge Martins and Paulo Rêgo.

The attractive Museu dos Azulejos (see the Things to See & Do chapter) has a small shop, which also includes more affordable azulejo souvenirs.

Among ceramic manufacturers, the most famous name is Vista Alegre (Map 11), whose finely crafted products can be found at a number of stores around the city including Rua Ivens 53 and Largo do Chiado 20.

BOOKS

Few of Lisbon's bookshops (livrarias) offer much of interest in English, aside from guidebooks. The city's biggest bookseller is Livraria Bertrand, with at least half a dozen shops, the original and biggest of which (Map 10; ☎ 342 19 41) is at Rua Garrett 73 in Chiado. You can find books in English and French here, and a good range of kids' books in both English and Portuguese. There are other branches of Bertrand in the Amoreiras shopping centre (Map 2) and the Centro Cultural de Belém (Map 13).

For second-hand books, there are two or three dusty shops along Calçada do Carmo as it climbs up behind Rossio train station and a couple of stalls in the arcade near the Praça do Comércio end of Rua Augusta. Other major bookshops are listed below.

Alcalá (Map 10), Rua Serpa Pinto 1A or Rua da Madalena 58; specialising in books in Spanish

Editorial Notícias (Map 9) at Rossio 23; limited range of French and English-language books

Librairie Française (Map 3), Avenida Marquês de Tomar 38; Lisbon's only exclusively French bookshop

Livraria Britânica (Map 6), Rua de São Marçal 83 (opposite the British Council); exclusively English-language books (including for kids)

Livraria Buchholz (Map 6), Rua Duque de Palmela 4 (metro: Rotunda); a huge literature collection in Portuguese, English, French and German

Livraria Diário de Notícias (Map 9), Rossio 11; modest range of English-language books, guides and maps

Livraria Municipal (Map 3), Avenida da República 21-A (metro: Saldanha); elegant shop devoted entirely to Lisbon, with books on city history, art and architecture (including a few titles in English), and easy chairs

Livraria Portugal (Map 9), Rua do Carmo 70; limited range of French and English-language books, especially art and history

Valentim de Carvalho (Map 9), Rossio 55 (and the Centro Cultural de Belém); best known for its CDs and cassettes, but a fair range of books on the 1st floor, too

CLOTHES

Some of the best buys in this department are stylish Portugal T-shirts (especially at places like Sintra which has its own range of designs) and children's clothes: thanks to the attention lavished on Portuguese kids, children's clothes shops seem to be everywhere. The following are some of the best:

Cenoura (Map 9), Rua Augusta 221; famous chain of children's shops, with zany designs for teenagers

Exclusivo bebé (Map 9), Rossio 86; a small but well-stocked shop with clothes not only for babies but up to 6 year olds, too

Maison Louvre (Map 9), Rossio 106; toddlers to 10-year-olds

My Store (Map 10), Rua do Alecrim 99 ; exclusively OshKosh clothes

O Palhaço (Map 11), Rua Augusta 97; up-market range of items for babies and toddlers

Rabimos (Map 9), Rossio 94; trendy gear for toddlers to teenagers

Tas Giro (Map 7), Largo da Graça 102; small shop with some bargain items

Zara, Rua Garrett 1-9 (and several other branches in and around Lisbon, including CascaiShopping); great range of bright, casual cotton clothes

Except during the summer sales, or at the outdoor 'gypsy' markets, you won't necessarily find great clothing bargains but the range is impressive. Worth a look, even if you're not digging deep enough into your pocket to actually buy anything, are some of

---

Markets

For something decidedly down-market, but more entertainment than bargain basement, browse the sprawling Feira da Ladra (Map 12) which materialises every Tuesday morning and all day Saturday at Campo de Santa Clara, beside the Igreja de São Vincent de Fora in the Alfama district. In addition to cheap clothes and old books, you'll find a motley array of junk, from nuts and bolts to old buttons and brassware, second-hand spectacles and old 78-rpm records. Popularly translated as 'Thieves' Market' (*ladra* means thief, the name is actually believed to come from *lada*, meaning margin, a reference to when the market moved, centuries ago, to the margin of the Rio Tejo.

Another regular Lisbon market is the Feira do Relógio (Map 1), held on Sundays on Rua Pardal Monteiro in the Bairro de Relógio district (take bus No 59 from Praça da Figueira or bus No 103 from Areeiro metro station).

For cheap shoes, clothes, toys and CDs, there's a rough-and-ready complex of market stalls open daily except Sunday on the north-west corner of Praça da Espanha (Map 2; metro: Palhava).

Markets outside Lisbon include Sintra's huge Feira de São Pedro market, held on the second and fourth Sunday of the month; the Feira de Cascais every Wednesday morning; the Feira de Carcavelos, en route to Cascais on Thursday mornings (great for cheap clothes); and the Feira de Oeiras on the last Sunday of the month (for bric-a-brac and antiques). ■

the imaginative haute couture designs by leading Portuguese designers. Check out the following for an idea of the latest fashions:

Ana Salazer (Map 11), Rua Nova do Almeda 89, Chiado; very feminine and distinctive designs, sold here and in Paris

Augustus (Map 11), Rua Augusta 55, Baixa; famous stylist of women's clothes

José António Tenente (Map 8), Travessa do Carmo 8, Chiado; avant garde sportswear designs for both men and women

Lena Aires (Map 8), Rua da Atalaia 96, Bairro Alto; leading name for women's fashions

Loja Branca (Map 6), Praça das Flores 48, Rato; avant-garde women's clothes, often in natural materials, by Manuela Gonçalves

SHOES

These are a bargain all over Portugal, and Lisbon abounds in *sapaterias* (shoe shops). Trawl Avenida de Roma in the north of the city (metro: Roma) to find renowned shops such as Hera at No 37-A, Mocci at No 61-A or Stivali at nearby Avenida João XXI 2. The Amoreiras shopping centre has branches of these shops as well as many others but you'll also find dozens of shoe shops in the Baixa district, especially along Rua Augusta.

Shoe Sizes

Confused about how big your feet are? Here's a table of comparative sizes for British, American and Portuguese feet.

Men

UK	USA	Europe
6	6½	39
7	7½	40
7½	8	41
8	8½	42
9	9½	43
10	10½	44

Women

UK	USA	Europe
3	4½	35½
4	5½	36½
5	6½	37½
6	7½	38½
6¼	8	39
7	8½	39½

HANDICRAFTS & TEXTILES

A fascinating (if rather overpublicised) *artesanato* is Santos Ofícios (Map 11), Rua da Madalena 87, at the edge of the Baixa district, with an eclectic range of folk art from all around Portugal. It's open daily, except Sunday, from 10 am to 8 pm. Another good source of select, high quality handicrafts from all over Portugal including straw dolls, hand-woven cotton and linen clothes, and ceramic and wooden objects is Pais em Lisboa (Map 8), Rua do Teixeira 25. Casa Regional (Map 10), at Rua Paiva Andrade 4, specialises in handicrafts from the Azores.

For hand-embroidered linen from its most famous source, Madeira, head for Madeira House (Map 11), at Rua Augusta 131, or Príncipe Real (Map 6) at Rua da Escola Politécnica 12. Teresa Alecrim (Map 11), at Rua Nova do Almeda 76, also has some excellent examples, not all from Madeira.

If you're around in July or August, you'll find a sizeable handicrafts fair at Estoril and Sintra (see the Excursions chapter) where you can pick up unique items handcrafted locally.

The following shops specialise in particular items:

Arte Rústica (Map 9), at Rua Áuea 246, Baixa; hand-painted ceramics, hand-embroidered items from Madeira and quality T-shirts

Casa Achilles (Map 6), Rua de São Marçal 194, Rato; bronzeware

Casa das Corticas (Map 6), Rua da Escola Politécnica 4, Bairro Alto; cork items, especially from cork's homeland, the Alentejo region

Caza das Vellas Loreto (Map 10), Rua do Loreto 53, Bairro Alto; venerable candle shop which has been around for two centuries

Casa Quintão, Rua Ivens 30, Chiado; traditional (and expensive) Arraiolos carpets and tapestries

MUSIC

Lisbon's longest established outlet for CDs and cassettes covering the whole spectrum of music from pop-rock, alternative and Brazilian strains to fado, jazz and classical music is Valentim de Carvalho at Rossio 57 (Map 9) and the Centro Cultural de Belém (Map 13). There's also a huge Virgin Megastore (Map 8) in the fabulous Art Deco Teatro Eden building

Speciality Shops

Searching for a satin glove? A made-to-measure shirt? Or a trilby hat with a red silk band? You won't have to go far to find them. Camisaria Pitta, at Rua Augusta 195, in the Baixa district, is one of the oldest shirt makers in Lisbon, with quality men's and women's clothes as well as superb made-to-measure shirts. At nearby Rossio 69 you'll find Azevedo Rua, the hat fanatic's haven, stocked with mostly men's hats for every occasion. And for elegant gloves in leather or lace, satin or silk, head for Luvaria Ulisses, at Rua do Carmo 87, the smallest and most exquisite little Art Deco shop in Lisbon. ■

in Praça dos Restauradores (next to the turismo). CDs range in price from around 1200$00 to 3600$00.

The following outlets are also worth checking out:

Loja da Música (Map 9), Rua Portas de Santo Antão 92
Discoteca Amália (Map 9), Rua Áurea 272; specialises in fado and cheap classic CDs
Contraverso (Map 8), Travessa da Queimada 33; rock, jazz and alternative music
Illegal, Rua 1 de Dezembro; hip, groovy stuff
The House of Rhythm, currently in a kiosk-shop by the turismo in Praça dos Restauradores

WINE & PORT

Portuguese wine of any variety – red, white or rosé; *maduro* (mature) or semi-sparkling young *vinho verde* – offers very good value.

And you needn't hunt for specialist shops: good stuff is available in supermarkets, and 800$00 to 900$00 will buy something to please the snobbiest taste buds. If it's port wine you're interested in, have a taste at the Solar do Vinho do Porto, Rua de São Pedro de Alcântara 45 in the Bairro Alto, and then head for the supermarket or one of the following shops which have an enormous array of both wine and port. It helps if you know roughly what you want, but staff can usually offer recommendations. Failing that, there's a shop run by the Instituto do Vinho do Porto in the international departures concourse at the airport.

Refer to Drinks in the Places to Eat chapter to learn more about Portuguese wines.

Napoleão, Rua dos Franqueiros 70; wide selection of port, wine and champagne, and excellent service from staff who really know their stuff
Manuel Tavares (Map 9), Rua da Betesga 1-A; lovely Art Deco shop crammed with wine, port and delicatessen items
Casa Macário, Rua Augusta 272; attractive little shop specialising in vintage ports (plus coffee and sweets)

Shop Names

Many small shops seem to have no name, only a sign indicating their generic speciality, so a few terms are worth learning – eg *artesanato* (handicrafts shop), *livraria* (bookshop), *papelaria* (stationery shop), *sapataria* (shoe shop) and *joalheria* (jewellery shop). ■

Excursions

Portugal is one of Europe's smallest countries (only 560km north to south and 220km east to west) with an efficient public transport system, so it doesn't take long to get to places from Lisbon, the hub of the transport network. An express coach to Porto in the north takes around 3½ hours, to the southern Algarve coast it's just under five hours, and three hours eastwards to the delightful town of Évora. But you don't even have to go this far to discover some great destinations: the following places can all be reached in under an hour, though Sintra and Setúbal warrant at least an overnight stay.

SINTRA
• pop 20,000 • postcode 2710 • area code ☎ 01
If you make only one side trip from Lisbon, Sintra should receive top priority. Cool and verdant, and just 28km north-west of Lisbon, Sintra is one of the most enchanting day trips

from the city and a worthwhile destination in its own right for several days exploration or relaxation.

Situated on the northern slopes of the craggy Serra de Sintra, its lush vegetation and spectacular mountaintop views towards the coast have lured admirers since the times of the early Iberians: they found the ridge so mystical they called it the Mountain of the Moon and made it a centre of cult worship. The Romans and Moors were equally captivated (the remains of a Moorish castle overlook the town). And for 500 years the kings of Portugal chose Sintra as their summer resort, and the nobility built extravagant villas and surrealist palaces on its wooded hillsides. Poets – especially the romantic English – were enraptured by its natural beauty. Even Lord Byron (who had few nice things to say about Portugal) managed to be charmed: 'Lo! Cintra's glorious Eden intervenes, in variegated maze of mount and glen,' he wrote in his famous travel epic, *Childe Harold*.

Arrive on a summer weekend and you may wonder where the romance has gone: the historical centre, Sintra-Vila, is crammed with restaurants, souvenir and handicraft shops catering to the 300,000 tourists a year who now descend on the town. But linger long enough and you'll still find a bewitching atmosphere and some fantastic walks and day trips: the Parque Natural de Sintra-Cascais encompasses both the Serra de Sintra and nearby coastal attractions (including Cabo da Roca, Europe's most westerly point).

Designated a UNESCO World Heritage Site in 1995, Sintra now faces ambitious eco-friendly plans by local authorities who are trying to combine its burgeoning tourism with its romantic heritage: cars are eventually to be prohibited from the historical centre, electric buses will be introduced, a funicular is to be built from Ribeira de Sintra to the centre and even a cable car installed

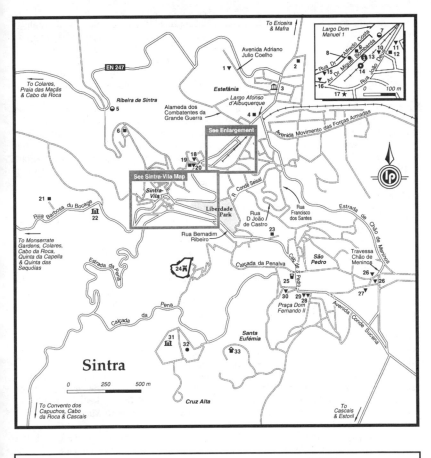

Sintra

PLACES TO STAY
- 2 Villa das Rosas
- 4 Pensão Nova Sintra
- 6 Casa Miradouro
- 9 Monte da Lua
- 12 Piela's
- 19 Casa de Hóspedes Adelaide
- 21 Hotel Palácio de Seteais
- 23 Residencial Sintra
- 33 Pousada de Juventude de Sintra

PLACES TO EAT
- 1 Orixás
- 10 Restaurante Parreirinha
- 11 O Tunel
- 15 Topico Bar & Restaurant & Snack Bar
- 16 Restaurante Apeadeiro
- 18 Restaurant Regional da Sintra
- 20 A Tasca do Manel
- 26 Adega do Saloio
- 27 Toca do Javali
- 28 Solar de São Pedro
- 29 Restaurante Pic Nic
- 30 Taverna dos Trovadores

OTHER
- 3 Museu de Arte Moderna
- 5 Tram to Praia das Maças
- 7 Bus Station
- 8 Lavandaria Teclava
- 13 Turismo
- 14 Train Station
- 17 Police Station
- 22 Quinta da Regaleira
- 24 Castelo dos Mouros
- 25 Mourisca Bar
- 31 Palácio Nacional da Pena
- 32 Pena Park

across the hills from São Pedro to the Pena Palace.

Orientation

Arriving at Sintra by train or bus you'll find yourself in Sintra's new town, Estefânia, where most of the cheap accommodation is located. It's 1.5km (about 15 minutes walk) away from the heart of Sintra's cultural attractions at Sintra-Vila (also called Vila Velha, Old Town). A couple of kilometres south-east of Sintra-Vila is the São Pedro district: you'll only need to go here if you're heading for the *pousada de juventude* nearby, want to visit the big fortnightly market (held on the second and fourth Sunday of the month), or if you'd like to check out some of São Pedro's excellent restaurants or antique shops.

Information

There are two turismos, one at the train station (☎ 924 16 23), and the main one (☎ 923 11 57 or 924 17 00; fax 923 51 76) at 23 Praça da República in Sintra-Vila, near the Palácio Nacional de Sintra (Sintra National Palace). This well-run office is open daily from 9 am to 7 pm (until 8 pm from June to September). It provides a free map (packed with information), as well as help with accommodation. Walkers might also be interested in the *Walking in Sintra* booklet (its poor maps are due for an update) and botanists in the detailed *Sintra: A Borough in the Wild*, both usually available at the turismo. The free TIPS booklet for the Costa do Estoril and Sintra region is worth picking up here, too: it lists transport, restaurants, hotels, banks, etc.

There are several laundrettes; the most convenient is Lavandaria Teclava (☎ 923 03 37), opposite the train station at 27D Avenida Miguel Bombarda. It's open weekdays from 8 am to 7.30 pm, and to noon on Saturdays.

There's a post office (open weekdays from 9 am to 12.30 pm and 2.30 to 6 pm) and bank (with ATM) in Sintra-Vila, near the turismo, and several more banks in Estefânia. The *centro de saúde*, or medical centre, (☎ 923 34 00) is at Rua Visconde de Monserrate 2,

but for medical emergencies it's advisable to head for Cascais Hospital (☎ 484 40 71). The police station (☎ 923 07 61) is at Rua João de Deus 6.

If you're arriving by car, note that driving and parking in Sintra-Vila can be murder on weekends and public holidays: it's often easier to park near the station and walk. Be sure to lock up well and keep valuables with you when you park at the Castelo dos Mouros and Monserrate Gardens. Note that private cars are no longer allowed up to Pena National Palace (see the Getting Around section for details of the bus service).

Palácio Nacional de Sintra

The Sintra National Palace (also known as the Paço Real or Palácio da Vila) dominates the town with its two huge, conical white chimneys. Of Moorish origins, the palace was greatly enlarged by João I in the early 15th century, adorned with Manueline additions by Manuel I the following century, and repeatedly restored and redecorated right up to the present day.

Historically, it's connected with a treasury of notable occasions: João I planned his 1415 Ceuta campaign here; the three-year-old Sebastião was crowned king in the palace in 1557; and the paralytic Afonso VI, who was effectively imprisoned here by his brother Pedro II for six years, died of apoplexy in 1683 while listening to Mass in the chapel gallery.

As for the palace's aesthetic appeal, the mixed styles create a muddled architectural result, but there are some fascinating decorations inside. The highlights are the palace's unrivalled display of 15th and 16th century azulejos, especially in the **Sala dos Árabes** (Arab Room), which are some of the oldest in Portugal; the **Sala das Armas** (Armoury Room, also called the Sala dos Brasões or Coat of Arms Room), with the heraldic shields of 74 leading 16th century families on its wooden coffered ceiling; and the delightful **El Sala dos Cisnes** (Swan Room), which has a polychrome ceiling adorned with 27 gold-collared swans.

Most memorable of all is the ground-floor

Top Left: Shop decoration near Castelo
Top Right: In case you're not sure what 'Urinol' means, check the sign!
Middle Right: Azulejo in Largo do Chafariz de Dentro
Bottom Left: Narrow laneway in the Castelo neighbourhood
Bottom Right: Azulejo on the wall of a building in Alfama

Top Left: Palácio Nacional de Sintra
Top Right: Looking down on Sintra-Vila from the castle
Bottom: Largo 5 de Outubro, Cascais

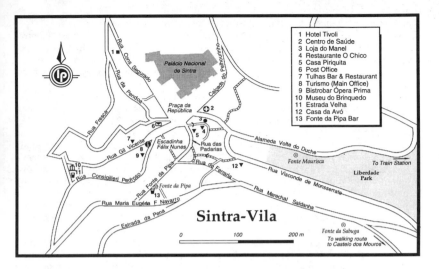

1 Hotel Tivoli
2 Centro de Saúde
3 Loja do Manel
4 Restaurante O Chico
5 Casa Piriquita
6 Post Office
7 Tulhas Bar & Restaurant
8 Turismo (Main Office)
9 Bistrobar Opera Prima
10 Museu do Brinquedo
11 Estrada Velha
12 Casa da Avó
13 Fonte da Pipa Bar

Sintra-Vila

Sala das Pêgas (Magpie Room), with a ceiling thick with painted magpies *(pêgas)*, each holding in its beak a scroll with the words *por bem* (in honour). The story goes that João I commissioned the cheeky decoration to represent all the court gossip about his advances toward one of the ladies-in-waiting. Caught red-handed by his queen, 'por bem' was the king's allegedly innocent response.

The palace is open Thursday to Tuesday, 10 am to 1 pm and 2 to 5 pm; entry is 400$00 (ticket sales stop 30 minutes before closing time). Try and avoid weekends and public holidays (especially during summer), when the place gets terribly crowded with tour groups.

Castelo dos Mouros

A steep 3km climb from Sintra-Vila leads to the ruins of this castle, which has battlements that snake over the craggy mountainside. First built by the Moors, the castelo was captured by Christian forces under Afonso Henriques in 1147. Much restored in the 19th century, it offers some wonderful panoramas: as long as Sintra's famous sea mists aren't rolling around, you should be able to

see as far as Cabo da Roca. Late afternoon is best for taking some spectacular photographs of the nearby Pena Palace. The castelo is open daily from 10 am to 7 pm (5 pm from October to May); admission is free.

Palácio Nacional da Pena

Another 20 minute walk up from the castelo is the most bizarre building in Sintra, the Pena National Palace. This extraordinary architectural confection, rivalling the best Disneyland castle, was cooked up in the fertile imagination of Ferdinand of Saxe Coburg-Gotha (artist-husband of Queen Maria II) and Prussian architect Ludwig von Eschwege. Commissioned in 1840 to build a 'romantic' or 'Gothick' baronial castle from the ruins of a 16th century Jeronimite monastery that still stood on the site, Eschwege delivered a Bavarian-Manueline fantasy of embellishments, turrets and battlements (and a statue of himself in armour, overlooking the palace from a nearby peak).

The interior is just as mind-boggling: the rooms have been left just as they were when the royal family fled on the eve of revolution in 1910. There's Eiffel-designed furniture, Ferdinand-designed china, and a whole room of naughty nude paintings. More serious artwork includes a 16th century carved alabaster altarpiece by Nicolas Chanterène in the original monastery's chapel.

The palace is open Tuesday to Sunday from 10 am to 1 pm and 2 to 6.30 pm (5 pm from 15 September to 30 June). Ticket sales stop 30 minutes before closing time. Entry is 400$00 (200$00 for senior visitors and those under 25; 160$00 if you have a student card). It's free on Sunday mornings.

Below the palace (en route from the castelo if you're walking) is the enchanting **Pena Park**, open daily from 10 am to 7 pm (5 pm from October to May); admission is free. It's packed with lakes and exotic plants, huge redwoods and fern trees, camellias and rhododendrons. Among the follies and cottages is a chalet built for Ferdinand's mistress, a German opera singer he titled Condessa d'Edla.

Convento dos Capuchos

For the biggest contrast in styles imaginable, head 5km along the main road that snakes south-west along the ridge below Pena National Palace and then turn right into the woods to reach this atmospheric Capuchin monastery.

A tiny troglodyte hermitage, buttressed by huge boulders and darkened by surrounding trees, the *convento* was built in 1560 to house 12 monks. Their dwarf-size cells (some little more than hollows in the rock) are lined with cork; hence the convento's popular name, Cork Convent. Visiting the place is an Alice-in-Wonderland experience as you squeeze through low, narrow doorways to explore the warren of cells, chapels, kitchen, and cavern where one recluse, Honorius, spent an astonishing but obviously healthy 36 years (he was 95 when he died in 1596). Hermits hid away here right up until 1834 when the monastery was finally abandoned. It's now open daily for visits from 10 am to 7 pm (5 pm from October to May); ticket sales stop 30 minutes before closing time; entry is 200$00.

Monserrate Gardens

Down from the ridge and 4km west of Sintra-Vila (about 50 minutes on foot) is another must-see spot: the Monserrate Gardens. Rambling and romantic, they cover 30 hectares of wooded hillside and feature everything from roses to conifers, tropical tree ferns to eucalypts, Himalayan rhododendrons to at least 24 species of palms.

The gardens were first laid out in the 1850s by the painter William Stockdale (with help from London's Kew Gardens), who imported many of the plants from Australasia and Mexico. Neglected for many years (the site was sold to the Portuguese government in 1949 and practically forgotten), its tangled pathways and aura of wild abandon are immensely appealing.

Recent EU funding can scarcely keep up with the garden's demands, although there's recently been a six month restoration stint. The local Amigos de Monserrate (Friends of Monserrate) group keeps the pressure on for continued maintenance, as well as for restoration of the garden's **quinta**. This bizarre Moorish-looking building – described by Rose Macauley in *They Went to Portugal* as a place of 'barbarous orientalism' – was constructed in the late 1850s by James Knowles for the wealthy merchant Englishman Sir Francis Cook. The quinta's previous incarnation was as a Gothic-style villa rented by the rich and infamous British writer William Beckford in 1794 after he fled Britain in the wake of a homosexual scandal. Beckford, who loved the 'beautiful Claude-like place', added his own touch of landscaping and even imported a flock of sheep from his estate in England. Today, there are various plans for restoring and opening it to the public: one of the most tasteful ideas is to turn it into a teahouse.

The gardens are open daily from 10 am to 6 pm (5 pm from October to May); entry is 200$00.

Museu do Brinquedo

Sintra has several art museums of rather specialist interest, but this toy museum is a delightful collection of lead soldiers, clock-

---

Parque Natural de Sintra-Cascais
The Sintra-Cascais Natural Park (14,583 hectares) is one of the most delightful areas in Portugal. Easily accessible from Lisbon, its terrain ranges from the verdant lushness of Sintra itself to the crashing coastline of Guincho (a champion site for modern surfers). Other coastal attractions include the lively coastal resort of Cascais and the wild and rugged Cabo da Roca, Europe's most westerly point. Sintra's mountains have exceptional climatic conditions enjoyed by dozens of plant and tree species; a large number of exotic species were also introduced to Pena Park and Monserrate Gardens during the 18th and 19th centuries. There are no official park trails, but there are plenty of walking routes in the parks and to the main points of interest. ■

---

work trains, Dinky toys and porcelain dolls. It's currently at Largo Latino Coelho and open Tuesday to Sunday, from 10 am to 12.30 pm and 2 to 6 pm; entry is 250$00 (100$00 students). It's due to move to a new Museu Infantil Technológico Lúdico (Children's Technology Museum) in the renovated former fire station on the corner of Volta do Duche and Rua Visconde de Monserrate.

Sintra Museu de Arte Moderna – Colecção Berardo

Sintra is putting itself on the international art map with this new museum, which opened in spring 1997 in the town's neoclassical former casino in Estefânia. This collection of some of the world's best postwar art has been built up by business tycoon, José Berardo and associate, Francisco Capelo. Among the 350 or so pieces there's a particularly strong selection of pop art by leading names such as Tom Wesselman, John Chamberlain and Lucas Samaras as well as works by Warhol, Lichtenstein, Pollock and Kossoff. Check out the top floor café, too, with its open-air terrace and views. The ground floor gift shop has some classy items.

The museum is open Wednesday to Sunday (including public holidays) from 10 am to 6 pm and Tuesdays from 2 to 6 pm; entry is 600$00 (students 300$00 and free for children up to 10). On Thursdays, admission is free for those under 18 and over 65.

Other Attractions

Between the gardens and Sintra-Vila you'll pass the brazenly luxurious **Hotel Palácio de Seteais**. Originally built in 1787 for the Dutch consul in Lisbon, its name (Palace of Seven Sighs) is said to refer to the Portuguese reaction to the 1808 Convention of Sintra (despatched from here), which gave the French reprehensibly lenient terms after their invasion. The interior has some fantastic murals (even piano lids are painted) but unless you can fork out for a room or a meal you probably won't get a foot past the snobby reception.

There's a string of lavish private villas on the way back to Sintra, notably the fairytale **Quinta da Regaleira**, known locally as Quinta dos Milhões because it cost so many millions to build. Built at the turn of the century for Carvalho da Silva, a Brazilian mining millionaire, this quinta was designed in pseudo-Manueline style by a stage designer. It now belongs to the Sintra town council. The **Museu Arqueológico de São Miguel de Odrinhas** – one of Portugal's most important archaeological collections – was due to re-open in late 1997 after improvement works. It's 15km north of Sintra (off the EN247 to Ericeira).

Activities

The Sintra region is increasingly popular for mountain-biking and hiking trips run by tour operators.

Sintraventura, an operation run by the Sintra town council's sporting division (☎ 920 40 37; fax 920 96 46; contact Carlos Pereira) offers occasional day-long mountain biking or walking trips for a mere

300$00 per person, but you need to contact the office in advance for exact dates and booking details. For details of other walks, see the following Getting Around section.

Wild Side Expedições e Excursões (mobile ☎ 0931 869010; fax 443 37 44) organises day-long hiking trips from April to June and September to October (around 4000$00 per person), mountain biking in the Peninha region of Sintra, Cabo da Roca or Guincho (6000$00) and kayaking along the Estoril Coast (6000$00). Half-day outings cost 40% less. If you want to bike it alone, head to Cascais to rent a bike.

Horse riding is best done in the grounds of Centro Hípico Penha Longa Country Club (☎ 924 90 33) for around 3500$00 an hour. The club is about 5km south of Sintra-Vila.

Special Events

Sintra's big annual event is a classical music festival, the Festival de Música, held from around mid-June to mid-July. It features international performers playing in the palaces and other suitably posh venues. It's followed by the equally international Noites de Bailado, a classical and contemporary dance festival that lasts until the end of August. Contact the turismo for details.

The far humbler Feira do Artesanato (Handicrafts Fair) takes place for two weeks in early August, on the shady Alameda dos Combatentes da Grande Guerra (near the train station). It features locally made ceramics, jewellery, Arraiolos carpets, clothes and charming model villages. Traditional song and dance performances also take place some evenings.

Places to Stay

Camping Praia Grande (see West of Sintra) is on the coast 12km from Sintra.

The youth hostel, *Pousada de Juventude de Sintra* (☎ 924 12 10), is at Santa Eufémia, 4km from Sintra-Vila and 2km south-west of São Pedro, which is the closest you'll get by bus. Along with dormitory beds, it has double rooms, which are good value at 3400$00. Advance bookings are essential.

Some of the cheapest accommodation in Sintra itself is in the 80 or so private quartos (rooms) that go for about 5000$00/3500 a double (with/without bath). Ask at the turismo for details. Also good value (especially for families) are the private one or two-bedroom apartments around town: they're about 8000$00 a day including kitchen facilities.

Most budget guesthouses are near the train station. *Casa de Hóspedes Adelaide* (☎ 923 08 73), Rua Guilherme Gomes Fernandes 11, a 10 minute walk from the station, is the kind of place where rooms are rented by the hour, but don't let that put you off: clean, simple doubles (without bath) go for 3500$00 per night. Closer to the station, at Largo Afonso d'Albuquerque 25, above the main road, *Pensão Nova Sintra* (☎ 923 02 20) was undergoing major renovations at the time of research: when finished, all rooms will have attached baths and there will also be a restaurant.

The popular *Piela's* (☎ 924 16 91), immediately across the railway at Rua João de Deus 70, was also planning an overhaul and major extensions. At the time of writing, its immaculate doubles were 6000$00/5000 with/without bath. The rooms are above Piela's café and snooker room. The charming *Monte da Lua* (☎ & fax 924 10 29), right opposite the station at Avenida Miguel Bombarda 51, has tastefully decorated doubles with TV and bath for 8000$00 or 7000$00 for the one room without bath. Try to get one of the quieter rooms at the back which overlook the wooded valley.

In an enviably picturesque position on the high road between Sintra-Vila and São Pedro, *Residencial Sintra* (☎ 923 07 38) is a big old mansion at Travessa dos Avelares 12, with 10 high-ceilinged and spacious rooms that go for 12,000$00. Perfect for families, there's an outdoor patio, rambling garden, swimming pool and children's swings and slides. Advance bookings are essential.

Among several Turihab properties in the area, the 19th century *Villa das Rosas* (☎ & fax 923 42 16), at Rua António Cunha 2-4, in Estefânia, boasts some splendid décor, with azulejos in the hall and dining room.

There's also a tennis court in the grounds. Doubles with breakfast cost 15,000$00. The candy-striped 19th century *Casa Miradouro* (☎ 923 59 00; fax 924 18 36), perched above Sintra-Vila at Rua Sotto Mayor 55, has grand views and six doubles at 17,500$00, including breakfast.

Top-end accommodation includes the ugly, modern *Hotel Tivoli* (☎ 923 35 05; fax 923 15 72), right in the centre of Sintra-Vila at Praça da República, where deluxe doubles will set you back 18,000$00. But it's worth splashing out 4000$00 more for the atmosphere and antiques in *Quinta das Sequóias* (☎ 924 38 21; fax 923 03 42), a superb manor house just beyond the Hotel Palácio de Seteais. Nearby, in the wooded valley below Monserrate Gardens, is a 16th century former farmhouse, *Quinta da Capella* (☎ 929 01 70; fax 929 34 25), where gorgeous rooms cost 24,000$00 a double.

Over-the-top luxury can be found at *Hotel Palácio de Seteais* (☎ 923 32 00; fax 923 42 77), Rua Barbosa du Bocage 8; the privilege of staying in this 18th century palace will cost you a mind-boggling 40,000$00 per night. Similarly priced are the rooms at the *Caesar Park Penha Longa Golf Resort* (☎ 924 90 11; fax 924 90 07), Estrada da Lagoa Azul, about 5km south of Sintra, which includes an 18-hole championship golf course, swimming pools, horse-riding, tennis, squash and health club facilities among its attractions.

Finally, if you're in a Byronic mood, ask about the place where he apparently stayed, the *Lawrence Hotel*. Built in 1786 (one of the first hotels in Portugal) and closed for the last 50 years, it's now being restored into a 17-room hotel and should be open by the time you read this.

Places to Eat

Estefânia Head for Rua João de Deus, on the other side of the railway line: in addition to *Piela's* café (see Places to Stay) there are three restaurants, including the *Restaurante Parreirinha* (☎ 923 12 07), a smoky locals' den at No 45, which has great grilled fish and chicken (try the succulent grilled garoupa);

and the smarter *O Tunel* (☎ 923 13 86), at No 86, where dishes such as arroz de pato no forno (roast duck and rice) are good value at about 950$00. It's closed on Saturday.

The unpretentious *A Tasca do Manel* (☎ 923 02 15), next to the ornate câmara municipal (town hall), at Largo Dr Vergílio Horta 5, has pratos do dia for an appetising 800$00 a dish. Across the square, at Travessa do Municipio 2, the classier *Regional de Sintra* (☎ 923 44 44) offers a choice of Portuguese provincial dishes for around 1500$00. Nearby, at Rua Dr Alfredo Costa 8, the *Topico Bar & Restaurant* (☎ 923 48 25) is more casual, with live music (Portuguese or Afro-Brazilian) on Fridays and Saturdays from 11 pm. Around the corner, at Avenida Miguel Bombarda 3-A, *Snack Bar-Restaurante Apeadeiro* (☎ 923 18 04) is popular with local students for its cheap 700$00 combinados snacks and generous 1500$00 main meals (and some half portions for 950$00).

For an up-market splurge in artistic surroundings, *Orixás* (☎ 924 16 72), at Avenida Adriano Julio Coelho 7, is an interesting Brazilian restaurant-cum-art gallery stuffed with wooden sculptures of nubile women. Dishes are exotic and expensive (at least 2200$00 each).

Sintra-Vila Many of the cafés and restaurants here are geared for the passing tourist trade, ie they are overpriced and soulless. But *Tulhas Bar & Restaurante* (☎ 923 23 78), a converted grain warehouse at Rua Gil Vicente 4, has maintained its character and quality. Specialities include an excellent bacalhau com natas (bacalhau in a cream sauce) for 1100$00, but expect to pay about 1500$00 for most other dishes. It's closed on Wednesdays. Cheaper and simpler is *Casa da Avó* (☎ 923 12 80), at Rua Visconde de Monserrate 46, which serves pratos do dia lunchtime dishes for under 1000$00 and main meals for around 1500$00. It's closed Mondays.

A classy new addition is the *Bistrobar Ópera Prima* (☎ 924 45 18), around the corner from the turismo at Rua Consiglieri

Pedroso 2-A. This cavernous bar and restaurant has been imaginatively designed by a local Belgian couple. The menu ranges from snacks, crêpes and home-made ice cream to Portuguese dishes for around 1500$00. It's open daily from 9 am to 2 am, and has live music some nights (see the following Entertainment section).

For Sintra's famous travesseiros (apple and almond pastries) and queijadas (sweet cheese cakes), head for the popular *Casa Piriquita* pastelaria at Rua das Padarias 1. Picnic supplies can be found at *Loja do Manel* grocery store in Rua do Arco do Teixeira (the lane near Casa Piriquita).

São Pedro In this area of town is a cluster of restaurants for meat-lovers, notably *Toca do Javali* (☎ 923 35 03; closed Wednesdays) at Rua 1 de Dezembro 12, where you can get your teeth into a chunk of javali (wild boar) for about 2100$00. Go early to get one of the few outdoor tables in the garden. Down the road, at Travessa Chão de Meninos, two outlets of *Adega do Saloio* (☎ 923 14 22; closed Tuesdays) have skinned goats on display, ready for grilling, as well as other standard grilled offerings. Dishes cost from 1500$00 to 2000$00, but some cheaper half-portions are also available.

Overlooking the huge cobbled Praça Dom Fernando II at the heart of São Pedro is the popular French restaurant *Solar de São Pedro* (☎ 923 18 60; closed Wednesdays), where you can find everything from frogs' legs Provençal (2500$00) to roast duck with orange (1900$00). The adjacent *Restaurante Pic Nic* (☎ 923 08 60), at Praça Dom Fernando II 10, offers cheaper, humbler fare with the added bonus of outdoor tables.

Entertainment

Fonte da Pipa (☎ 923 44 37), Rua Fonte da Pipa 11-13, is a cosy bar with snacks and inexpensive drinks; it's open nightly from around 9 pm. The central *Estrada Velha* (☎ 923 43 55), at Rua Consiglieri Pedroso 16, is another popular bar, usually open until around 2 am. Check out Bistrobar Ópera Prima (see Places to Eat) for its live jazz, soul

and blues music on Tuesday, Wednesday and Thursday from around 10.30 pm to 1 am.

Restaurante O Chico (☎ 923 15 26) in Rua Arco do Teixeira has some rather touristy fado nightly during July to September, from around 8 pm to midnight. There's no admission charge, but meals are pricey.

São Pedro also has a lively bunch of bars: just off the square, *Taverna dos Trovadores* (☎ 923 35 48) is an up-market tavern with fado on Fridays (minimum charge 1500$00) and other types of live music on Thursdays. A more casual dive popular with locals is *Mourisca Bar* (☎ 923 52 53), at Calçada de São Pedro 56, where you can play snooker, darts or chess.

Getting There & Away

Bus Buses run by Stagecoach (☎ 486 76 81) or Mafrense (☎ 923 09 71) leave from Sintra's train station regularly for popular destinations such as Cascais (direct 390$00; or via Cabo da Roca, 480$00), Estoril (390$00), Mafra (375$00), Ericeira (375$00), and the nearby beach of Praia Grande (290$00) via Colares. Services are reduced on Sundays and public holidays. Ask for the Stagecoach timetable booklet from its office opposite the train station or from turismo.

Most of the Lisbon regional bus tours (see Organised Tours in the Getting Around chapter) include Sintra in their itineraries, though usually only a visit to the Pena or Sintra National Palace.

Tram There's a recently renovated 50 minute tram service running from Ribeira de Sintra (1.5km from Sintra-Vila) to the beach of Praia das Maçãs, about 12km to the west, via Colares. Originally opened in 1904 to connect Sintra to this popular bathing resort, the line was also used to transport wine and other goods from Colares. It now runs two to three times daily (except Monday and Tuesday). Tickets cost 500$00 one way.

Train Trains run every 15 minutes between Lisbon (Rossio station) and Sintra (the last train back to Lisbon is at 1.23 am). The 45 minute run costs 185$00. There are also regular connections to/from Apeadeiro 5 de Outubro station (near Entre Campos) and Sintra, with a change of train at Queluz-Massamá or Cacém.

Getting Around

Bus Stagecoach bus No 435 runs regularly from the station to São Pedro via Sintra-Vila (180$00). To get to Pena National Palace, catch Stagecoach bus No 434 which runs at least twice an hour daily from the train station via a stop at the turismo in Sintra-Vila (500$00).

For 1200$00 you can buy a Day Rover Ticket which allows a day's unlimited bus travel on the Stagecoach network. A weekly network ticket costs 3000$00 (both available at Stagecoach offices near Cascais, Estoril and Sintra train stations).

Car The nearest car-rental outfits are in Cascais, but the turismo can arrange to have a car delivered to Sintra without extra charge.

Taxi Taxis are expensive but useful for one-way trips to the start of a walk or for quick one-day tours. Available at the train station and outside the Palácio Nacional de Sintra, they aren't metered so check first what the fare should be with the turismo (which has a comprehensive price list). For a return trip to Pena Palace, the Castle or Monserrate, figure on about 2000$00 (including one hour waiting time). From the train station to Sintra-Vila, it's around 500$00. There's a 20% supplement on weekends and holidays.

Horse & Carriage Getting around by horse and carriage is the most romantic option. Operated by Sintratur (☎ 924 12 38) they clip-clop all over the place, even as far as Praia das Maças. A popular trip is to Monserrate (11,000$00 return). The cheapest quick clop is around town (*Volta da Vila*) to Estefânia and back (7500$00). Weekend prices are higher. The turismo has a full list of prices; or check the table of prices on each carriage (*trens*). The carriages wait in the square just below the Pálacio Nacional de Sintra.

Walking Walkers will get itchy feet just sniffing Sintra. The most popular walking route is from Sintra-Vila to the ruined Castelo dos Mouros above town, a relatively easy 40 minute hike. The energetic can continue up to Palácio Nacional de Pena (another 20 minutes) and to the Serra de Sintra's highest point, the 529m Cruz Alta, with its spectacular views.

Less well trodden (and harder to follow) is the 3km path from Monserrate Gardens to the forest hideaway of Convento dos Capuchos (also accessible by walking 5km along the road from Pena Palace). Beware of getting stranded here late in the day: there's no public transport back to Sintra. And walking the roads (especially to Monserrate) can be nerve-wracking on a busy weekend when mammoth tour buses squeeze close to the roadside to get past each other.

Pick up a copy of the *Landscapes of Portugal: Sintra, Cascais, Estoril* by Brian & Eileen Anderson for more detailed descriptions of off-road walks (and car tours). See Activities for information on organised walks.

WEST OF SINTRA

The most alluring day-trip destinations out of Sintra are to the **beaches** of Praia das Maças and Praia Grande, about 12km to the west. Praia Grande, as its name suggests, is a big sandy beach with ripping breakers, backed by ugly apartments and a few cafés. There's also an open-air swimming pool here, open daily from June to September (900$00 adults and 1100$00 at weekends; 500$00/550 for children aged five to 10 years). Praia das Maças is more popular with Sintra's youth for its late-night revelries.

En route to the beaches, 8km west of Sintra, is the ancient ridge-top village of **Colares** (not to be confused with traffic-clogged Várzea de Colares on the main road below). It's a laid-back spot with spectacular views and has been famous for its wines since the 13th century: these were the only vines in Europe to survive the 19th century phylloxera plague, thanks to their deep roots and the local sandy soil. Call in advance to visit the Adega Regional de Colares (☎ 929 12 10) and taste some of the velvety reds.

Attracting all the tour buses, however, is **Cabo da Roca** (Rock Cape), about 18km west of Sintra. This sheer cliff plunging 150m to the roaring sea below is Europe's westernmost point. A wild and rugged spot, it's surprisingly uncommercialised, perhaps because it feels too uncomfortably remote: there are only a couple of stalls, a café and a tourist office where you can buy a certificate (500$00, or 800$00 for the deluxe version) to show you've been here.

Touch Rugby

This popular game has become a big hit on beaches along the Estoril coast and west of Sintra. If you see huge crowds gathered at Cascais' Praia da Ribeira, chances are they're watching a touch rugby tournament. And if you're in Praia Grande around noon on 23 August, you can join in one of the biggest tournaments in the area. It's open to anyone over nine years old and the only rule is to have fun! ■

Places to Stay & Eat

Colares has several places to stay, though none are very cheap: the most reasonable is *Residencial Conde* (☎ 929 16 52; fax 929 16 02), at Rua Quinta do Conde 32, with doubles for around 8000$00. There's one camping ground in Praia Grande, *Camping Praia Grande* (☎ 929 05 81). Also here is the classy *Conjunto Turístico das Arribas* (☎ 929 21 45), with doubles for around 12,000$00. In Praia das Maçãs, there's the *Residencial Oceano* (☎ 929 23 99) or *Residencial Real* (☎ 929 20 02) – both charging around 6500$00 a double. For cheaper alternatives, check out the private quartos signs on the road to Praia das Maçãs.

Restaurants are best at Praia das Maçãs: for seafood specialities *Buzio* (☎ 929 21 72) and *Cai Ao Mar* (☎ 928 23 74) are popular; both are on the main street above the beach.

Entertainment

At last count, there were three discos at Praia das Maçãs: *Concha* (☎ 929 20 67), on the left by the GALP station; *Casino Monumental* (☎ 929 20 24) in the centre; and *Quivuvi* (☎ 929 12 17) further along on the right, in a modern shopping mall. They can keep you bopping till 4 am on weekends.

Getting There & Away

Stagecoach bus No 441 runs from Sintra train station directly to Praia Grande beach about eight times daily. There's also a tram service between Ribeira de Sintra and Praia das Maçãs, which runs two or three times daily.

You can reach Cabo da Roca from Sintra or Cascais on bus No 403 which runs between the two towns via the cape eight times daily.

ESTORIL
• *postcode 2765* • *area code* ☎ *01*

This beach resort 26km west of Lisbon along the Costa do Estoril has long been a favoured haunt of the rich and famous. It has Europe's biggest casino, a mild climate and a genteel ambience that smothers any hint of unruly excitement (for that, as well as a cheaper and wider range of accommodation, bars and restaurants, head to Cascais, a couple of kilometres further west along the coast). But if you fancy a quiet break gambling away the escudos, or playing golf on one of half a dozen top-notch courses near Estoril, there's accommodation to suit most pockets (the deeper the better).

Orientation & Information

Arriving by train, you'll be on Avenida Marginal right across from Estoril's central attraction: the pleasantly shady Parque do Estoril, with the casino at the top. Buses also stop at the train station.

The turismo (☎ 466 38 13; fax 467 22 80) is at Arcadas do Parque, on the left side of the park

---

Golf on the Estoril Coast

As far as beach resorts go, Estoril is one of the dullest places west of Lisbon. But if you're a gambler or golfer (and preferably rich) you'll be in seventh heaven: Estoril not only has Europe's biggest casino, it's also got half a dozen spectacular golf courses within 25km.

The closest is just 2km north: Golf do Estoril (☎ 468 01 76; fax 468 27 96) has two courses overlooking the sea – one 18-hole, par 69, and the second 9 holes and par 34. The Quinta da Marinha course (☎ 486 98 81; fax 486 90 32), 9km west, was designed by Robert Trent Jones to give both high handicappers and scratch golfers a challenge, with the course rolling over wind-blown dunes and rocky outcrops.

Ten km north-west is the 18-hole, par 72 Penha Longa Golf Club (☎ 924 00 14; fax 924 90 24), a well-equipped Trent Jones Jr creation with superb views of the Serra de Sintra and Atlantic Ocean. Nearby are Golf Estoril-Sol (☎ & fax 924 03 31), designed by John Harris and Ron Fream, and the 18-hole Quinta da Beloura (☎ 924 00 21; fax 924 00 61), designed by Rocky Roquemore, who's also responsible for the newest course in the region, the 18-hole Belas Clube de Campo (☎ 962 35 36), 22km north-east of Estoril in the Carregueira hills. Estoril's turismo has full details. ■

---

opposite the train station. It's open daily from 9 am to 7 pm (Sunday 10 am to 6 pm).

Swimming

Estoril's most enjoyable attraction is its small sandy beach, Praia Estoril Tamariz, behind the train station (accessible from the turismo via an underpass). Recently spruced up with a new promenade and ocean swimming pool, it has shower facilities (250$00), a trio of bar-cafés open till late, and an Italian restaurant. The Piscina do Tamariz ocean swimming pool is open daily in summer from 10 am to 8.30 pm. Admission for adults/children (from four to nine years old) is 1100$00/800 (1600$00/1000 at weekends) for an afternoon session (2 to 7 pm) or 1400$00/950 for a whole day (1800$00/1200 weekends).

Tennis

The Clube de Ténis do Estoril (☎ 466 27 70), at Avenida Conde de Barcelona on the northern outskirts of the town, has 13 floodlit slow courts and four fast courts. It's open daily from 9 am to 10 pm. Call ahead to book a court.

Special Events

The Festival de Música da Costa do Estoril is held throughout July and features classical concerts in both Estoril and Cascais. The Estoril Festival de Jazz, also held in July, is actually held mostly in Cascais, at the Auditório Parque Palmela. The turismo offices have details.

A Feira do Artesanato (Handicrafts Fair) is held in Estoril throughout July and August beside the casino, from 6 pm to midnight daily. As well as stalls of ceramics, rugs, sculpture, embroidery etc, there are also open-air food stalls selling Portuguese snacks.

Racing fanatics may like to check whether the Grand Prix Formula One World & European Championships are back on track at the Autodromo do Estoril, 9km north of town. Usually held in late September or early October, the races weren't held in 1997, due to track repairs and lack of interest from the competing teams.

Places to Stay

The nearest youth hostel is the Pousada de Juventude de Catalazete (☎ 443 06 38) at Oeiras, 9km east of Estoril, near Oeiras train station.

The pick of the pensões is *Pensão Smart* (☎ 468 21 64), at Rua José Viana 3 (entrance on Rua Maestro Lacerda 6), in a quiet residential area 10 minutes walk from the station. Doubles with breakfast start at 7000$00. Cheaper digs can be found nearby at *Casa de Hóspedes Paula Castro* (☎ 468 06 99), on Rua da Escola 4, where basic doubles without bath go for about 5000$00.

An even better deal is *Pensão Costa* (☎ 468 16 99) at Rua de Olivença 2 (a quiet residential road just above the beach): doubles are 5000$00/4500 with/without showers. Ask for a room overlooking the sea.

More up-market residenciales can be found along the busy Avenida Marginal a few minutes walk east of the station (turn right when you exit): *Residencial São Mamede* (☎ 467 10 74; fax 467 14 18) has comfortable doubles with breakfast for 8500$00. Almost next door, the recently renovated and very welcoming *Residencial São Cristóvão* (☎ & fax 468 09 13) has doubles without bath for 8000$00 and 10,000$00 with shower (the spacious triple for 15,000$00 is great for families). All include breakfast.

A good 20 minute walk north of the centre, at Rua de São Pedro, Porta B, Bairro de Santo António, is the popular *Toca dos Grilos* guesthouse (☎ 467 47 03; fax 467 46 92), a modern seven-room house with garden and swimming pool. Doubles are around 9000$00. For a grand old seaside hotel that fits Estoril's ambience to a tee, head for *Hotel Inglaterra* (☎ 468 44 61; fax 468 21 08) at Rua do Porto 1. Its doubles (a bargain 11,550$00 in low season) soar to 23,200$00 in high season.

The cheapest of the apartment hotels is *Hotel Apartamento Estoril Eden* (☎ 467 05 73; fax 467 08 48), at Avenida de Sabóia, near the sea en route to Cascais. Singles/doubles are 13,500$00/17,000. The smaller, more up-market *Hotel Apartamento Clube Mimosa* (☎ 467 00 37; fax 467 03 74), further inland at Avenida do Lago 4, has doubles from around 20,000$00. Both have swimming pools.

Places to Eat

Restaurants here are ridiculously pricey – even the deceptively cheap-looking ones in the Arcadas do Parque (the arcade near the turismo). You're better off heading for Cascais. If you don't mind parting with your escudos, a few worthwhile places are *Casabranca* (☎ 467 29 98), a trendy place in an elegant old house at Avenida Biarritz 8;

the *English Bar* (☎ 468 04 13), at Avenida Sabóia 9, near Monte Estoril train station (15 minutes walk along the seafront towards Cascais), which is especially popular for its excellent seafood; and *Frolic* (☎ 468 12 19), by the Hotel Palácio on Avenida Clotilde, on the eastern side of the park, which serves pizzas and Portuguese dishes and is open till at least midnight. Cheaper fare in more casual surroundings can be found in the underpass to the beach and at the beachfront bar-cafés.

Entertainment

The best late-night entertainment in summer is probably at the Praia do Tamariz. The seaside *Absurdo Bar* (☎ 467 54 18) here is open daily from 10 am to around 4 am and there's live music some Friday nights.

Gambling The casino is open daily from 3 pm to 3 am. In addition to the gaming rooms (everything from roulette to baccarat, slot machines to blackjack, 21 and the popular dice game of French bank), there's a vast restaurant (☎ 468 45 21) where you can have dinner before watching the international floor show at 11 pm (9000$00 per person including dinner, 5000$00 without dinner but with two free drinks). If you don't fancy forking out for this or the gambling (there's an entrance fee of 500$00 to the gaming room, though it's free to play the slot machines and bingo), at least try to get a look at the lobby, which doubles as an art gallery.

Getting There & Away

From Cais do Sodré train station in Lisbon it's a half-hour trundle on the Linha de Cascais to Estoril (185$00). There are frequent buses between Sintra and Estoril. For Cascais you can hop on the train or, more pleasantly, walk along the seafront for about an hour.

Lisbon regional bus tours, such as Grayline, include a quick visit to Estoril's casino. Cityrama (☎ 355 85 69) organises an evening outing (11,900$00 per person) with time to visit the floor show and gambling rooms.

CASCAIS
• *pop 19,000* • *postcode 2750* • *area code* ☎ *01*

This former fishing village has been tuned into tourism since 1870 when the royal court first came here for the summer, bringing a train of nobility in its wake. It's now the liveliest beach resort on the Estoril Coast, attracting a young and international crowd, especially Brits (all year) and French and Italians in August. If you like your home comforts (John Bull pubs, McDonald's, even Marks & Spencer), you'll be happy in the touristy pedestrianised centre or on the three small beaches nearby. But there's a surpris-

ingly unspoilt old town area, which provides a pleasant afternoon's meander, and some remnants of traditional fishing activity that carries on regardless of the tourists.

Orientation & Information
Everything of interest is within easy walking distance. The train station (where buses for nearby destinations also congregate) is on Avenida Marginal, a 10 minute walk north of the pedestrianised Rua Frederico Arouca, where you'll find most of the tourist-oriented shops and restaurants. Near the western end of this street is the informative turismo

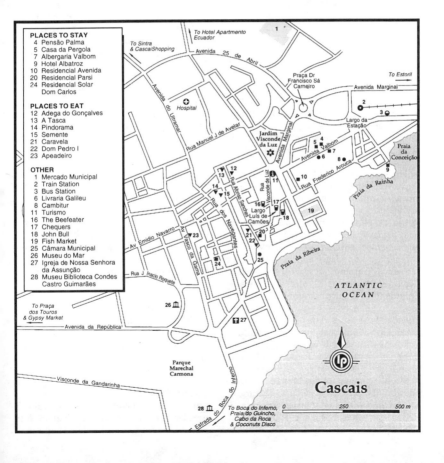

PLACES TO STAY
4   Pensão Palma
5   Casa da Pergola
7   Albergaria Valbom
9   Hotel Albatroz
10 Residencial Avenida
20 Residencial Parsi
24 Residencial Solar
    Dom Carlos

PLACES TO EAT
12 Adega do Gonçalves
13 A Tasca
14 Pindorama
15 Semente
21 Caravela
22 Dom Pedro I
23 Apeadeiro

OTHER
1   Mercado Municipal
2   Train Station
3   Bus Station
6   Livraria Galileu
8   Cambitur
11 Turismo
16 The Beefeater
17 Chequers
18 John Bull
19 Fish Market
25 Câmara Municipal
26 Museu do Mar
27 Igreja de Nossa Senhora
    da Assunção
28 Museu Biblioteca Condes
    Castro Guimarães

Cascais

(☎ 486 82 04), at Rua Visconde de Luz 14. It's open daily from 9 am to 8 pm (to 7 pm from October to May; Sunday from 10 am to 6 pm). You can pick up a copy of the free *Estoril Coast* magazine here, which gives details of special events, museums, restaurants and entertainment.

Most banks in town have Multibanco facilities for credit card cash advances.

A good source of second-hand books in English, Spanish, Italian, French and German is Livraria Galileu, at Avenida Valbom 24-A.

For medical problems, there's both the Cascais Hospital (☎ 484 40 71) and a private International Health Centre (☎ 484 53 17) whose doctors speak English, Dutch and German.

Old Cascais

To catch a hint of Cascais' former life as a fishing village, head for the **fish market** between Praia da Ribeira and Praia da Rainha at about 6 pm every day (except Sunday) when an auctioneer sells off the daily catch in an unintelligible rapid-fire lingo.

The atmospheric back lanes and alleys to the west of the *câmara municipal* (town hall) are also well worth exploring. In a shady square just south-west of the town hall is the **Igreja de Nossa Senhora da Assunção** with azulejos that predate the 1755 earthquake that destroyed most of the town.

Nearby, the large and leafy Parque Marechal Carmona contains the **Museu Biblioteca Condes Castro Guimarães**. This late 19th century mansion of the Counts of Castro Guimarães is now a museum displaying the family's furnishings (especially pretty Indo-Portuguese furniture), paintings and books, as well as archaeological finds from the area. It's open Tuesday to Sunday from 10 am to 5 pm; entry is 400$00.

More intriguing is the **Museu do Mar**, north of the park on Rua Julio Pereira de Melo (the other side of the Avenida da República), which has a small, quality collection of model boats and marine artefacts.

It's open Tuesday to Sunday from 10 am to 5 pm; admission costs 400$00.

Beaches

Most of the activity in Cascais centres around its restaurants and bars, but there are beaches if you want them: three sandy stretches (Praia da Ribeira is the largest and closest) tucked into little bays just a few minutes walk south of the main drag, Rua Frederico Arouca. They're nothing to write home about but they make pleasant suntraps if you can find an empty patch.

Cascais' most famous tourist attraction is **Boca do Inferno** (literally, 'mouth of hell'), a couple of kilometres west of the centre, where the sea roars into an abyss in the coast. You can walk there in about 20 minutes (or take the electric train – see the following Getting Around section) and join the crowds pouring out of their tour buses, but don't expect anything dramatic unless there's a storm raging.

Far more exciting waves are made at **Praia do Guincho**, 9km north-west of Cascais. This long, wild beach is a surfer's and windsurfer's paradise (the 1991 World Surfing Championships were held here), with massive crashing rollers. But there's a strong undertow which can be dangerous for swimmers and novice surfers.

Bullfighting

Cascais also boasts Portugal's largest praça de touros (bullring) where bullfights take place regularly (at least every weekend during summer). Check with the turismo for dates and times.

Horse-Riding

There are horse-riding facilities at the Centro Hípico da Quinta da Marinha (☎ 487 14 03), a couple of kilometres inland from Praia do Guincho, where you can rent horses for around 4000$00 an hour, with guide.

Special Events

Summertime musical events include a popular international jazz festival in July (see the Estoril section for details of a joint classical music festival, too). In late July (though not every year), Cascais honours the patron saint of its fisherfolk, the Senhora dos Navegantes, with a day-long procession through the streets. And in August, there's a Verão de Cascais (Cascais Summer) programme of free outdoor music and dance events, usually at Largo de Camões or Largo da Misericórdia at 10 pm. Ask the turismo for details.

Places to Stay

Camping Orbitur do Guincho (☎ 487 10 14; fax 487 21 67) is in Areia, about a kilometre inland from Praia do Guincho and 9km from Cascais. Hourly buses run to Guincho from Cascais train station.

Accommodation prices in Cascais soar in summer, and in August you'll be hard pushed to find a place at all without advance reservations. The best budget bets are private rooms (quartos), usually available for about 5000$00 a double. The turismo can help you locate them if the touts lingering outside the turismo don't find you first.

The popular *Residencial Avenida* (☎ 486 44 17), at Rua da Palmeira 14, is the best budget bet in town, with just four prettily decorated doubles (without bath) for 5000$00. *Residencial Parsi* (☎ 484 57 44; fax 483 71 50), Rua Afonso Sanches 8, is a crumbling old building overlooking the waterfront that has doubles (without private bath) from 6000$00.

Closer to the station is the *Pensão Palma* (☎ 483 77 97; fax 483 79 22), at Avenida Valbom 13. It's one of a pair of dainty town villas and is as pretty as a doll's house, with a fragrant flower garden and tiny swimming pool out the front. Doubles range from 6500$00 (no bath) to an overpriced 11,500$00 (with bath and breakfast). Next door, *Casa da Pergola* (☎ 484 00 40; fax 483 47 91) is a much more up-market Turihab establishment with an ornate façade decorated with hand-painted tiles. Doubles with bath and breakfast range from 15,500$00 to 17,500$00 in high season. More modern and less inspired accommodation can be found across the road at *Albergaria Valbom* (☎ 486

58 01; fax 486 58 05), at No 14, where comfortable doubles (including breakfast) go for 11,500$00.

In a quiet part of the old town, at Rua Latino Coelho 8, *Residencial Solar Dom Carlos* (☎ 486 84 63; fax 486 51 55) is a 16th century former royal residence that features a chapel where Dom Carlos used to pray. Rooms are 20th century (all with private bath) and cost 12,000$00.

Top of the range is *Hotel Albatroz* (☎ 483 28 21; fax 484 48 27), a former 19th century ducal palace overlooking the sea at Rua Frederico Arouca 100. High season doubles with a sea view go for a staggering 42,000$00 (low season land-view rooms are half the price).

There are several *hotel apartamentos* (apartment hotels) if you want your own cooking facilities. One of the most reasonably priced is *Hotel Apartamento Ecuador* (☎ 484 05 24; fax 484 07 03) at Alto da Pampilheira. Singles/doubles in this high-rise on the town's northern outskirts are 10,780$00/14,200.

Places to Eat

There are plenty of restaurants serving unmemorable tourist-oriented stodge and overpriced seafood and burgers in the town centre. It's worth heading away from the crowds for something better. *Dom Pedro I* (☎ 483 37 34), tucked into a backstreet corner of the old town at Beco dos Invalides 5, serves tasty and reasonably priced dishes from 800$00; go early to grab one of the few prized outdoor tables on the cobbled steps.

Further west, *Apeadeiro* (☎ 483 27 31), at Avenida Vasco da Gama 32, is locally famous for its grilled fish. Another popular haunt is the more up-market *Adega do Goncalves* (☎ 483 02 87), at Rua Afonso Sanches 54, where hearty servings cost around 1400$00 a dish. Simpler and cheaper is *A Tasca*, almost opposite at No 61; try the delicious fish kebabs. Seafood splurges are best had at *Caravela* (☎ 483 02 80), Rua Afonso Sanches 19, where you can indulge in crab, lobster or prawns. Expect to pay at least 1300$00 a dish.

The only vegetarian restaurant in town is the modest *Semente* snack bar (☎ 483 23 92), at Rua Poco Novo 65, where you can find tofu pies, quiches, millet salads and fresh fruit juices. It's open Monday to Saturday. Around the corner, at Rua Alexandre Herculano 25, there's another unusual restaurant, the *Pindorama* (☎ 482 20 85) which serves Brazilian fare from around 1500$00 per dish. It's closed on Monday.

Entertainment
There's no lack of bars to keep the nights buzzing, especially in Rua Frederico Arouca and the Largo Luís de Camões area, just down the road from the turismo, where the bars triple as cafés, restaurants and discos. For British-style establishments with imported beers and bopping music, check out *John Bull*, on Praça Costa Pinto 32, *Chequers* (☎ 483 09 26), in Largo Luís de Camões, and the *Beefeater* (☎ 484 06 96) on Rua Visconde da Luz 1. The most popular disco around is *Coconuts* (☎ 484 41 09), at Avenida Rei Humberto II de Itália 7, which has seven bars, two dance floors and an esplanade by the sea. It's open daily from 11 pm to 4 am. Wednesday is Ladies' Night, featuring a male striptease act.

Things to Buy
Serious shoppers should head straight for CascaiShopping, a massive shopping complex en route to Sintra. Bus No 417 passes by regularly.

The town's *mercado municipal* (munici-

pal market), off Avenida 25 de Abril on the northern outskirts of town, takes place on Wednesday and Saturday mornings (Wednesday is best), while a Gypsy market fills the area next to the Praça dos touros, a couple of kilometres west of town on the first and third Sunday of the month.

Getting There & Away
Trains from Lisbon's Cais do Sodré station run every 20 minutes (from 5 am to 2.30 am) for the 25 minute trip to Cascais (185$00). Buses run regularly throughout the day from outside Cascais train station to Sintra and Cabo de Roca, and every hour to Praia do Guincho and Mafra. Cascais is also included in most regional bus tours from Lisbon (see Organised Tours in the Getting Around chapter).

Getting Around
Daily throughout the summer a free electric train ferries tourists on a 45 minute round trip to Boca do Inferno, leaving every hour between 7 am and 10 pm from the Jardim Visconde da Luz (just up the road from the turismo). Sometimes it goes to the Parque Marechal Carmona and up to the Hotel Citadela on the north-western outskirts of town.

There's also a couple of horse and carriages which do half-hour trips to Boca do Inferno for about 4000$00 return (15,000$00 for a trip to Guincho and back). They wait beside the Jardim Visconde da Luz.

There are several car rental agencies, including Cambitur (☎ 486 75 28), at Rua Frederico Arouca 73-A, which also organises sight-seeing trips; Auto Jardim (☎ 483 10 73) and Transrent (☎ 486 45 66) with rates from around 6600$00 per day or from 15,000$00 for three days. To rent bikes or motorcycles contact Gesrent (☎ 486 45 66) at Centro Comercial Cisne, Loja 15, Avenida Marginal; or AA Castanheira (☎ 483 42 59) at Edificio Sol de Cascais, Loja 11, Avenida 25 de Abril. Prices range from about 1500$00 per day for a mountain bike to 5500$00 for a Honda 125. You have

---

Fun & Fireworks
If you're hanging around Largo de Camões in Cascais around 10 pm on a Thursday or Friday night during the summer, keep an eye and ear out for the live bands and street entertainers strolling around the largo. And at midnight every Saturday during July and August, drag yourself out of the pubs to see the town's brightest night-time event: a free firework display over the Praia da Ribeira beach. ■

to be 21 to rent a motorcycle (25 for motor-bikes over 500cc) and have had a motorcycle licence for at least a year.

QUELUZ
• *pop 42,900 • postcode 2745 • area code ☎ 01*

The only reason to stop at this dull town 5km north-west of Lisbon, en route to Sintra, is to see the pink-hued **Palácio de Queluz**, which was converted in the late 18th century from a hunting lodge to a summer residence for the royal family. It's the most elegant example of rococo architecture in Portugal, a miniature Versailles with feminine charm and formal gardens of whimsical fancy. One wing of the palace is often used to accommodate state guests and visiting dignitaries but the rest is open to the public Wednesday to Monday from 10 am to 1 pm and 2 to 5 pm; entry is 400$00.

The palace has witnessed some extraordinary royal scenes. Built for Prince Dom Pedro between 1747 and 1752 and designed by the Portuguese architect Mateus Vicente de Oliveira and French artist Jean-Baptiste Robillon, it was Dom Pedro's niece and wife, Queen Maria I, who inspired the most scintillating gossip about the place: she lived here for most of her reign, going increasingly mad. Her fierce, scheming daughter-in-law, the Spanish Carlota Joaquina, supplied even more bizarre material for the wealthy British visitor William Beckford to write about – most famously, an occasion when she insisted that Beckford run a race with her maid in the garden and then dance a bolero (which he did, he relates, 'in a delirium of romantic delight').

Today the interior still has hints of its owners' eccentric characters, though the furnishings are typical of the time, including English and French-style furniture, Arriaolos carpets, porcelain Chinoiserie and floors inlaid with exotic woods. Highlights are the Ambassador's Room with a floor of chequered marble and ceiling painting of the royal family attending a concert, the mirror-lined Throne Room, a wood-panelled Music Room (still used for concerts), and Pedro IV's 'circular' bedroom (actually a circular

JULIA WILKINSON

Pálacio de Queluz

ceiling over a square room) with scenes from *Don Quixote* on the walls. The palace's vast kitchens have been converted into an expensive restaurant, *Cozinha Velha*.

The garden is a delightful medley of box hedges, fountains and lead statues, and features an azulejo-lined canal where the royal family went boating.

Getting There & Away
It's a 20 minute train ride (155$00) on the Sintra line from Lisbon's Rossio station to Queluz-Belas, followed by a 15 minute walk downhill (follow the signs) to the palace.

MAFRA
• *postcode 2640* • *area code ☎ 061*
The unremarkable town of Mafra, 39km north-west of Lisbon, is famous for its massive Palácio-Convento de Mafra, the most awesome of the many extravagant monuments created in the 18th century reign of Dom João V, when money was no problem. There's nothing else of interest in town, so it's best to come here on a day trip from Lisbon, Sintra or Ericeira.

Orientation & Information
You can't miss the palace: its huge grey façade dominates the town. The poorly signposted turismo (☎ 81 20 23; fax 521 04) is on Avenida 25 de Abril, five minutes walk north down the main street from the palace, beside the Auditorio Municipal Beatriz Costa. It's open weekdays from 9.30 am to 7 pm and on weekends from 9.30 am to 1 pm and 2.30 to 7.30 pm (to 6 pm in winter). The turismo has a decent map (300$00) of the Mafra area and useful information on nearby attractions.

Palácio Nacional de Mafra
The Mafra National Palace is a combination of palace, monastery and basilica – a huge baroque and neoclassical monument covering 10 hectares. It was begun in 1717, to fulfil a prior vow by Dom João V should he be granted a male heir. As the king's coffers filled with newly discovered gold from Brazil, the initial design – meant for 13 monks – was expanded to house 280 monks and 140 novices, and to incorporate two royal wings. No expense was spared to build its 880 halls and rooms, 5200 doorways, 2500 windows and two bell towers boasting the world's largest collection of bells (57 in each). Indeed, when the Flemish bell-founders queried the extravagant order for a carillon of bells, Dom João V is said to have immediately doubled the order and to have sent the money in advance.

Under the supervision of the German architect Friedrich Ludwig, up to 20,000 artisans (including Italian masons and carpenters) worked on the monument. That figure rose to a mind-boggling 45,000 workers in the last two years of construction, all of them kept in order by 7000 soldiers. The presence of so many outstanding artists spurred Dom João V to establish a school of sculpture in the palace; this functioned from 1753 to 1770 and employed many of Portugal's most important sculptors. Though the building may have been an artistic coup, the expense of its construction and the use of such a large workforce helped destroy the country's economy.

It was only briefly used as a palace – in 1799, as the French prepared to invade Portugal, Dom João VI and the royal family fled to Brazil, taking most of Mafra's furniture with them. In 1807, General Junot put his troops in the monastery, followed by Wellington and his men. From then on, the palace became a favourite military haven. Even today, most of it is used as a military academy.

One-hour tours (excluding the basilica) take you through innumerable galleries of polished wooden floors, down 230m-long corridors, through interminable salons and apartments and up dozens of flights of stairs – and this is only a fraction of the place.

It's easy to get dazed by it all, but a few things stand out, including some amusing 18th century pinball machines in the games room; grotesque hunting décor in the dining room, where chandeliers are made of antlers' horns and chairs are upholstered in deerskin; and the monastery's infirmary where insane

Wolf Recovery Centre

Some 10km north-east of Mafra is the Centro de Recuperação de Lobo Ibérico (Iberian Wolf Recovery Centre), established in 1988 to provide a home for wolves that have been trapped, snared or kept in dire conditions and are unable to function in the wild any longer. Kept 'in the most naturalistic surroundings possible', there are now some 22 wolves at the centre, all from the north of the country where Portugal's last 300 Iberian wolves roam.

Recent reports suggest that the centre – under new management – has now become very commercialised, with group tours and school visits encouraged and little genuine care given to the wolves. If you want to see for yourself, take a bus from Mafra to Malveira, then pick up any Torres Vedras-bound bus and get off at Vale de Guarda (about 4km from Malveira). See Endangered Species under Flora & Fauna in the Facts about Lisbon chapter for more on the Iberian wolf. ■

monks were locked away. Most impressive is the magnificent barrel-vaulted baroque library, housing nearly 40,000 books from the 15th to the 18th century. At 88m it's the longest room in the building. According to the original plan, its ceiling was to have been gilded, but at this point the money ran out.

The central basilica, with its two bell towers, is wonderfully restrained by comparison with the rest of the palace, featuring multihued marble floors and panelling and Carrara marble statues.

The palace-monastery is open Wednesday to Monday (closed public holidays), from 10 am to 6 pm (closed from 1 to 2 pm in winter); entry is 400$00. The one hour guided tours are actually little more than an 'escort' by a (Portuguese-speaking) guard; tours in English, French or German have to be booked in advance.

Tapada de Mafra

The palace's park and hunting ground, Tapada de Mafra, originally enclosed by a wall 20km long, is also open for guided tours. The tours take place at 10 am, 2.45 and 3.45 pm on Saturdays and Sundays (at 10 am and 3 pm in winter). The 90 minute tours (call ☎ 511 00 a day ahead to reserve a place) take visitors to see the park's deer and wild boar and its falcon-recuperation centre (the former royal hunting lodge is currently being converted into a pousada and tearoom). The tours are a combination of bus transport and walking and cost 950$00 for adults and 500$00 for children under 10.

Sobreiro

Another unusual excursion from Mafra is to the village of Sobreiro, about 4km north-west (take any bus heading to Ericeira), where sculptor José Franco has created a craft village with a traditional bakery and cobbler's and clockmaker's shops, as well as several small wind and watermills. Kids love it here; so do adults, especially when they discover the rustic *adega* (bar) with good red wine, snacks and meals.

Horse-Riding

Horse-lovers can go to the Escola de Equitação de Alcainça (☎ 966 21 22) about 5km south-east of Mafra at Rua de São Miguel, Alcainça, where you can rent horses for around 3500$00 an hour. You can also take an intensive four-day riding course on Lusitanos horses for 19,000$00 per day (including meals and accommodation).

Portuguese windmill

Getting There & Away

There are regular buses to Mafra from Ericeira (20 minutes) and Sintra (45 minutes, 375$00). Hourly buses from Lisbon take 1½ hours (530$00) and leave from the minuscule Mafrense bus company terminal at Rua Fernandos da Fonseca 18 (right by the Socorro metro station), going via the main bus station on Avenida Casal Ribeiro.

SETÚBAL PENINSULA

The Setúbal Peninsula – the northern spur of the region the tourist board calls the Costa Azul – is an easy hop from Lisbon by ferry across the Rio Tejo, with regular bus connections to all the major points of interest. You can laze on the vast beaches of Costa da Caparica, join trendy lisboêtas in Sesimbra's beach resort further south or eat great seafood in nearby Setúbal. Setúbal's express bus connections make it a convenient stopover if you're heading south or east. There are two major nature reserves as well – the Reserve Natural do Estuário do Sado and Parque Natural da Arrábida, both worth exploring if you have your own transport.

Cacilhas

This suburb across the Rio Tejo from Lisbon is notable mainly for its fish restaurants and the **Cristo Rei**, the immense statue of Christ with outstretched hands visible from almost everywhere in Lisbon. The 28m-high statue (a small version of the one in Rio de Janeiro) was built in 1959 and partly paid for by Portuguese women grateful for the country having been spared the horrors of WWII. A lift (operating from 9 am to 7 pm in summer) takes you right to the top from where you can gasp at the panoramic views.

Getting There & Away Ferries to Cacilhas (90$00) run every 10 minutes from Lisbon's Cais da Alfândega river terminal by Praça do Comércio. The trip takes about 10 minutes, with the last boat leaving at around 10.30 pm. A car ferry also runs every 20 minutes from Cais do Sodré (this one runs all night). To reach the statue, take the bus from stand No 9 at the bus station opposite Cacilhas' ferry terminal. Or you can take bus No 52 or 53 directly from Lisbon's Praça de Espanha (get off just after the bridge).

Costa da Caparica

This 8km stretch of beach on the west coast of the peninsula is Lisbon's favourite weekend escape, with cafés, restaurants and bars catering to every age group. During the summer a narrow-gauge railway runs along the entire length of the beach, giving you the option of jumping off at any one of 20 stops; earlier stops attract families, later ones gays and nudists. The turismo (☎ 290 00 71) at Praça da Liberdade can fill you in on accommodation options (including several camping grounds), but these are expensive.

Getting There & Away Buses run to the Costa da Caparica regularly from Lisbon's

---

Reserva Natural do Estuário do Sado

The Sado Estuary Natural Reserve encompasses a vast coastal area (23,160 hectares) around the Sado River and estuary, stretching from Setúbal in the north to near Alcácer do Sal in the south-east. Its mud banks and marshes, lagoons, dunes and former salt pans are a vitally important habitat for mammals, molluscs and migrating birds. The mammal species that attracts the most attention is *Tursiops truncatus*, a species of dolphin (known in Portuguese as Roaz-Corvineiro) often found in coastal waters. There are thought to be only about 50 dolphins left in this area, fighting for survival as the mouth of the estuary becomes increasingly developed. Among the 100 or so bird species worth looking out for are flamingoes (over a thousand of the birds usually winter here), white storks (spring and summer) and resident marsh harriers and little egrets.

Without your own transport, explorations of the park are inevitably limited. The *Walking Guide to Arrábida & Sado* details several hikes but they start several kilometres from any bus routes. ■

Praça de Espanha (taking about an hour) and from Cacilhas' bus terminal (stand No 17 or 25).

Setúbal
• pop 80,000 • postcode 2900 • area code ☎ 065
Once an important Roman settlement, Setúbal is now the largest town on the Setúbal Peninsula and Portugal's third-largest port (after Lisbon and Porto). Situated on the north bank of the Sado estuary, some 50km south of Lisbon, it's refreshingly untouristy – concentrating more on its fishing, commercial port and industries (sardine-canning, cement and salt), than on visitors. But with its easy-going atmosphere, beaches and good cheap restaurants, it makes an ideal weekend escape from Lisbon. It's also a suitable base for exploring the Parque Natural da Arrábida, though you'll need your own transport unless you take one of the adventure trips mentioned below.

Orientation & Information There are two train stations. The one opposite Praça do Brasil, 700m north of the city centre, serves trains from Lisbon, while the local station is centrally located at the eastern end of Avenida 5 de Outubro. The main bus station is also on this avenida, five minutes walk from the municipal turismo (☎ 53 42 22) on Praça do Quebedo. The turismo is open weekdays only from 9 am to 12.30 pm and 2 to 5.30 pm.

For more comprehensive information head for the regional turismo (☎ 52 42 84; fax 367 45). It's at Travessa Frei Gaspar 10, near the town's pedestrianised shopping centre (around 10 minutes walk south of the bus station). It's open from 9 am to 7 pm daily (closed 12.30 to 2 pm on Monday and Saturday, and on Sunday afternoons). Brisk and efficient, the office has stacks of publications about the Setúbal region and a touch-screen information terminus outside.

Banks and shops are plentiful in the pedestrian area near the regional turismo office. The main post office is further north, on Avenida 22 de Dezembro, a few minutes walk from the Igreja de Jesus.

Igreja de Jesus There's only one major cultural site in Setúbal: the Igreja de Jesus in Praça Miguel Bombarda (at the western end of Avenida 5 de Outubro). Constructed in 1491, it was designed by Diogo de Boitac, better known for his later work on Belém's Mosteiro dos Jerónimos. The small church itself is late Gothic in style but walk inside and you'll see the earliest examples of Manueline decoration – extraordinary twisted pillars, like writhing snakes, made from delicately coloured Arrábida marble. The walls of the nave and chancel are more conservative, decorated with fine 18th century azulejos on the life of the Virgin Mary. The church is open Tuesday to Saturday from 9 am to 12.30 pm and 2 to 5.30 pm.

Museu de Setúbal Around the corner from the Igreja de Jesus, on Rua Balneários Dr Paula Borba, is the town's major museum. It

---

Stressed Out?
If you've arrived in Lisbon stressed-out or overloaded with sight-seeing, there's an unusual cure at hand: thalassotherapy. A treatment using minerals from the sea, including iodine, calcium and sulphur, thalassotherapy helps alleviate stress, fatigue and insomnia as well as rheumatism, circulatory problems and obesity.

The Centro Thalasso da Costa de Caparica (☎ 290 56 55; fax 291 26 57) at Avenida 1 de Maio 25-A, Costa de Caparica, offers various treatments including hydro-massage (in a bath of seaweed), marine hydro-therapy and aqua-gymnastics well as straightforward massage, sauna and solarium. Prices range from 1500$00 just for the solarium and 2500$00 for the sauna to 8500$00 per day for a two to five-day treatment. The centre is open Monday to Saturday from 10 am to 2 pm and 3 to 7 pm. ∎

houses a renowned collection of 15th and 16th century Portuguese paintings, azulejos, and ecclesiastic gold and silver. It's open Monday to Friday from 9 am to 12.30 pm and 2 to 5.30 pm.

Museu de Arqueologia e Etnografia The Archaeological & Ethnographic Museum, at Avenida Luísa Todi 162, houses an impressive collection of Roman remains. Setúbal was founded by the Romans at the beginning of the 5th century AD after their fishing port of Cetobriga (now Tróia), on the opposite side of the river mouth, was destroyed by an earthquake in 412. The museum opens its doors Tuesday to Saturday from 9.30 am to 12.30 pm and 2 to 5 pm, and on Sunday from 9.30 am to 12.30 pm.

Castelo São Filipe Worth the half-hour stroll to the west of town is this castle built by Filipe I in 1590 to fend off an English attack on the invincible Armada. Converted into a pousada in the 1960s, its ramparts are still huge and impressive and its chapel boasts 18th century azulejos on the life of São Filipe.

Beaches For good beaches, head west of Setúbal along the coast road until you reach Figuerinha, Galapos or Portinho da Arrábida – all fine beaches, accessible by buses from Setúbal in summer. More crowded are the beaches of Sesimbra and Tróia (across the mouth of the Sado estuary), which has become hideously developed.

Organised Tours For active exploration of the Parque Natural da Arrábida and Reserva Natural do Estuário do Sado, contact Planeta Terra (☎ 53 21 40; fax 52 79 21), Praça General Luiz Domingues 9, which organises canoe day-trips on the Sado Estuary and mountain biking in the Arrábida area (both for around 5000$00 per person) plus various trekking trips. It's best to reserve three days in advance. Mil Andanças (☎ 53 29 96; fax 396 63), Rua de Traz da Guarda 40, also organises a combination of boat and off-road safari trips in the Setúbal and Sesimbra areas,

lasting seven hours. Cost (including lunch) is 8000$00 for adults, 6000$00 for children up to 12.

The US-based Easy Rider Tours (see Organised Tours in the Getting There & Away chapter) has a Costa Azul biking tour that includes a day's biking through the Serra da Arrábida.

Another unusual way to experience the area is aboard a modern galleon, the *Riquitum*, which sails along the Sado Estuary on four-hour trips (6500$00 per person) leaving every Friday at 9 am from the Cais de Embarque, just west of the Doca do Comércio (commercial dock). The trips are organised by Troiacruze (☎ 28482), which also offers short scuba-diving courses. Bookings can also be made through Pestana Tour (☎ 30325 or ☎ 36759).

Wine buffs may be interested in the free wine-cellar tours of the José Maria da Fonseca adega (☎ 218 02 27), at Rua José Augusto Coelho 11, Vila Fresca de Azeitão, where the famous *moscatel* of Setúbal is made. Catch any Sesimbra-bound bus from Setúbal to reach Vila Fresca de Azeitão. The adega is open on weekdays from 9 am to noon and 2 to 5 pm, with tours several times daily.

Places to Stay The adequate *Toca do Pai Lopes* (☎ 52 24 75) municipal camping ground is 1.5km west of the town centre on Rua Praia da Saúde (near the shipyards). During the summer, a regular bus to Figuerinha beach passes close by both this camping ground and the one (☎ 383 18) a couple of kilometres further along the coast at Outão.

In Setúbal itself, the *centro de juventude* in Largo José Afonso has dorm beds for 1300$00 (although they're often booked out by youth groups).

There are several other reasonably priced options: the friendly *Residencial Todi* (☎ 205 92), at Avenida Luísa Todi 244, has tatty but clean doubles from 3000$00/4000 without/with bath; a triple here is good value at 4500$00. Another attractive bargain, though less welcoming, is the central *Pensão*

Bom Regresso (☎ 298 12) overlooking the pleasant Praça de Bocage. It offers doubles with bath from around 3500$00.

Up several notches is the comfortable *Residencial Bocage* (☎ 215 98; fax 218 09), on the pedestrianised Rua São Cristovão at No 14, where singles/doubles with breakfast are 5500$00/6500. The smart, pretentious *Residencial Setúbalense* (☎ 52 57 90; fax 52 57 89), in another central pedestrianised lane at Rua Major Afonso Pala 17, offers deluxe rooms with breakfast for 7500$00. A more attractive choice in this bracket is the four-star *Albergaria Solaris* (☎ 52 21 89; fax 52 20 70) on Praça Marquês de Pombal 12, where rooms with all the frills cost 8000$00/10,000.

Most luxurious of all is the *Pousada de São Filipe* (☎ 52 38 44; fax 53 25 38), within the walls of the town's hilltop castle (some of the rooms are in the old dungeons). Doubles will set you back a tidy 28,500$00.

Places to Eat There are lots of cheap little eateries in the lanes just east of the regional turismo office. *Neca's Snack Bar* (☎ 377 13), at Rua Dr António Joaquim Granjo 10, is a welcoming little place which (despite its name) serves regular meals including bargain pratos do dia (eg a dozen sardines) for 700$00 and special titbits such as a delicious queijo de ovelha (sheep's cheese). In the nearby Rua Arronches Junqueiro, locals cram into the *Snack-Bar A Telha Azul* (☎ 373 71) at lunch time for its cheap, filling meals.

A more mainstream restaurant in the pedestrian area is *O Escondidinho* (☎ 52 34 08; closed Sundays), at Rua José António Januario da Silva 4-6, which has several tables outside and meia doses (half-portions) from 850$00. For excellent seafood and fish dishes, head for the western end of Avenida Luísa Todi, where there's a string of seafood restaurants. *Casa do Chico* (☎ 395 02; closed Mondays), at No 490, is small and friendly and offers weekend specialities such as arroz de tamboril (monkfish with rice) and caldeirada à Setúbalense (Setúbal-style seafood stew).

Getting There & Away From Lisbon, train connections are complicated since you must first cross the Rio Tejo to Barreiro. Far easier are the buses that leave every hour from Praça de Espanha, or from Cacilhas (stand No 13), a quick ferry-hop from Lisbon's Cais de Alfândega terminus.

For buses from Setúbal to Sesimbra, go to the stop outside the office of the Covas & Filhos bus company on Avenida Alexandre Herculano 5-A (five minutes walk from the main bus station), where buses leave around nine times a day. This is also the place to get Solexpresso bus tickets to the Algarve, Elvas, Peniche and Portalegre.

Parque Natural da Arrábida

The Arrábida Natural Park stretches along the south-east coast of the Setúbal Peninsula, from Setúbal to Sesimbra. Covering the 35km-long Serra da Arrábida mountain ridge, with its sweeping views of the Atlantic, this is an area rich in Mediterranean thickets and plants (over 1000 different species), butterflies, beetles and birds (especially birds of prey). Even seaweed comes in 70 different varieties here.

The variety of flora makes for great local honey, especially in the gardens of the Convento da Arrábida, a 16th century former convent overlooking the sea just north of Portinho. Cheese and wine are other famous local products (see Setúbal – Organised Tours for details of wine cellar tours).

There's little public transport through the park (buses between Setúbal and Sesimbra mostly skirt its northern boundary), so your best option is to rent a car or motorcycle and walk. For ideas of where to go, see the *Walking Guide to Arrábida and Sado* (no maps), published by the Região de Turismo da Costa Azul. It's available at the regional turismo in Setúbal and from park headquarters (☎ 52 40 32) at Praça da República, Setúbal. ∎

Ferries to the Tróia Peninsula depart every 30 to 45 minutes daily. The fare is 120$00 per person (520$00 for a car).

Car-rental agencies include Avis (☎ 52 69 46), at Avenida Luísa Todi 96, and Alucar (☎ 53 32 85; fax 52 54 05) at Avenida Combatentes da Grande Guerra 60.

Sesimbra
• pop 7300 • postcode 2970 • area code ☎ 01

This former fishing village sheltering under the Serra da Arrábida, at the western edge of the Arrábida Natural Park, some 30km west of Setúbal, has become a favourite seaside resort with lisboêtas (it's only about an hour and a half away from the city). At weekends and in high season, the traffic, jet skis and bar music hardly provide a tonic of tranquility but if you like your beaches to buzz, this little resort may fit the bill.

Orientation & Information The bus station is on Avenida da Liberdade, five minutes walk up from the seafront. Turn right when you reach the bottom of the avenida, pass the small 17th century Forte do Santiago (not open to the public) and you'll reach the turismo (☎ 223 57 43) at Largo da Marinho, just off the main Avenida dos Náfragos. It's open daily from 9 am to 8 pm in summer (from 10 am to 12.30 pm and 2 to 5.30 pm in winter) and can help with accommodation.

Things to See & Do Eating and drinking seem to be the main activities in Sesimbra, though **water sports** attract a few sober souls during the day: windsurfers and paddle boats can be rented along the beach in summer, and swimming is good on either side of the Forte do Santiago.

The unusually energetic can hike up to the ruined Moorish **castelo** (allow at least an hour), which was taken from the Moors by Dom Afonso Henriques in the 12th century, retaken by the Moors, and finally snatched back by the Christians under Dom Sancho I in the following century. Perched 200m above the town, it's a great spot for coastal panoramas.

To see the last vestiges of Sesimbra's traditional fishing lifestyle, head for the **Porto de Abrigo**, a kilometre or so west of the town centre, where fisherfolk auction off their catch in the late afternoon.

Places to Stay The nearest camping ground (☎ 223 36 97) is at Forte de Cavalo, just a kilometre west of town, but it's often packed out in summer. The next nearest options are the municipal camping ground (☎ 268 53 85) at Maçã, 4km north (take any Lisbon or Setúbal bus) or the better equipped Valbom camping ground (☎ 268 75 45) at Cotovia, only a kilometre further north.

Although accommodation here is generally expensive, it's always worth enquiring at the turismo about private rooms (quartos), which are often available in summer for around 5500$00 a double. Some of the most obvious are the well-signposted rooms of *Senhora Garcia* (☎ 223 32 27) at Travessa Xavier da Silva 1; these are pricey at 7000$00 a double (with bath) but spacious and clean. Alternatively, try *Residencial Chic* (☎ 223 31 10), opposite at No 6, where adequate rooms (without bath and with noisy night-time music from the downstairs café) are 3500$00/6000.

In the upper price bracket, there's the comfortable *Residencial Nautico* (☎ 223 32 33), a 10 minute walk uphill from the waterfront, at Bairro Infante Dom Henrique 3, which has doubles with breakfast for 9000$00. More attractive is the *Casa da Terrina* (☎ 268 02 64), a 19th century converted farmhouse about 3km from Sesimbra at Quintola de Santana (take the bus to Cabo Espichel). There are five doubles here for 10,500$00 (one larger room with verandah for 12,500$00), and a swimming pool in the grounds.

Places to Eat You're spoilt for choice with fish restaurants, especially along Avenida 25 de Abril, east of the Forte do Santiago. Prices aren't cheap, though, and can often escalate alarmingly if you make anything other than a run-of-the-mill choice. Along the waterfront in the other direction, a pleasant option is *Restaurant Baia* (☎ 223 20 12) at No 45 next to the Hotel do Mar. For cheaper fare, head for the backstreets around the bus station.

Entertainment Among the many bars and cafés on the waterfront, *Sereia* (☎ 223 20 90), at Avenida dos Náufragos 20, attracts a lively crowd and is open until at least 2 am.

Getting There & Away Buses to Sesimbra depart from Lisbon's Praça de Espanha three to four times a day and about nine times a day from Setúbal and Cacilhas (bus stand No 11).

Glossary

See the Food Glossary in the Places to Eat chapter for words and terms to do with eating and drinking.

adega – a cellar, especially a wine cellar; also means a winery, or a traditional wine bar likely to serve wine from the barrel

Age of Discoveries – the period during the 15th and 16th centuries when Portuguese explorers ventured across the seas, 'discovering' and colonising various territories, exploring the coast of Africa, and finally charting the sea route to India

aguardente – strongly alcoholic firewater

albergaria – an up-market inn

arco – arch

armazém – riverside warehouses and stores

artesanatos – handicraft shops

autos-da-fé – judgements handed down by the Inquisition

azulejos – hand-painted tiles, often blue and white, used to decorate buildings

bagagem – baggage office

bairro – town district

balcão – counter in a bar or café

beco – cul de sac

câmara municipal – town hall

cartões telefónicos – plastic phonecards

casa de banho – public toilets; also known as *sanitários*

castelo – castle

centro de saúde – state-administered medical centre

chafariz – fountain

cidade – city

claustro – cloisters

coro alta – choir stalls overlooking the nave in a church

correios – post office

direita – right (direction); abbreviated as D, dir or Dta

Dom, Dona – honorific titles (Sir, Madam)

traditionally given to kings, queens and other nobles

duplo – room with twin beds

elevador – lift (elevator) or funicular

esplanada – terrace or seafront promenade

esquerda – left; abbreviated as E, esq or Esqa

estação – station (usually train station)

fado – the haunting, melancholy Portuguese equivalent of blues music

farmácia – pharmacy

feira – fair

festa – festival

fortaleza – fort

freguesia – parish

GNR – Guarda Nacional Republicana, the national guard; acting police force in major towns

Gypsy markets – huge outdoor markets specialising in cheap clothes and shoes, and largely operated by Portugal's Gypsies

hipermercado – hypermarket

horário – timetable

ICEP – Investimentos, Comércio e Turismo de Portugal; the government umbrella organisation for Portugal's national tourism body; there are ICEP *turismos* in most major cities (in addition to the municipal turismos)

igreja – church

igreja matriz – parish church

intercidade – express intercity train

interregional – fairly fast train without too many stops

IVA (Imposto sobre Valor Acrescentado) – VAT (value added tax)

jardim – garden

judiaria – a Jewish quarter where Jews were once segregated

junta de turismo – see *turismo*

largo – small square

lavandaria – laundry
lisboêtas – what the inhabitants of Lisbon call themselves
livraria – bookshop

Manueline – a unique and elaborate style of art and architecture that emerged during the reign of Manuel I in the 16th century
mercado municipal – municipal market
minimercado – grocery or small supermarket
miradouro – lookout
mosteiro – monastery
mouraria – Moorish quarter where Moors were segregated after the Christian *Reconquista*
mudéjar – Moorish-influenced art or decoration
museu – museum

paços de concelho – town hall (an older name for a *câmara municipal*)
parque de campismo – camping ground
parque infantil – children's playground
pastelaria – cake shop; confectionary
pelourinho – stone pillory, often ornately carved; from the 13th to the 18th century, pillories were used, particularly in northern Portugal, not only as a symbol of justice but also to chain up criminals for whipping and abuse
pensão (s), **pensões** (pl) – guesthouse; the Portuguese equivalent of a bed and breakfast (B&B), but breakfast is not always included
portagem – toll road
posto de turismo – see *turismo*
pousada de juventude – youth hostel
pousada – government-run hotel (in a programme called Pousadas de Portugal) offering up-market accommodation, often in a converted castle, convent or palace

praça – square
praça de touros – bullring
praia – beach
PSP – Polícia de Segurança Pública; the local police force

quarto de casal – room with a double bed
quarto individual – single room
quarto particular (or simply **quarto**) – room in a private house

Reconquista – Christian reconquest of Portugal begun in 718 and completed in 1249
rés do chão – ground floor; abbrieviated as R/C
residencial (s), **residenciais** (pl) – guesthouse; often slightly more expensive than a *pensão* and usually serving breakfast
rio – river
romaria – religious pilgrimage

sanitários or **casas de banho** – public toilets
sé – cathedral, from the Latin for 'seat' *(sedes)*, implying an episcopal seat
selos – stamps
sem chumbo – unleaded petrol
supermercados – supermarket

talha dourada – gilded woodwork
tourada – bullfight
Turihab – short for Turismo Habitação, an association marketing private accommodation in country cottages, historic buildings and manor houses
turismo – tourist office

vila – town
vinho da casa – house wine
vinho verde – semi-sparkling young wine

Index

LONELY PLANET PHRASEBOOKS

Nepali phrasebook

Ethiopian Amharic phrasebook

Latin American Spanish phrasebook

Ukrainian phrasebook

Greek phrasebook

Vietnamese phrasebook

Building bridges,
Breaking barriers,
Beyond babble-on

Listen for the gems

Speak your own words

Ask your own questions

Master of your own image

- handy pocket-sized books
- easy to understand Pronunciation chapter
- clear and comprehensive Grammar chapter
- romanisation alongside script to allow ease of pronunciation
- script throughout so users can point to phrases
- extensive vocabulary sections, words and phrases for every situation
- full of cultural information and tips for the traveller

'...vital for a real DIY spirit and attitude in language learning' – Backpacker

'the phrasebooks have good cultural backgrounders and offer solid advice for challenging situations in remote locations' – San Francisco Examiner

'...they are unbeatable for their coverage of the world's more obscure languages' – The Geographical Magazine

---

Arabic (Egyptian)
Arabic (Moroccan)
Australia
  Australian English, Aboriginal and Torres Strait languages
Baltic States
  Estonian, Latvian, Lithuanian
Bengali
Brazilian
Burmese
Cantonese
Central Asia
Central Europe
  Czech, French, German, Hungarian, Italian and Slovak
Eastern Europe
  Bulgarian, Czech, Hungarian, Polish, Romanian and Slovak
Ethiopian (Amharic)
Fijian
French
German
Greek

Hindi/Urdu
Indonesian
Italian
Japanese
Korean
Lao
Latin American Spanish
Malay
Mandarin
Mediterranean Europe
  Albanian, Croatian, Greek, Italian, Macedonian, Maltese, Serbian and Slovene
Mongolian
Moroccan Arabic
Nepali
Papua New Guinea
Pilipino (Tagalog)
Quechua
Russian
Scandinavian Europe
  Danish, Finnish, Icelandic, Norwegian and Swedish

South-East Asia
  Burmese, Indonesian, Khmer, Lao, Malay, Tagalog (Pilipino), Thai and Vietnamese
Spanish (Castilian)
  Basque, Catalan and Galician
Sri Lanka
Swahili
Thai
Thai Hill Tribes
Tibetan
Turkish
Ukrainian
USA
  US English, Vernacular, Native American languages and Hawaiian
Vietnamese
Western Europe
  Basque, Catalan, Dutch, French, German, Irish, Italian, Portuguese, Scottish Gaelic, Spanish (Castilian) and Welsh

LONELY PLANET JOURNEYS

JOURNEYS is a unique collection of travel writing – published by the company that understands travel better than anyone else. It is a series for anyone who has ever experienced – or dreamed of – the magical moment when they encountered a strange culture or saw a place for the first time. They are tales to read while you're planning a trip, while you're on the road or while you're in an armchair, in front of a fire.

JOURNEYS books catch the spirit of a place, illuminate a culture, recount a crazy adventure, or introduce a fascinating way of life. They always entertain, and always enrich the experience of travel.

THE GATES OF DAMASCUS
Lieve Joris

Translated by Sam Garrett

This best-selling book is a beautifully drawn portrait of day-to-day life in modern Syria. Through her intimate contact with local people, Lieve Joris draws us into the fascinating world that lies behind the gates of Damascus. Hala's husband is a political prisoner, jailed for his opposition to the Assad regime; through the author's friendship with Hala we see how Syrian politics impacts on the lives of ordinary people.

Lieve Joris, who was born in Belgium, is one of Europe's leading travel writers. In addition to an award-winning book on Hungary, she has published widely acclaimed accounts of her journeys to the Middle East and Africa. *The Gates of Damascus* is her fifth book.

'Expands the boundaries of travel writing' – **Times Literary Supplement**

KINGDOM OF THE FILM STARS
Journey into Jordan
Annie Caulfield

Kingdom of the Film Stars is a travel book and a love story. With honesty and humour, Annie Caulfield writes of travelling in Jordan and falling in love with a Bedouin. Her book offers fascinating insights into the country – from the traditional tent life of nomadic tribes to the first woman MP's battle with fundamentalist colleagues. *Kingdom of the Film Stars* unpicks some of the tight-woven Western myths about the Arab world, presenting cultural and political issues within the intimate framework of a compelling love story.

Annie Caulfield, who was born in Ireland and currently lives in London, is an award-winning playwright and journalist. She has travelled widely in the Middle East.

'Annie Caulfield is a remarkable traveller. Her story is fresh, courageous, moving, witty and sexy!' – **Dawn French**

LONELY PLANET TRAVEL ATLASES

Lonely Planet has long been famous for the number and quality of its guidebook maps. Now we've gone one step further and in conjunction with Steinhart Katzir Publishers produced a handy companion series: Lonely Planet travel atlases – maps of a country produced in book form.

Unlike other maps, which look good but lead travellers astray, our travel atlases have been researched on the road by Lonely Planet's experienced team of writers. All details are carefully checked to ensure the atlas corresponds with the equivalent Lonely Planet guidebook.

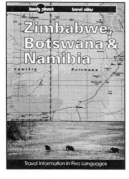

The handy atlas format means no holes, wrinkles, torn sections or constant folding and unfolding. These atlases can survive long periods on the road, unlike cumbersome fold-out maps. The comprehensive index ensures easy reference.

- full-colour throughout
- maps researched and checked by Lonely Planet authors
- place names correspond with Lonely Planet guidebooks
  – no confusing spelling differences
- legend and travelling information in English, French, German, Japanese and Spanish
- size: 230 x 160 mm

Available now:
Chile & Easter Island • Egypt • India & Bangladesh • Israel & the Palestinian Territories •Jordan, Syria & Lebanon • Kenya • Laos • Portugal • South Africa, Lesotho & Swaziland • Thailand • Turkey • Vietnam • Zimbabwe, Botswana & Namibia

---

LONELY PLANET TV SERIES & VIDEOS

Lonely Planet travel guides have been brought to life on television screens around the world. Like our guides, the programmes are based on the joy of independent travel, and look honestly at some of the most exciting, picturesque and frustrating places in the world. Each show is presented by one of three travellers from Australia, England or the USA and combines an innovative mixture of video, Super-8 film, atmospheric soundscapes and original music.

Videos of each episode – containing additional footage not shown on television – are available from good book and video shops, but the availability of individual videos varies with regional screening schedules.

Video destinations include: Alaska • American Rockies • Australia – The South-East • Baja California & the Copper Canyon • Brazil • Central Asia • Chile & Easter Island • Corsica, Sicily & Sardinia – The Mediterranean Islands • East Africa (Tanzania & Zanzibar) • Ecuador & the Galapagos Islands • Greenland & Iceland • Indonesia • Israel & the Sinai Desert • Jamaica • Japan • La Ruta Maya • Morocco • New York • North India • Pacific Islands (Fiji, Solomon Islands & Vanuatu) • South India • South West China • Turkey • Vietnam • West Africa • Zimbabwe, Botswana & Namibia

The Lonely Planet TV series is produced by:
Pilot Productions
The Old Studio
18 Middle Row
London W10 5AT UK

For video availability and ordering information contact your nearest Lonely Planet office.

Music from the TV series is available on CD & cassette.

PLANET TALK

Lonely Planet's FREE quarterly newsletter

We love hearing from you and think you'd like to hear from us.

When...is the right time to see reindeer in Finland?
Where...can you hear the best palm-wine music in Ghana?
How...do you get from Asunción to Areguá by steam train?
What...is the best way to see India?

For the answer to these and many other questions read PLANET TALK.

Every issue is packed with up-to-date travel news and advice including:

* a letter from Lonely Planet co-founders Tony and Maureen Wheeler
* go behind the scenes on the road with a Lonely Planet author
* feature article on an important and topical travel issue
* a selection of recent letters from travellers
* details on forthcoming Lonely Planet promotions
* complete list of Lonely Planet products

To join our mailing list contact any Lonely Planet office.

Also available: Lonely Planet T-shirts. 100% heavyweight cotton.

LONELY PLANET ONLINE

Get the latest travel information before you leave or while you're on the road

Whether you've just begun planning your next trip, or you're chasing down specific info on currency regulations or visa requirements, check out Lonely Planet Online for up-to-the minute travel information.

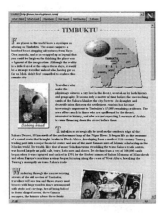

As well as travel profiles of your favourite destinations (including maps and photos), you'll find current reports from our researchers and other travellers, updates on health and visas, travel advisories, and discussion of the ecological and political issues you need to be aware of as you travel.

There's also an online travellers' forum where you can share your experience of life on the road, meet travel companions and ask other travellers for their recommendations and advice. We also have plenty of links to other online sites useful to independent travellers.

And of course we have a complete and up-to-date list of all Lonely Planet travel products including guides, phrasebooks, atlases, Journeys and videos and a simple online ordering facility if you can't find the book you want elsewhere.

www.lonelyplanet.com
or
AOL keyword: lp

LONELY PLANET PRODUCTS

Lonely Planet is known worldwide for publishing practical, reliable and no-nonsense travel information in our guides and on our web site. The Lonely Planet list covers just about every accessible part of the world. Currently there are eight series: *travel guides, shoestring guides, walking guides, city guides, phrasebooks, audio packs, travel atlases* and *Journeys* – a unique collection of travel writing.

EUROPE

Amsterdam • Austria • Baltic States phrasebook • Britain • Central Europe on a shoestring • Central Europe phrasebook • Czech & Slovak Republics • Denmark • Dublin • Eastern Europe on a shoestring • Eastern Europe phrasebook • Estonia, Latvia & Lithuania • Finland • France • French phrasebook • Germany • German phrasebook • Greece • Greek phrasebook • Hungary • Iceland, Greenland & the Faroe Islands • Ireland • Italian phrasebook • Italy • Lisbon • Mediterranean Europe on a shoestring • Mediterranean Europe phrasebook • Paris • Poland • Portugal • Portugal travel atlas • Prague • Russia, Ukraine & Belarus • Russian phrasebook • Scandinavian & Baltic Europe on a shoestring • Scandinavian Europe phrasebook •Slovenia • Spain • Spanish phrasebook • St Petersburg • Switzerland •Trekking in Spain • Ukrainian phrasebook •Vienna •Walking in Britain • Walking in Switzerland • Western Europe on a shoestring • Western Europe phrasebook

Travel Literature: The Olive Grove: Travels in Greece

NORTH AMERICA

Alaska • Backpacking in Alaska • Baja California • California & Nevada • Canada • Florida • Hawaii • Honolulu • Los Angeles • Mexico • Miami • New England • New Orleans • New York City • New York, New Jersey & Pennsylvania • Pacific Northwest USA • Rocky Mountain States • San Francisco • Southwest USA • USA phrasebook • Washington, DC & the Capital Region

CENTRAL AMERICA & THE CARIBBEAN

Bermuda • Central America on a shoestring • Costa Rica • Cuba •Eastern Caribbean •Guatemala, Belize & Yucatán: La Ruta Maya • Jamaica

SOUTH AMERICA

Argentina, Uruguay & Paraguay • Bolivia • Brazil • Brazilian phrasebook • Buenos Aires • Chile & Easter Island • Chile & Easter Island travel atlas • Colombia • Deep South • Ecuador & the Galápagos Islands • Latin American Spanish phrasebook • Peru • Quechua phrasebook • Rio de Janeiro • South America on a shoestring • Trekking in the Patagonian Andes • Venezuela

Travel Literature: Full Circle: A South American Journey

ANTARCTICA

Antarctica

ISLANDS OF THE INDIAN OCEAN

Madagascar & Comoros • Maldives• Mauritius, Réunion & Seychelles

AFRICA

Africa - the South • Africa on a shoestring • Arabic (Moroccan) phrasebook • Cape Town • Central Africa • East Africa • Egypt • Egypt travel atlas• Ethiopian (Amharic) phrasebook • Kenya • Kenya travel atlas • Malawi, Mozambique & Zambia • Morocco • North Africa • South Africa, Lesotho & Swaziland • South Africa, Lesotho & Swaziland travel atlas • Swahili phrasebook • Trekking in East Africa • West Africa • Zimbabwe, Botswana & Namibia • Zimbabwe, Botswana & Namibla travel atlas

Travel Literature: The Rainbird: A Central African Journey • Songs to an African Sunset: A Zimbabwean Story

MAIL ORDER

Lonely Planet products are distributed worldwide. They are also available by mail order from Lonely Planet, so if you have difficulty finding a title please write to us. North American and South American residents should write to Embarcadero West, 155 Filbert St, Suite 251, Oakland CA 94607, USA; European and African residents should write to 10a Spring Place, London NW5 3BH; and residents of other countries to PO Box 617, Hawthorn, Victoria 3122, Australia.

NORTH-EAST ASIA

Beijing • Cantonese phrasebook • China • Hong Kong • Hong Kong, Macau & Guangzhou • Japan • Japanese phrasebook • Japanese audio pack • Korea • Korean phrasebook • Mandarin phrasebook • Mongolia • Mongolian phrasebook • North-East Asia on a shoestring • Seoul • Taiwan • Tibet • Tibet phrasebook • Tokyo

Travel Literature: Lost Japan

MIDDLE EAST & CENTRAL ASIA

Arab Gulf States • Arabic (Egyptian) phrasebook • Central Asia • Central Asia phrasebook • Iran • Israel & the Palestinian Territories • Israel & the Palestinian Territories travel atlas • Istanbul • Jerusalem • Jordan & Syria • Jordan, Syria & Lebanon travel atlas • Lebanon • Middle East • Turkey • Turkish phrasebook • Turkey travel atlas • Yemen

Travel Literature: The Gates of Damascus • Kingdom of the Film Stars: Journey into Jordan

ALSO AVAILABLE:

Travel with Children • Traveller's Tales

INDIAN SUBCONTINENT

Bangladesh • Bengali phrasebook • Delhi • Hindi/Urdu phrasebook • India • India & Bangladesh travel atlas • Indian Himalaya • Karakoram Highway • Nepal • Nepali phrasebook • Pakistan • Rajasthan • Sri Lanka • Sri Lanka phrasebook • Trekking in the Indian Himalaya • Trekking in the Karakoram & Hindukush • Trekking in the Nepal Himalaya

Travel Literature: In Rajasthan • Shopping for Buddhas

SOUTH-EAST ASIA

Bali & Lombok • Bangkok • Burmese phrasebook • Cambodia • Ho Chi Minh City • Indonesia • Indonesian phrasebook • Indonesian audio pack • Jakarta • Java • Laos • Lao phrasebook • Laos travel atlas • Malay phrasebook • Malaysia, Singapore & Brunei • Myanmar (Burma) • Philippines • Pilipino phrasebook • Singapore • South-East Asia on a shoestring • South-East Asia phrasebook • Thailand • Thailand's Islands & Beaches • Thailand travel atlas • Thai phrasebook • Thai audio pack • Thai Hill Tribes phrasebook • Vietnam • Vietnamese phrasebook • Vietnam travel atlas

AUSTRALIA & THE PACIFIC

Australia • Australian phrasebook • Bushwalking in Australia • Bushwalking in Papua New Guinea • Fiji • Fijian phrasebook • Islands of Australia's Great Barrier Reef • Melbourne • Micronesia • New Caledonia • New South Wales • New Zealand • Northern Territory • Outback Australia • Papua New Guinea • Papua New Guinea phrasebook • Queensland • Rarotonga & the Cook Islands • Samoa • Solomon Islands • South Australia • Sydney • Tahiti & French Polynesia • Tasmania • Tonga • Tramping in New Zealand • Vanuatu • Victoria • Western Australia

Travel Literature: Islands in the Clouds • Sean & David's Long Drive

THE LONELY PLANET STORY

Lonely Planet published its first book in 1973 in response to the numerous 'How did you do it?' questions Maureen and Tony Wheeler were asked after driving, bussing, hitching, sailing and railing their way from England to Australia.

Written at a kitchen table and hand collated, trimmed and stapled, *Across Asia on the Cheap* became an instant local bestseller, inspiring thoughts of another book.

Eighteen months in South-East Asia resulted in their second guide, *South-East Asia on a shoestring*, which they put together in a backstreet Chinese hotel in Singapore in 1975. The 'yellow bible', as it quickly became known to backpackers around the world, soon became *the* guide to the region. It has sold well over half a million copies and is now in its 9th edition, still retaining its familiar yellow cover.

Today there are over 240 titles, including travel guides, walking guides, language kits & phrasebooks, travel atlases and travel literature. The company is the largest independent travel publisher in the world. Although Lonely Planet initially specialised in guides to Asia, today there are few corners of the globe that have not been covered.

The emphasis continues to be on travel for independent travellers. Tony and Maureen still travel for several months of each year and play an active part in the writing, updating and quality control of Lonely Planet's guides.

They have been joined by over 70 authors and 170 staff at our offices in Melbourne (Australia), Oakland (USA), London (UK) and Paris (France). Travellers themselves also make a valuable contribution to the guides through the feedback we receive in thousands of letters each year and on our web site.

The people at Lonely Planet strongly believe that travellers can make a positive contribution to the countries they visit, both through their appreciation of the countries' culture, wildlife and natural features, and through the money they spend. In addition, the company makes a direct contribution to the countries and regions it covers. Since 1986 a percentage of the income from each book has been donated to ventures such as famine relief in Africa; aid projects in India; agricultural projects in Central America; Greenpeace's efforts to halt French nuclear testing in the Pacific; and Amnesty International.

'I hope we send people out with the right attitude about travel. You realise when you travel that there are so many different perspectives about the world, so we hope these books will make people more interested in what they see. Guidebooks can't really guide people. All you can do is point them in the right direction.'

– Tony Wheeler

LONELY PLANET PUBLICATIONS

Australia
PO Box 617, Hawthorn 3122, Victoria
tel: (03) 9819 1877 fax: (03) 9819 6459
e-mail: talk2us@lonelyplanet.com.au

USA
Embarcadero West, 155 Filbert St, Suite 251,
Oakland, CA 94607
tel: (510) 893 8555 TOLL FREE: 800 275-8555
fax: (510) 893 8563
e-mail: info@lonelyplanet.com

UK
10a Spring Place,
London NW5 3BH
tel: (0171) 428 4800 fax: (0171) 428 4828
e-mail: go@lonelyplanet.co.uk

France:
71 bis rue du Cardinal Lemoine, 75005 Paris
tel: 1 44 32 06 20 fax: 1 46 34 72 55
e-mail: 100560.415@compuserve.com

World Wide Web: http://www.lonelyplanet.com
or *AOL keyword: lp*

Top: Praia da Conceição, Cascais
Bottom: Praça da Repúlica, Sintra

MAP 1

Greater Lisbon

MAP 2
MAP 5
MAP 4
MAP 13

0   0.5   1 km

To Torres Vedras

Campo Grande

To Queluz & Sintra

Avenida General Norton de Matos

Colégio Militar

9

Alto dos Moinhos

Cidade Universitária

To Queluz & Sintra

14

Avenida das

Laranjeiras

12

10

13

Aqueduto das Águas Livres

11

Parque Florestal de Monsanto

Sete-Rios

Pahlava

Campolide

22

23

Auto Estrada

N7

Auto Estrada

To Estoril & Cascais

Avenida da Ceuta

Rato

Estrela

Lapa

Avenida das Descobertas

Restelo

Ave Ilha da Madeira

24 25

26

27

Ajuda

Alcântara

Belém

To Estoril & Cascais

To Setúbal   Ponte 25 de Abril

MAP 1

EXPO '98 SITE

PLACES TO STAY
10 Quinta Nova da Conceição
19 Pensão Louro
23 Campismo de Câmara
   Municipal de Lisboa

OTHER
1 Museu Nacional do Teatro
2 Museu Nacional do Traje
3 Estádio José
  de Alvalade
4 Olivais Swimming Pool
5 Expo '98 Headquarters,
  Parque Expo
6 Feira do Relógio
7 Museu da Cidade
8 Campo Grande Swimming Pool
9 Estádio da Luz
11 Palácio dos Marquêses
   da Fronteira
12 Jardim Zoológico
13 US Embassy & Consulate
14 Santa Maria Hospital School
15 Biblioteca Nacional
16 Jumbo Expresso
17 Teatro Maria Matos
18 Areeiro Swimming Pool
20 Igreja de Penha de França
21 Museu Nacional do Azulejo
22 Highest point in Lisbon
24 Aquaparque
25 Turkish Embassy
26 Museu Nacional de Etnologia
27 Museu do Palácio
   Nacional da Ajuda

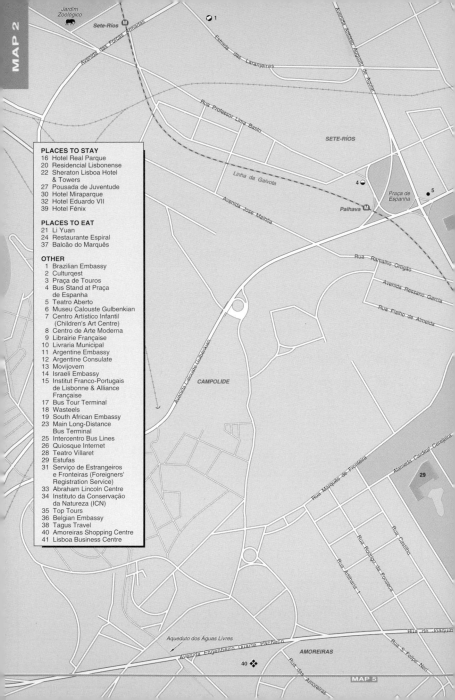

MAP 2

Jardim
Zoológico

Sete-Rios Ⓜ

Avenida das Forças Armadas

Estrada das Laranjeiras

Avenida António Augusto de Aguiar

Rua Professor Lima Basto

SETE-RÍOS

Linha da Gaivota

Avenida José Malhoa

Palhava Ⓜ

Praça de
Espanha

Rua Ramalho Ortigão

Avenida Ressano Garcia

Rua Fialho de Almeida

PLACES TO STAY
16 Hotel Real Parque
20 Residencial Lisbonense
22 Sheraton Lisboa Hotel
   & Towers
27 Pousada de Juventude
30 Hotel Miraparque
32 Hotel Eduardo VII
39 Hotel Fénix

PLACES TO EAT
21 Li Yuan
24 Restaurante Espiral
37 Balcão do Marquês

OTHER
1 Brazilian Embassy
2 Culturgest
3 Praça de Touros
4 Bus Stand at Praça
   de Espanha
5 Teatro Aberto
6 Museu Calouste Gulbenkian
7 Centro Artístico Infantil
   (Children's Art Centre)
8 Centro de Arte Moderna
9 Librairie Française
10 Livraria Municipal
11 Argentine Embassy
12 Argentine Consulate
13 Movijovem
14 Israeli Embassy
15 Institut Franco-Portugais
   de Lisbonne & Alliance
   Française
17 Bus Tour Terminal
18 Wasteels
19 South African Embassy
23 Main Long-Distance
   Bus Terminal
25 Intercentro Bus Lines
26 Quiosque Internet
28 Teatro Villaret
29 Estufas
31 Serviço de Estrangeiros
   e Fronteiras (Foreigners'
   Registration Service)
33 Abraham Lincoln Centre
34 Instituto da Conservação
   da Natureza (ICN)
35 Top Tours
36 Belgian Embassy
38 Tagus Travel
40 Amoreiras Shopping Centre
41 Lisboa Business Centre

Avenida Calouste Gulbenkian

CAMPOLIDE

Rua Marquês de Fronteira

Alameda Cardeal Cerejeira

29

Rua Castilho

Rua Rodrigo da Fonseca

Rua Artilharia I

Rua da Joaquim

Rua S. Felipe Neri

Aqueduto dos Águas Livres

Avenida Engenheiro Duarte Pacheco

AMOREIRAS

40 ❖

Rua das Amoreiras

MAP 5

JULIA WILKINSON

Doca de Santo Amaro

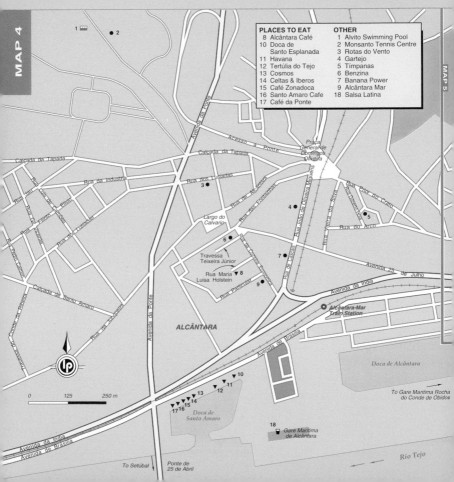

MAP 4

MAP 5

PLACES TO EAT
8 Alcântara Café
10 Doca de
   Santo Esplanada
11 Havana
12 Tertúlia do Tejo
13 Cosmos
14 Celtas & Iberos
15 Café Zonadoca
16 Santo Amaro Cafe
17 Café da Ponte

OTHER
1 Alvito Swimming Pool
2 Monsanto Tennis Centre
3 Rotas do Vento
4 Gartejo
5 Tímpanas
6 Benzina
7 Banana Power
9 Alcântara Mar
18 Salsa Latina

Calçada da Tapada

Rua da Indústria

Acesso à Ponte

Calçada da Tapada

Praça General de Domingos Oliveira

Avenida da Ponte

Rua dos Lusíadas

Rua de Alcântara

Rua Prior do Crato

Rua do Arco

Rua João de Oliveira Miguéns

Largo do Calvário

Rua das Fontainhas

Travessa Teixeira Júnior

Rua Maria Luísa Holstein

Rua Particular

Avenida 25 de Julho

Avenida da Índia

Alcântara-Mar Tram Station

ALCÂNTARA

Avenida da Ponte

Avenida de Brasília

Doca de Alcântara

To Gare Marítima Rocha do Conde de Óbidos

Calçada de Santo Amaro

Rua de Maquina

0   125   250 m

Doca de Santo Amaro

Gare Marítima de Alcântara

Avenida da Índia
Avenida de Brasília

To Setúbal   Ponte de 25 de Abril

Rio Tejo

MAP 5

MAP 2

MAP 6

MAP 4

PLACES TO STAY
14 Hotel da Lapa
19 York House
28 Janelas Verdas

PLACES TO EAT
2 Real Fábrica
20 Sua Excelência
22 Picanha

OTHER
1 Austrian Embassy
3 British Hospital
4 British Consulate
5 Swiss Embassy
6 Basílica da Estrela
7 Irish Embassy
8 Discoteca A Lontra
9 Palácio da Assembleia
   da República
10 Finnish Embassy
11 Swedish Embassy
12 Senhor Vinho
13 Netherlands Embassy
15 UK Embassy
16 Álcool Puro
17 French Embassy
18 Até Qu'Enfim
21 Stones bar
23 Kremlin
24 Kapital
25 Cervejinhas
26 Paulinha
27 Luxembourg Embassy
29 Décibel
30 Metalúrgica
31 Museu Nacional de Arte Antiga
32 Café Central
33 Jardim 9 de Abril
34 Gringo's Café
35 Speakeasy
36 Ultramar
37 Dock's Club
38 Blues Café
39 Discoteca Kings & Queens

Praça das Amoreiras

Rua Tr Fábrica dos Pentes

Rua das Amoreiras

Rua Campo de Ourique

Rua Dom João V

CAMPO DE OURIQUE

Rua Ferreira Borges

Rua da Arrábida

Largo do Rato

RATO

R de Infantaria Dezasseis

Rua Saraiva de Carvalho

Rua de São João

Rua de São Paulo

Rua Quatro de Infantaria

Rua Almeida e Sousa

Rua Coelho da Rocha

Cemitério dos Ingleses

Rua de São Jorge

ESTRELA

Rua Domingos Sequeira

Rua da Estrela

Jardim da Estrela

Praça da Estrela

Rua de São Bernardo

Rua de Santo Amaro

Rua do Jardim

Rua do Patrocínio

Rua de São António à Estrela

Calçada da Estrela

Rua de Possidónio

Rua dos Navegantes

Rua de Borges Carneiro

Miguel Lupi

Avenida Dom Carlos

Rua do Borja

Avenida Infante Santo

Tapada das Necessidades

Rua de São Caetano

Rua de São Domingos

Rua de Buenos Aires

Rua da Lapa

Rua de São João da Mata

Rua do Quelhas

LAPA

Rua do Sacramento à Lapa

Rua de São Filipe Neri

Rua das Praças

Rua Garcia da Horta

Rua das Trinas

Rua Melo e Lapa

Calçada Marquês de Abrantes

Rua de Santos o Velho

Calçada Ribeiro Santos

Rua do Prior

Rua Borges

Rua do Olival

Rua das Janelas Verdes

Avenida 24 de Julho

Santos Train Station

Rua Presidente Arriaga

Rua Nova do Calvário

Doca de Alcântara

0   125   250 m

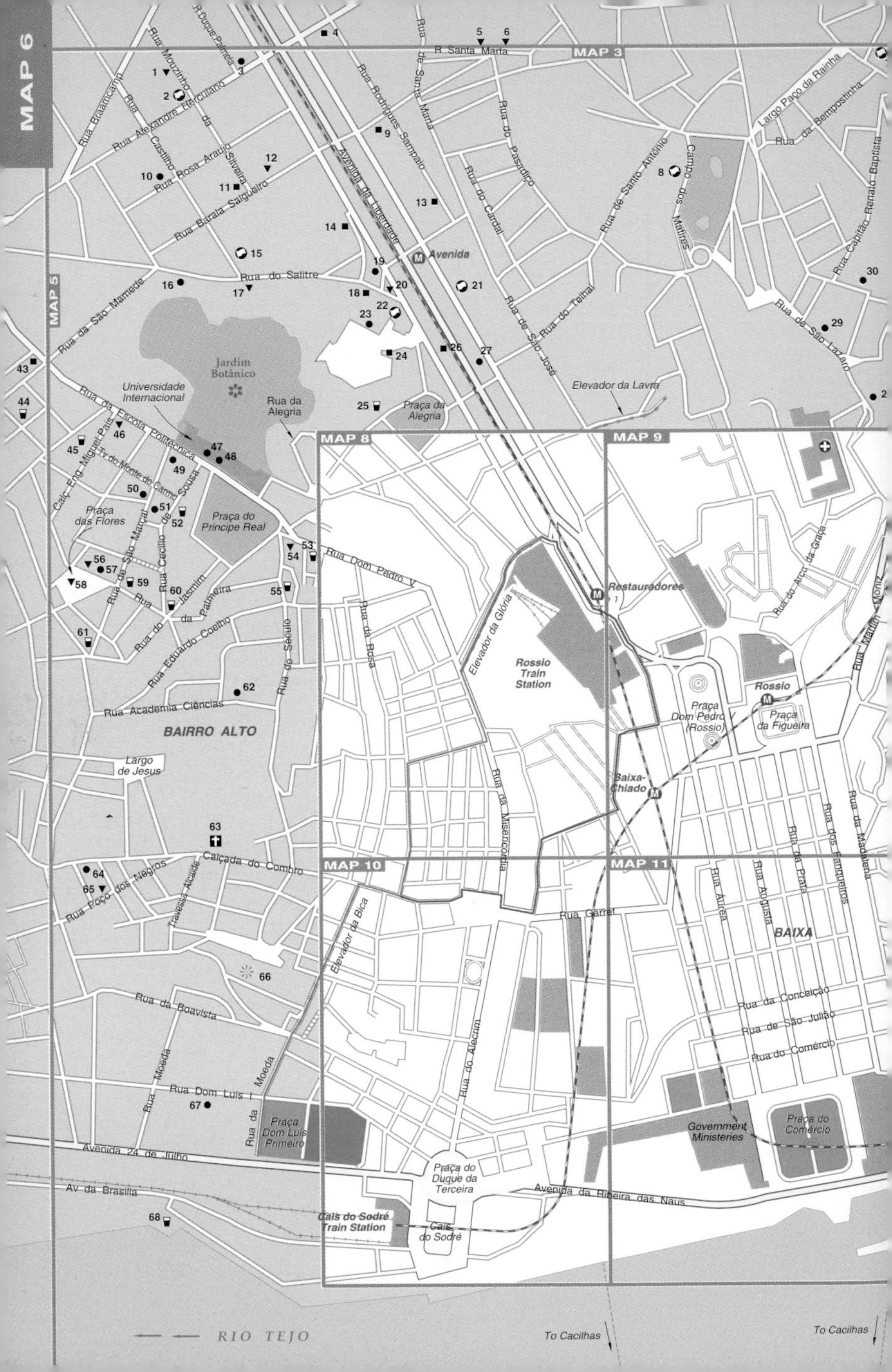

MAP 6

MAP 3
MAP 5
MAP 8
MAP 9
MAP 10
MAP 11

R. Santa Maria

Rua Santa Maria

Rua Dona Estefânia

Rua Braancamp

Rua Marquês

Rua Alexandre Herculano

Rua Castilho

Rua Rosa Araújo

Rua Rodrigues Sampaio

Rua Barata Salgueiro

Avenida da Liberdade

Rua do Passadiço

Rua do Salitre

Rua de Santo António

Rua de Santo Antão

Campo dos Mártires

Largo Paço da Rainha

Rua da Bempostinha

Rua Capitão Renato Baptista

Rua de São Lázaro

Avenida

Rua de São José

Rua de São Tiago

Elevador da Lavra

Jardim Botânico

Universidade Internacional

Rua da Alegria

Praça da Alegria

Rua da Escola Politécnica

Calç. Eng. Miguel Pais

Trav. do Monte do Carmo

Praça das Flores

Praça do Príncipe Real

Rua Dom Pedro V

Rua da Rosa

Rua da Misericórdia

Elevador da Glória

Restauradores

Rossio Train Station

Praça Dom Pedro V (Rossio)

Praça da Figueira

Rossio

Baixa-Chiado

Rua do Século

Rua da Palmeira

Rua Eduardo Coelho

Rua Academia Ciências

BAIRRO ALTO

Largo de Jesus

Calçada do Combro

Rua do Loreto

Rua Garrett

Rua Áurea

Rua da Prata

Rua dos Fanqueiros

Rua dos Correeiros

BAIXA

Rua da Conceição

Rua de São Julião

Rua do Comércio

Rua Poço dos Negros

Trav. Água da Flor

Rua da Boavista

Rua da Moeda

Elevador da Bica

Rua do Alecrim

Rua Dom Luís I

Praça Dom Luís Primeiro

Avenida 24 de Julho

Av da Brasília

Praça do Duque da Terceira

Cais do Sodré Train Station

Cais do Sodré

Avenida da Ribeira das Naus

Government Ministeries

Praça do Comércio

RIO TEJO

To Cacilhas

To Cacilhas

MAP 7

PLACES TO STAY

4 Hotel Presidente
9 Hotel Lisboa
11 Hotel Jorge V
13 Hotel Britânia
14 Hotel Tivoli Jardim
18 Pensão Residencial
   13 da Sorte
24 Hotel Lisboa Plaza
26 Hotel Sofitel
33 Albergaria Senhora do Monte
43 Casa de São Mamede

PLACES TO EAT

1 Centro de Alimentação
   e Saúde Natural
5 Restaurante Estrela
   de Santa Marta
6 O Coradinho
12 Big Apple Restaurante & Ad Lib
17 Restaurante Os Tibetanos
20 Cervejaria Ribadouro
45 Confeitaria Cister
54 Tascardoso
56 Conventual
58 Casa de Pasto Flores
65 Cantinho do Paz
70 Hua Ta Li

OTHER

2 Japanese Embassy
3 Livraria Buchholz
7 Italian Embassy & Consulate
8 German Embassy
10 Automóvel Club
   de Portugal (ACP)
12 Ad Lib & Big Apple Restaurante
15 Danish Embassy
16 Quercus
19 Cambridge School
21 Canadian Embassy
22 Spanish Embassy & Consulate
23 Teatro Maria Vitória
25 Hot Clube de Portugal
27 Regus Business Centre
28 Gay & Lesbian Community Centre
29 Os Ferreiras
30 Olaria do Desterros
31 Cerâmica Viúva Lamego
32 Miradouro da Senhora do Monte
34 Museu da Água
35 Tas Giro
36 Military Barracks
37 Voz do Operário
38 Ópera
39 Miradouro da Graça

40 Anos 60
41 Lavandaria Sous'ana
42 Mafrense Bus Terminal
44 Memorial
45 Trumps
47 Príncipe Real
48 Casa das Cortiças
49 Casa Achilles
50 Livraria Britânica
51 British Council
52 Brica Bar
53 Pavilhão Chinês
55 Snob Bar
57 Loja Branca
59 Bar 106
60 Finalmente
61 Tatoo
62 Ratton
63 Igreja de Santa Catarina
64 Incógnito
66 Miradouro de Santa Catarina
67 Absoluto
68 Rock City
69 Igreja da Conceição Velha
71 Renex Bus Stop
72 Cruises on the Tejo

WALKING TOURS

Red Tour: Largo dos Portas do Sol to Alfama
Green Tour: From Cathedral to Castle
Blue Tour: From Turismo to Avenida 24 de Julho
Purple Tour: From Turismo and back

Castelo de
São Jorge

CASTELO

ALFAMA

GRAÇA

Largo
da Graça

Largo do
Terreirinho

Campo de Santa Clara

Santa Apolónia
Train Station

Campo das
Cebolas

Government
Ministeries

Terreiro
do Paço

Ferreiro do Paço
Ferry Terminal

MAP 12

To Montejo
& Seixal

To Barreiro

Tn Mucou
Nacional do
Azulejo

0   125   250 m

MAP 9

3

12

13

14

17

24

23

22

25

21

26

28

27

Largo de
Domingos

51

44 Praça
Dom João
da Câmara

47

48

45

49

Rossio

46

Praça
Dom Pedro V

52

Travessa Nova De São Domingos

50

54

(Rossio)

55

Praça
da Figueira

82

56

81

57

80

83

79

85

84

Rua Betesga

53

78

58

59

77

76

60

62

Baixa-Chiado

63

61

73

74

75

Rua de Santa Justa

Elevador de Santa Justa

71

72

BAIXA

64

70

69

68

65

Largo
do Carmo

111

66

112

Rua da Assunção

MAP 11

67

Largo Chão do
Loureiro

MAP 11

MAP 12

Key for Maps 8 & 9 on the previous pages

PLACES TO STAY

1 Residencial Nova Avenida
2 Residencial Roma
8 Pensão Perola de Baixa
9 Pensão Monumental
10 Hotel Suiço-Atlântico
11 Pensão Iris
12 Pensão Florescente
17 Pensão Imperial
19 Orion Eden Lisboa
24 Residencial Campos
29 Pensão Londres
31 Pensão Globo
52 Pensão Residencial
    Alcobia
54 Hotel Lisboa Tejo
63 Pensão Moderna
66 Pensão Insulana
76 Pensão Arco da
    Bandeira
84 Pensão Estação Central
85 Residencial Estrêla do
    Mondego
87 Pensão Duque
88 Pensão Estrêla de Ouro

PLACES TO EAT

7 Restaurante O Brunhal
15 Casa do Alentejo
22 Pinóquio
26 Gambrinus
30 Restaurante Novo
    Bonsai
33 O Cantinho da Rosa
35 Até Lá Lá
36 Cafétaria Brasil
38 Restaurante O Tacão Pequeno
53 Algures na Mouraria
55 Casa Suiça
59 Restaurante João do Grão
62 Restaurante São Cristóvão
64 Restaurante Ena Pãi
65 Lagosta Vermelha
70 Chiadomel
75 Casa Chineza
79 Café Nicola
83 Celeiro
86 Casa Transmontana
93 Ali-a-Papa
94 Bota Alta
98 Vá e Volte
103 Pap'Açorda
109 Henry J Bean's
110 Cervejaria da Trinidade
112 Leitaria Académica
115 Tavares Rico
117 Tasca do Manel
120 O Catinho do Bem Estar

OTHER

3 São José Hospital
4 Banque Nacional de Paris
5 Banco Borges e Irmão
6 Ritz Clube
13 Loja da Música
14 Câmara do Comércio e
    Portuguesa
16 Post Office
18 Turismo
20 Virgin Megastore
21 ABEP Ticket Agency
23 Lisboa Card Office
25 Palácio dos Condes de
    Almada
27 Teatro Nacional de Dona
28 Multibanco ATM
32 Nova
34 Pais em Lisboa
37 Solar do Vinho do Porto
39 O Forcado
40 Primas
41 Frágil
42 Igreja de São Roque &
    de São João Baptista
43 Museu de Arte Sacra
44 Portugal Telecom
45 Farmácia Estácio
46 Valentim de Carvalho
47 Azevedo Rua
48 Exclusivo bebé
49 Rabimos
50 Dolls Hospital
    (Hospital das Bonecas)
51 Igreja de São
    Domingos
56 Maison Louvre
57 Carris Ticket Office
58 Manuel Tavares
60 Casa Macário
61 Farmácia Homeopática Santa
    Justa
67 Camisaria Pitta
68 Cenoura
69 Arte Rústica
71 Livraria Portuga
72 Discoteca Amália
73 Luvaria Ulisses
74 Cota Câmbios
77 Livraria Diário de Notícias
78 Tabacaria Adamastor
80 Tabacaria Mónaco
81 Editorial Notícias
82 Gabriel de Carvalho
89 Café Luso
90 O Velho Sapateiro
91 Arroz Doce
92 Portas Largas

Continued next page...

Key for Maps 10 & 11 on the following pages

MAP 10

MAP 8

Rua do Diário de Notícias — 1

2

3

Rua da Salgadeiras

Rua do Loreto
4 ▼ 5

6 ●

Elevador da Bica

7 ▼

Rua da Bica
Duarte Belo

11 ◨

Praça de
Luís Camões

Largo
do Chiado

16 ▼

Rua Garret

17

15 ⊞

8
9 ▼

Travessa do Sequeiro

Rua da Horta Seca

12 ▼

13 ●

14 ●

Travessa da Laranjeira

10 ▼

Rua da Emenda

Travessa do Portuguaza

Largo de
São Carlos

Travessa do Cabral

Largo do
Barão
de Quintela

Rua Paiva de Andrada

Travessa de Guilherme Coussul

39 ●

38 ● 37 ▼

36 ▼

Rua Capelo

35 ★

Rua António Maria Cardoso

40

41

Beco das Arcosfras

Rua do Ataíde

Rua do Alecrim

Rua dos Duques de Bragança

Rua Serpa Pinto

43 �🏛

42 ●

Rua de São Paulo

50 ▼

Travessa Carvalho

Travessa do
Alecrim

Rua Vítor Cordon

49

Rua Ribeira Nova

Rua da Moeda

Rua Nova do Carvalho

Rua de São Paulo

Rua Ferragial

51 ●

Rua do Corpo Santo

52

53 ▼ 54

55 ▼

56

57 ▼

Rua Bernardino Costa

58 ▼

59 ●

Travessa dos Remolares

Praça do
Duque da
Terceira

60

Avenida 25 de Julho

Cais do Sodré

Cais do Sodré
Train Station

Cais do
Sodré

61 ●

62 ⎈

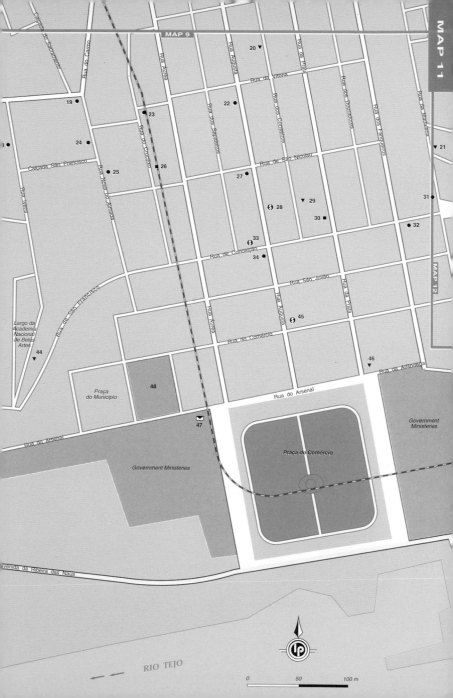

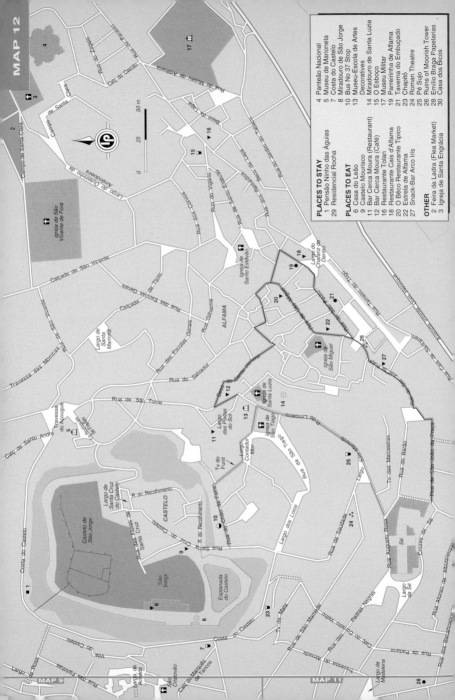

MAP 12

PLACES TO STAY
1 Pensão Ninho das Águias
29 Residencial Rocha

PLACES TO EAT
6 Casa do Leão
9 Castelo Mourisco
11 Bar Cerca Moura (Restaurant)
12 Bar Cerca Moura (Café)
16 Restaurante Tolan
18 Restaurante Cais d'Alfama
20 O Beco Restaurante Típico
22 Estrela de Alfama
27 Snack-Bar Arco Íris

4 Panteão Nacional
5 Museu de Marioneta
7 Costa do Castelo
8 Miradouro de São Jorge
10 Bus No 37 Stop
13 Museu-Escola de Artes
     Decoratives
14 Miradouro de Santa Luzia
15 O Esboço
17 Museu Militar
19 Parreirinha de Alfama
21 Taverna do Embuçado
23 Chapitô
24 Roman Theatre
25 Pé Sujo
26 Ruins of Moorish Tower
28 Emílio Braga Papelarias
30 Casa dos Bicos

OTHER
2 Feira da Ladra (Flea Market)
3 Igreja de Santa Engrácia

CASTELO
ALFAMA

Castelo de São Jorge
São Jorge
Esplanada do Castelo

Igreja de São Vicente de Fora
Igreja de Santo Estêvão
Igreja de São Miguel
Igreja de Santa Luzia
Igreja de São Tiago
Sé

Largo da Sé
Largo de Madalena

MAP 9
MAP 11

TONY WHEELER

Monument to the Discoveries

BETHUNE CARMICHAEL

Mosteiro dos Jerónimos

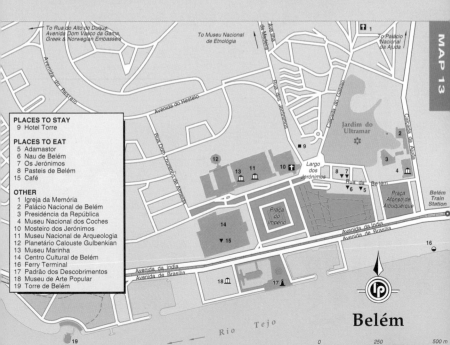

PLACES TO STAY
9 Hotel Torre

PLACES TO EAT
5 Adamastor
6 Nau de Belém
7 Os Jerónimos
8 Pasteis de Belém
15 Café

OTHER
1 Igreja da Memória
2 Palácio Nacional de Belém
3 Presidência da República
4 Museu Nacional dos Coches
10 Mosteiro dos Jerónimos
11 Museu Nacional de Arqueologia
12 Planetário Calouste Gulbenkian
13 Museu Marinha
14 Centro Cultural de Belém
16 Ferry Terminal
17 Padrão dos Descobrimentos
18 Museu de Arte Popular
19 Torre de Belém

MAP 13

Belém

MAP 14

Expo '98 Site

0   100   200 m

P
Visitors
Parking

North Entrance ▼

West
Entrance ▶

River
Entrance

Oriente Station

Cable Car

Doca dos
Olivais

P

P
Visitors
Parking

South
Entrance

P
VIP
Parking

PLACES OF INTEREST
2   Video Stadium
4   North International Area
6   Utopia Pavilion
7   Open Air Amphitheatre
8   Portuguese Pavilion
10 Pavilion of the Future
11 South International Area
12 Knowledge of the Seas Pavilion
13 Oceans Pavilion
15 Jules Verne Auditorium
16 Virtual Reality Pavilion
18 Nautical Exhibition

OTHER
1   Vasco da Gama Tower
3   Garcia da Orta Gardens
5   International Organisations Area
9   Ceremonial Plaza
14 Water Gardens
17 Press Centre

RESTAURANT GUIDE
▼   High level restaurants
▼   Family type restaurants
▼   Take-away
▼   Self Service
▼   Kiosks

LEGEND
●   Performance Areas / Small Stages
    Pavilions
    Restaurants
    Other Buildings
    Water Gardens
    Water
    Park / Garden area
─── Shuttle Bus

"Dive into the Future" at EXPO '98

MAP 15

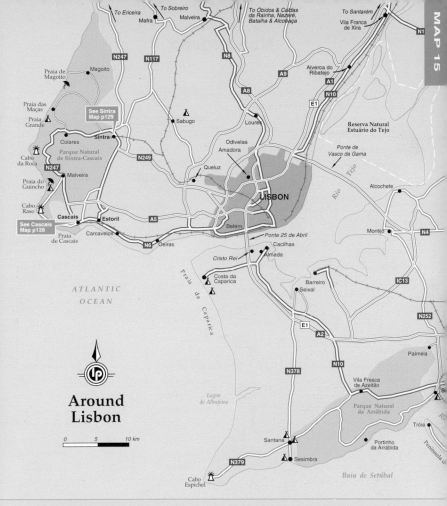

Around Lisbon

0   5   10 km

To Ericeira

To Sobreiro

To Óbidos & Caldas
da Rainha, Nazaré,
Batalha & Alcobaça

To Santarém

Mafra

Malveira

Vila Franca
de Xira

N1

N247

N117

N8

Alverca do
Ribatejo

A9

A8

A1

N10

E1

Magoito

Praia de
Magoito

Praia das
Maças

Praia
Grande

Cabo
da Roca

Praia do
Guincho

Cabo
Raso

Colares

Sabugo

Sintra

Loures

Reserva Natural
Estuário do Tejo

Parque Natural
de Sintra-Cascais

Odivelas
Amadora

Ponte de
Vasco da Gama

N249

Queluz

Rio Tejo

Alcochete

Malveira

LISBON

Cascais

Estoril

A5

Belém

Montijo

N4

Carcavelos

N6

Oeiras

Ponte 25 de Abril

IC13

Praia
de Cascais

Cacilhas

Cristo Rei

Almada

Barreiro

Seixal

N252

ATLANTIC
OCEAN

Praia da Caparica

Costa da
Caparica

E1

A2

N10

Palmela

N378

Vila Fresca
de Azeitão

S

Lagoa
de Albufeira

Parque Natural
da Arrábida

Tróia

Santana

Portinho
da Arrábida

R

N379

Sesimbra

Baía de Setúbal

Península d

Cabo
Espichel

JULIA WILKINSON

Cabo da Roca

Map Legend

BOUNDARIES

.... International Boundary
.... Provincial Boundary

ROUTES

A25 ...... Freeway, with Route Number
.... Major Road
.... Minor Road
.... Minor Road - Unsealed
.... City Road
.... City Street
.... City Lane
.... Train Route, with Station
.... Metro Route, with Station
.... Cable Car or Chairlift
.... Ferry Route
.... Walking Track

AREA FEATURES

.... Building
.... Cemetery
.... Hotel
.... Market
.... Park, Gardens
.... Pedestrian Mall
.... Urban Area

HYDROGRAPHIC FEATURES

.... Canal
.... Coastline
.... Creek, River
.... Lake, Intermittent Lake
.... Rapids, Waterfalls
.... Salt Lake
.... Swamp

SYMBOLS

✪ **CAPITAL** ...... National Capital	✈ .... Airport	⌂ .... Museum
◉ **CAPITAL** ...... Provincial Capital	⌐ ... Ancient or City Wall	← .... One Way Street
● **CITY** .... City	⁘ ... Archaeological Site	⊡ .... Parking
● **Town** .... Town	ϴ .... Bank	★ .... Police Station
● Village .... Village	卍 .... Buddhist Temple	▭ .... Post Office
	舟 .... Castle or Fort	❖ .... Shopping Centre
■ .... Place to Stay	✝ .... Church	血 .... Stately Home
	≈ .... Cliff or Escarpment	▭ .... Swimming Pool
▼ .... Place to Eat	◒ .... Embassy	✡ .... Synagogue
▌ .... Pub or Bar	▥ .... Hindu Temple	☎ .... Telephone
	✚ .... Hospital	□ .... Tomb
	☼ .... Lookout	❶ ...... Tourist Information
	▲ .... Monument	⬤ .... Transport
	☾ .... Mosque	🐘 .... Zoo

Note: not all symbols displayed above appear in this book